Traces of War

Edited by
Birger Stichelbaut

With contributions from
Thomas Apers
Jean Bourgeois
Maarten Bracke
Piet Chielens
Jan Decorte
Marc Dewilde
Anton Ervynck
Wouter Gheyle
Bert Heyvaert
Koen Himpe
Johan Hoorne
An Lentacker
Nicolas Note
Timothy Saey
Birger Stichelbaut
Hanne Van den Berghe
Veerle Van Eetvelde
Yannick Van Hollebeeke
Marc Van Meirvenne
Annick Vandenbilcke
Simon Verdegem
Franky Wyffels

Traces of War

The Archaeology of the First World War

HANNIBAL

CONTENTS

FIG. 1

Crenellated trench in Heuvelland, visible as cropmarks during the 2017 summer drought.

This book is the first of its kind, a compendium of the findings of ten years of First World War (WW1) archaeology in Belgium. Published to coincide with the exhibition of the same name in the In Flanders Fields Museum in Ypres, *Traces of War* is an important milestone for the museum, and by extension for all those involved in the study of the First World War. Over the last twenty years we have witnessed – at first unwillingly but ultimately very gratefully – a major evolution. Together with our first chairman, Alderman Frans Lignel, we spent the last years of the last century searching for ways to dig up and preserve human remains in a decent and fitting manner. Then Paul Breyne, the governor of the Province of West Flanders, came up with a protocol enabling the more than 200 fallen soldiers unearthed by the Diggers, a team of amateur archaeologists headed by Patrick Van Wanzeele who have spent years of their free time excavating WW1 remains, to be given a final resting place.

This was the period in which official, academically trained archaeologists had no time or resources for, or interest in researching the First World War. Things are now completely different. Under our current chairman, Alderman Jef Verschoore, we have been able to set up and consolidate the Centre for Historical & Archaeological Aerial Photography/ *Centrum voor Historische & Archeologische Luchtfotografie* (CHAL), together with Ghent University and the Province of West Flanders. Under the dynamic leadership of Dr Birger Stichelbaut, the editor of this book and curator of the exhibition, CHAL is working on developing non-invasive forms of archaeology. This work is multidisciplinary, combining the academic fields of archaeology, history, geography and soil science. The research team is in permanent contact with archaeologists in the government and in the field. In addition, CHAL is developing, in conjunction with the In Flanders Fields Museum, visual tools such as films and apps to enable the public to take a closer look at the historical context of the present-day landscape. This interaction is bearing fruit, with the insights provided by WW1 archaeology contributing to the classical historical study of the period.

While obviously not rewriting the history of the First World War, this book highlights the fact that WW1 archaeology is a new and supplementary source that can add new aspects and depth to that history. For the public at large, this archaeological project makes it clear that the war is not far below the ground of the former front-line zone – and not only there. In 2006, the museum launched the slogan that the contemporary landscape is the last witness of the war, a fact repeatedly proven and reinforced by our archaeological research.

For all this new knowledge – the subject of this book and the exhibition – we are indebted to Professor Jean Bourgeois and Birger Stichelbaut from Ghent University and their colleagues Wouter Gheyle, Professor Marc Van Meirvenne and Professor Veerle Van Eetvelde; to the Flemish Heritage Agency and in particular Marc Dewilde, Franky Wyffels, Anton Ervynck and Koen Himpe; to archaeologist Jan Decorte from CO7, the cooperation partnership of Southern Westhoek local authorities; to on-the-ground archaeologists Simon Verdegem, Maarten Bracke and Bert Heyvaert; and to Johan Hoorne, Yannick Van Hollebeeke, Nicolas Note, Timothy Saey, Hanne Van den Berghe, Thomas Apers and An Lentacker. Many thanks for their contributions to this book, and also many thanks to Bart Biesbrouck for his exceptional text editing.

Over the past ten years, more than 150 archaeological contracts have been put out for tender. The whole sector has worked together in a most positive manner to come up with improved techniques and insights: the government archaeologists from the heritage agency, the CHAL desktop studies, private companies such as Ruben Willaert bvba, Group Monuments archaeology department, landowners – both private and public – and major project developers such as Fluxys.

Without their efforts, this book would never have appeared. There was a time when we had to go abroad to gain expertise in this domain. Today we possess this knowledge ourselves. There will undoubtedly be more, but now we already have a very rich, new source for historical research into a period that drastically changed our landscape.

On behalf of the In Flanders Fields Museum
Piet Chielens and Annick Vandenbilcke

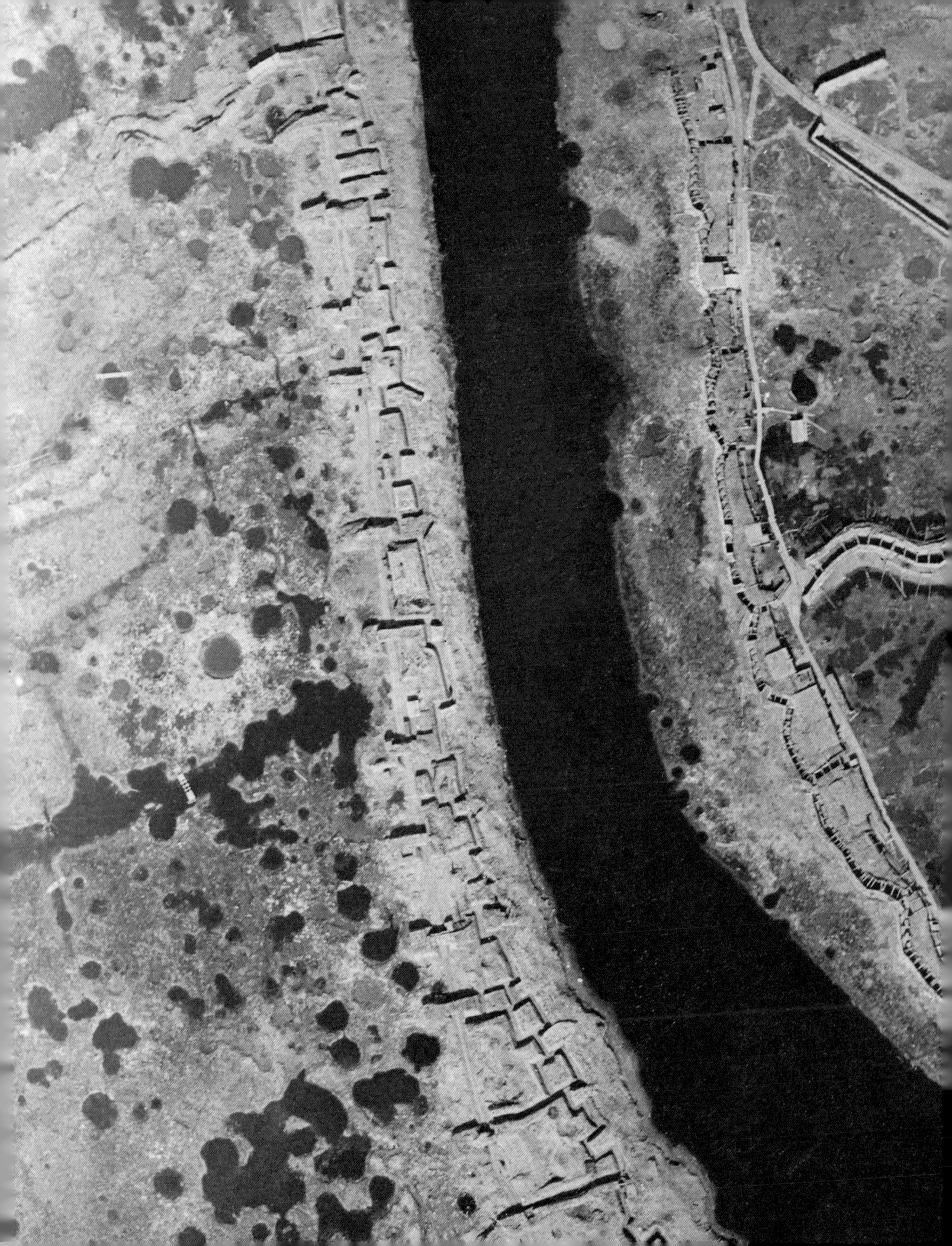

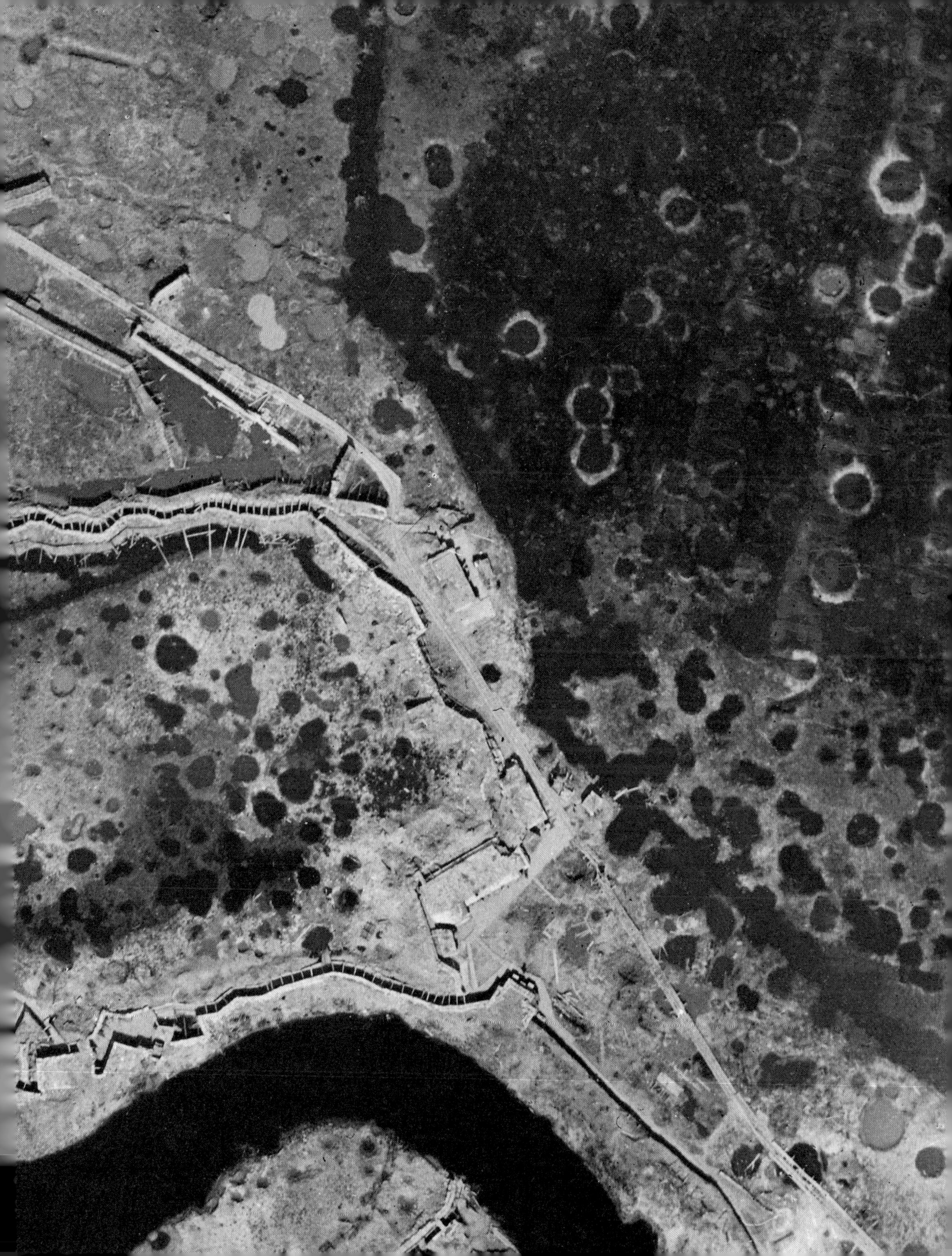

The Archaeology of the First World War

Birger Stichelbaut
Simon Verdegem
Yannick Van Hollebeeke
Marc Dewilde
Franky Wyffels
Anton Ervynck
Maarten Bracke
Jan Decorte
Wouter Gheyle

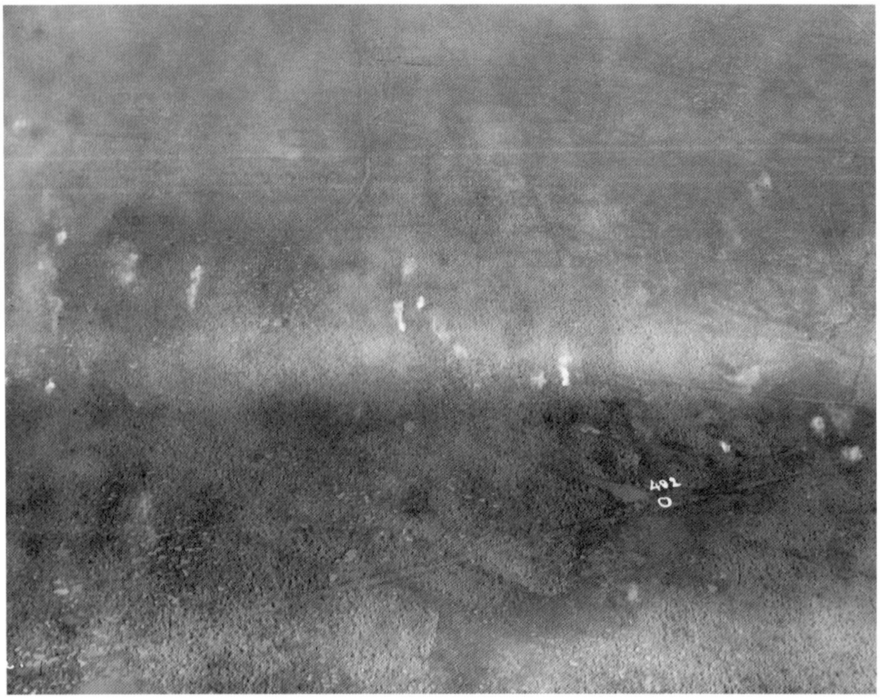

3

FIG. 2 (pp. 10-11)
Belgian-German front lines separated by the Yser in Diksmuide.

FIG. 3
German aerial photo dated 11 September 1917 showing the devastated terrain along the front near Sint-Juliaan.

FIG. 4
German prisoners of war and Chinese workers at the end of the war in the Ypres Salient.

FIG. 5 (pp. 14-15)
Reconstruction work in the devastated region, 15 September 1921.

The First World War was the first worldwide conflict conducted on an industrial scale. Never before had so many troops been deployed, so many men killed or wounded, so many shells and bullets fired. Never before had the landscape been devastated on such a scale than in the four years of trench warfare (**FIG. 2 & 3**). At the end of it, the front line was little more than a vast barren waste. Villages had been erased from the face of the earth, fields and meadows were littered with craters, the landscape was criss-crossed with trenches and military roads, railways and camps.

After the war, what remained of the local population moved back in dribs and drabs, faced with the daunting challenge of rebuilding the region and making it inhabitable again. They were helped by the military. Colonial troops, workers from the Chinese Labour Corps and even prisoners of war were deployed to clear up the battlefields. The Chinese worker Gu Xingqing described the immense challenge in the following words: "With the announcement of the Armistice, all hostilities ceased, and obviously no more war-related work was needed. But the former battle theatre was now nothing more than an unimaginable ghastly mess, needing to be cleaned up as quickly as possible. The English and French governments therefore called in all Chinese units to do this work. (…) The cleaning-up was not just a case of removing shells, grenades and barbed wire. The corpses of the fallen English soldiers had to be dug up and given a proper burial. The battlefield alone was vast, and finding the dead was no simple task."[1]

[1] Xingqing 1938

Miles and miles of trenches and thousands of craters were filled in, and the military infrastructure largely dismantled, wiping out any traces of the war. The material remains of the war were buried, becoming part of the underground archaeological archive (**FIG. 5**).

THE LANDSCAPE AS THE LAST REMAINING WITNESS

A century later, the last living witnesses are no longer with us. Younger generations have no direct connection to the war and personal links are fading with the passing of time.

All that is left is the landscape: contours and slopes that dictated where the front lines ran; smaller landscape features, such as hedges or rows of trees that hid the gun emplacements and trenches from enemy sight; farms and castles that were transformed into shelters, first-aid stations and headquarters; rivers and submerged polders that formed natural barriers; strategic heights

4

PHOTO
ANTONY
150921-12

that quickly came under barrages of fire. Everywhere along the Western Front, the landscape dictated the course of the war.

Conversely, the battles had an enormous impact on the landscape. Although the superficial traces were erased in the post-war years and one can no longer see where the front lines ran, many traces of the war remain. Some are landmarks and have become tourist attractions or memorials. Others are visible only to the trained eye. Spectacular relics in the landscape, such as the mine craters with their deep and impressive scars, appeal to the imagination of thousands of visitors. Bunkers (also called pillboxes) are tangible witnesses of long-gone positions (**FIG. 7**).

More often the traces are subtle, hidden from view by vegetation or hardly visible due to their low height. In the woodlands of the Westhoek, the area around Ypres that bore the brunt of the fighting in Flanders (the Ypres Salient), thousands of now grown-over shell craters and miles and miles of trenches can still be found (see Chapter 9). Further away from the front, where forests survived the shelling, one can see graffiti on signposts or markings carved by soldiers in the trees (**FIG. 8**). The impact of the war is evident in the jet-black spots in the annual rings of old trees[2].

And in the ground, some 30 centimetres down and invisible to the naked eye, another source can be found. Everywhere in the Westhoek, and in surprisingly many places deep in the hinterland, a wealth of archaeological information lies just under the surface (**FIG. 9**).

[2] Chielens, Dendooven et al. 2012, Haneca 2014

A

One of the most poignant exhibits in the In Flanders Fields Museum is the cross-section of an oak tree which grew in the park of Elverdinge between 1760 and 1994. The annual rings added during the war show jet-black traces of war stress caused by the explosions of German shells. Following the war, the tree continued to grow, preserving the scars. The cross-section symbolises the landscape as the last witness of the war, showing how the war is part and parcel of the region's DNA.

FIG. 6
The landscape as the last remaining witness: the Bellewaarde ridge is a complex landscape riddled with dozens of deep mine craters. After the war, a layer of monuments was added. Barely 30 centimetres under the surface, an invisible layer of archaeological information lies dormant.

FIG. 7
British bunker in Polygon Wood in Zonnebeke.

FIG. 8
De Galgebossen (Gallows Woods) near Poperinge was a place behind the front for rest and recuperation. Several trees still display the carvings of British soldiers.

FIG. 9
Bird's-eye view of a team of archaeologists excavating a meandering Belgian trench in Diksmuide.

6

7

8

9

THE TANGIBLE WAR

Twenty-first-century archaeology goes a lot further than just finding artefacts. The scale of any research varies from studying objects found in a pit or trench, via the analysis of site structures, to a synthesis of the information for an entire region. The focus is on the people involved and how they interacted with their environment. WW1 archaeology involves the study of the material and structural remains of men's deeds under very unique and specific war circumstances.

In the early days, the question was sometimes raised: "These days, we know so much about the war. What's the point of archaeological research?" The action on the battlefields and the course of the battles are known through official documents and regimental histories. Fragments of film and photographs provide glimpses of the war. Thousands of trench maps and aerial photos show the landscape as it was then, revealing where action took place. How can archaeological research add to these already-known sources of information?

Obviously, archaeology does not rewrite history. But it can make the past tangible, illustrating day-to-day life in the trenches and military camps behind the front; the continual battle against the elements; coping with death. It shows us how the construction of trench networks, bunkers and tunnels evolved, and enables us to compare these real-life situations with 'the ideal battlefield' outlined in military manuals. Archaeology shows us how improvised the construction methods were, for example to win the fight against groundwater. It also unearths (in the true sense of the word!) short-lived battles barely mentioned or not mentioned at all in the historical sources.

A NEW DISCIPLINE

The years just after the war were dominated by the reconstruction of the devastated regions, but reminders of the war remain anchored in the landscape in the form of dozens of monuments and graveyards. The returning population often went out in search of war scrap (**FIG. 10**). Lead, copper and iron were recovered and sold[3]. Interest in the war slowly dissipated, not least due to the outbreak of the Second World War twenty years later. In the 1960s, interest picked up for a short period, in commemoration of the 50th anniversary of the Great War.

The material heritage of the First World War proved to be a great attraction for collectors of military memorabilia. Treasure hunters scoured the battlefields with metal detectors, searching for war artefacts. The book *Battlefield Archaeology*[4] was published in 1987, a typical product of the zeitgeist at the time. A practical guide to finding artefacts from both world wars, it was aimed at attracting more 'battlefield archaeologists' to the former front-line regions. The book, devoid of any archaeological expertise or concern, played on an interest in military history.

Interest in the First World War started growing again in the 1990s, as witnessed by the 1992 opening of a large museum dedicated to the Battle of the Somme in Péronne in France. Six years later, the In Flanders Fields Museum opened its doors in Ypres. In the same period, associations of enthusiastic First World War battlefield archaeologists started springing up, with their members devoting their free time to excavating the former battlefields. This work helped raised awareness of the rapidly disappearing archaeological heritage. One of the groups of amateur archaeologists working in the battlefields around Boezinge and Ypres called itself 'the Diggers'[5]. They unearthed trenches

[3] Debaeke 2010
[4] Laffin 1987
[5] De Diggers 2001
[6] Doyle, Barton et al. 2006
[7] Saunders 2007

10

FIG. 10
Drawing by Joe English warning of the danger of unexploded ordnance in 1918.

The reuse of ancient siege techniques, such as undermining each other's positions, and the ever-increasing impact of the murderous shelling, made troops seek protection below ground. They dug into the heavy Flanders clay, creating an extensive network of mine shafts and tunnels. Five metres beneath the church in Zonnebeke, a 'deep dugout' was located: an underground shelter 30 metres long with five rooms furnished with wooden beams and metal profiles. The Zonnebeke Church Dugout is still in an exceptionally good condition. The entrance tunnel runs under the church's foundations. After the war, the tunnel became filled with water, helping to preserve the wood. In 2017, the decision was taken to temporarily open it to the public.

B

and explored 'deep dugouts', such as the Yorkshire Trench and Dugout in Boezinge (**FIG. 11 & 12**), also coming across more than 200 war victims. Another organisation established in the late 1990s was the Association for Battlefield Archaeology in Flanders (ABAF). This spent its time excavating, among other things, the German Bayernwald trenches in Heuvelland and the Beecham Dugout in Zonnebeke[6]. The ABAF was superseded by the Association for Battlefield Archaeology and Conservation (ABAC), whose best-known Belgian project was the excavation of the Vampire Dugout in Zonnebeke in 2008. These projects all helped make public authorities realise that the material remains of the war were valuable[7].

Professional archaeologists were initially not very interested in investigating the First World War, as the period was considered too recent to be a suitable subject. When any investigation of First World War remains took place, it was usually done by the Flemish government's Institute for Archaeological Patrimony (IAP), after these remains had been unearthed during excavations of 'real' archaeological sites. For instance, the British dugout beneath the Augustine abbey in Zonnebeke was registered as a 'recent disturbance' of the soil.

FIG. 11
Discovery of the Yorkshire Trench and Dugout. An amateur archaeologist descends into the metre-deep underground shelter.

FIG. 12
Amateur excavation of the German Fortin 17 bunker in Boezinge industrial park.

11

12

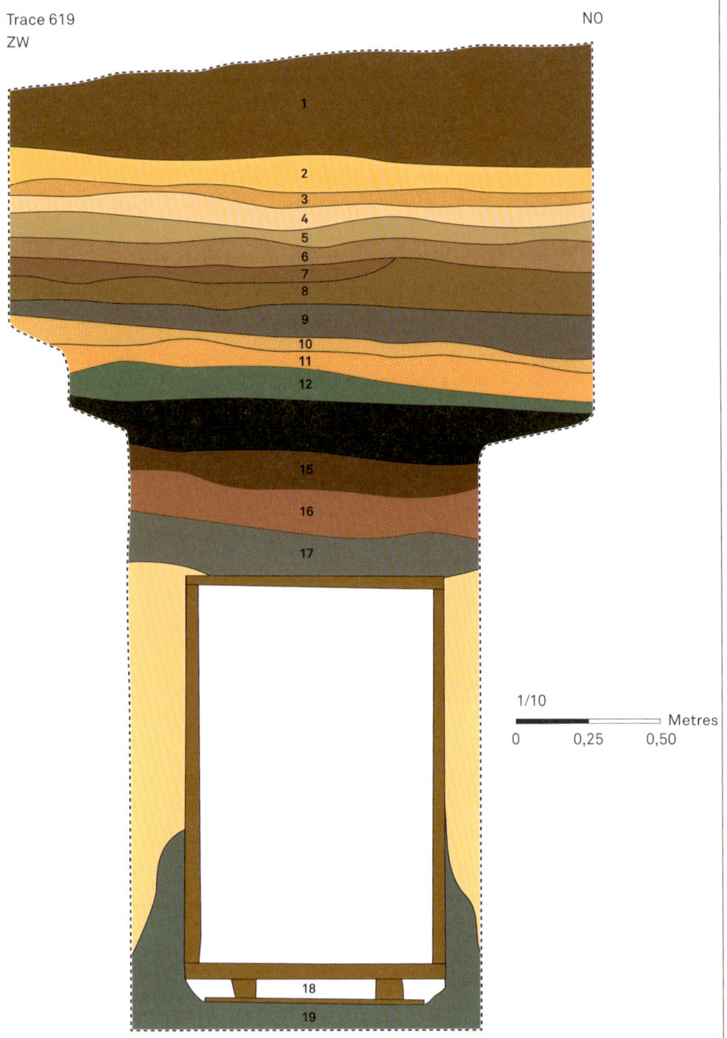

1 Brown sandy loam. The present-day humus layer.
2 Yellow, brown sandy loam with fragments of bricks.
3 Grey, brown sandy loam with yellow spots. Iron concretions.
4 Grey, beige marbled sandy loam. Small layer of rust above and below the layer. Fragments of iron. Possibly left behind by the war.
5 Grey, brown sandy loam. Iron concretions. Fragments of brick and bioturbation.
6 Cf. 5. Browner.
7 Cf. 6. Homogeneous and without fragments of bricks.
9 Brown, grey sandy loam. Fragments of bricks. Iron concretions and bioturbation.
10 A yellow, brown compact layer of sandy loam. Iron concretions and bioturbation.
11 Green, grey sandy loam. Grey spots. Bioturbation, bricks.
12 Cf. 11. Without grey spots.
13 Black layer. A lot of bricks and stone.
14 Layer of white and red bricks.
15 Hard brown layer of sandy loam. Stones.
16 Red layer with large pieces of brick and stone.
17 Greyish-blue layer. Fragments of brick.
18 Hollow space under the tunnel floor planks.
19 Stamped topsoil.

13

The turn of the century proved to be a turning point, with professional archaeologists in France and Britain becoming interested in the archaeological heritage of the First World War[8]. In France, the excavation of the Grimsby Chums, a mass grave of British soldiers, got the ball rolling. The 20 corpses were found arm in arm, a hitherto unknown form of burial. The investigation also showed that their fellow soldiers had made great efforts to give them as decent a funeral as possible. All that remained of some soldiers were a few fragments of bone, which their comrades had carefully laid out in the form of a human body[9].

Thanks to close contacts between archaeologists, the idea gained ground that there was potential in such research in Flanders too. The date 6 February 2002 marked an official starting point, the day when Minister Paul Van Grembergen, responsible for the region's heritage, entrusted the IAP with the task of archaeologically evaluating the former battlefields. There were plans to extend the A19 motorway, and the authorities wanted to check whether any remains of the war were still left along its planned route. During a so-called 'ground prospecting', a mechanical excavator made trial ditches in the ground to document any remains. The results were astounding, an eye-opener not just for the professional archaeologists who had little experience in this field, but also for the policymakers. The proposed motorway project was stopped.

Immediately, potential new lines of research opened up, while at the same time urgent ethical, practical and deontological questions arose. What was the added value of archaeological research? In what state were the remains and what influence did they have on today's land usage? How great was the chance of finding the remains of fallen soldiers? What would be done with them? How dangerous was unexploded ordnance for archaeologists? How were we going to combine the many maps, aerial photos and written sources with the archaeological fieldwork? The whole research field needed to be professionalised. This was the period when First World War archaeology found its way into the academic world[10].

FIG. 13
Cross-section of a German tunnel found near Messines.

FIG. 14
Aerial photo of the excavation of the gas pipeline cutting across the former front.

UPSCALING

Starting in 2006, the Flemish archaeological world underwent a fundamental change. Through a stricter interpretation of European archaeological legislation – the Treaty of Malta concluded in 1992 – and the deregulation of the archaeological sector, archaeological research in Flanders, and in the Westhoek in particular, experienced exponential growth. In addition to purely scientific research into a specific problem, the focus is now on preventive archaeology: surveys preceding large-scale earthworks, such as expansions of industrial sites, the laying of new cables and the construction of gas pipelines. Since then, the principle of 'he who destroys shall pay' applies: the site developer has to finance the archaeological survey. Various shared local government archaeological departments have been set up, together with the first commercial archaeological consultancies. This increase has resulted in more systematic research and in many cases in larger-scale projects.

One of the first projects undertaken by a commercial company was an excavation in 2009 in the Kriekstraat in Reningelst, where, among other things, the remains of buried horses were found (see Chapter 5)[11]. Later projects included the excavation of a British hospital near Lijssenthoek (see Chapter 4), the first project focused on military structures in the hinterland[12]. Another investigation in 2012 involved excavating more than 3 hectares of a British logistics centre and a trench network. That same year, an excavation in Messines studied the evolution of the German trench network between 1915 and 1917, unearthing a number of shallow tunnels (FIG. 13 & 18)[13].

The expansion of an industrial park in Pilkem (2013-2014) was an incentive to probe the British back line, with the archaeologists documenting well-developed and previously unresearched dugouts incorporated into the trench parapets[14]. Even more impressive in its scale is the recent survey conducted prior to the laying of a 79-kilometre gas pipeline between Alveringem and Maldegem, with a 7.5-kilometre branch between Houthulst and Langemark-Poelkapelle (FIG. 14). This project gained the attention of the Flemish public via the successful TV series *Ten oorlog special: Onder Vlaamse velden* (At War Special: Beneath Flanders Fields). The three-part documentary also won international fame due to the identification of the fallen New Zealand officer Henry Walker (see Chapter 3).

The idea that the war heritage deserved protection has since gained ground. Together with Wallonia and France, the Flemish government has worked hard to get the former Western Front recognised as a UNESCO World Heritage Site (see Chapter 11). Although the findings of the archaeological and historical research were promising and evidence showed enormous potential, the landscape and the archaeological heritage were omitted when the application for recognition was finally submitted in 2016.

14

[8] Desfossés 1998, Saunders 2002
[9] Desfossés, Jacques et al. 2008
[10] Stichelbaut 2004, Wackenier 2004, Verdegem 2007
[11] Bouckaert, Bracke et al. 2009
[12] Bracke 2011, Bracke 2013
[13] Verdegem, Billemont et al. 2013
[14] Verdegem & Van Goidsenhove 2016

FROM BATTLEFIELD ARCHAEOLOGY TO CONFLICT ARCHAEOLOGY

War archaeology is often referred to as 'battlefield archaeology', though the term is too restrictive. It springs from the Anglo-Saxon research tradition and its studies of older battlefields, which involved analysing artefacts discovered by metal detectors, such as arrowheads, musket balls and cannonballs. But interest in the archaeological remains of the First World War is no longer limited to the battlefield. The military camps, practice trenches, airfields and other military infrastructure elements in the hinterland are also included, as is daily life in the trenches, shelters and dugouts. Originally confined to the Westhoek, the research has steadily been extended to the rest of the country, the military hinterland and the occupied areas (see Chapter 7). A term that better suits the extent of the research is 'conflict archaeology'.

More than ever, the research has become interdisciplinary, characterised by a wide variety of available sources. Regimental histories, diaries, photographs, trench maps and even film fragments set the historical context. An analysis of historical aerial photos reveals what the ground holds in store for the archaeologists (see Chapter 8). Digital terrain models reveal what is still left on the surface (see Chapter 9), while geophysical soil sensors are now used by archaeologists to 'see' what is still in the soil without having to dig it up (see Chapter 10). Archaeological fieldwork – the traditional excavation – can thus zoom in much more accurately on the artefacts remaining in the ground, constantly unearthing hitherto unknown structures. In short, the discipline has become characterised by great interaction between archaeology, geography, military history and cultural anthropology. Conflict archaeology is increasingly becoming a science that combines the knowledge and techniques of these different disciplines to gain an insight into what happened in the past.

INDUSTRIAL SCALE AND MASS PRODUCTION

One specific characteristic of WW1 was its industrial scale, with consequences for the heritage and the material remains, which are discovered on an equally large scale. Finds such as military equipment, bayonets, guns and ammunition usually stem from mass production. As these are well documented in the literature, further finds of such material offer little addi-

C

Close to the Belgian front line along the Yser, archaeologists excavated a Belgian support trench in 2016. They were very surprised to come across a British battery of Livens projectors. These were simple steel tubes used as mortars to launch large containers filled with flammable or toxic chemicals at the enemy. A unique find, indicating for the first time that gas attacks also took place on the Belgian front. Special British units belonging to the Royal Engineers were temporarily posted to the Belgian army for this purpose. Between 26 October and 11 November 1917, more than 1,000 projectors filled with phosgene projectiles were buried and fired towards the Minoterie, the flours mills in Diksmuide where the Germans had dug in. After this action, the intention was to use them elsewhere, but apparently something went wrong. Several projectors exploded on the spot, while others sank deep into the swampy soil.

FIG. 15
A find of four Lee Enfield rifles in almost perfect condition just under the street surface in Wieltje.

FIG. 16
Excavation of a shell crater used as a fortified position, with German hand grenades, bullets and the remains of a rifle on the ground. A plank and cartwheel ensured a sure footing in the mud.

tional information. But this makes it all the more important to recognise those artefacts whose study will lead to new insights, possibly testifying to improvisation, reuse and/or a soldier's individual creativity and experience – that is, artefacts with an individual tale to tell within the war's industrial context.

Millions of shells were fired during the war. The empty casings were often used to produce trench art (see Chapter 4). Excavations have revealed letter openers made out of the driving bands of shells, fuses with words carved into them, casings turned into ashtrays, and even a crucifix cut from a shell. Of more importance than actually finding an artefact is its association with the place where it is found – referred to by archaeologists as the 'context'.

15

16

[15] Desfossés, Jacques et al. 2007, de Meyer 2009

TIME IS RUNNING OUT

The heavy and sticky clay soil of Ypres, cursed during the war by British tunnel-diggers who nicknamed it 'blue bastard clay', is today a boon for archaeologists. Objects and constructions buried in it, and consequently not exposed to daylight, are well conserved. Metal and organic artefacts such as wood, leather and even paper often emerge from the blue clay in a condition that's as good as new (**FIG. 15**). In fact, it's often hard to believe that certain artefacts have been buried for a century.

It is therefore very unfortunate that their excellent condition is threatened by the use of fertilisers and chemical products on fields. The acids in the fertilisers make metals degrade faster, to such an extent that there may be little or nothing left of any metal artefacts in the coming decades. Metal items seem to last longer in pasture, precisely because this is less fertilised. For this reason, we must step up our archaeological efforts.

WHAT A SHELL CRATER CAN TELL US

The need to study trenches, dugouts, hospital sites and military camps is obvious. But opinions differ with regard to other structures. For instance, a shell crater, one of the most common traces found, is a pit created by the explosion of an artillery shell. Millions of craters turned the region into a lunar landscape. Some were used later in the war for specific purposes, suddenly making them very interesting for today's archaeologists. Groups of craters were sometimes linked together, turning them into strongholds in the crater-filled landscape. Individual craters were sometimes used as machine gun emplacements or as temporary shelters during an offensive (**FIG. 16**). Or they may have been used as a rubbish dump, also after the war had ended, to get rid of waste. Some became burial sites for soldiers, either as the result of a direct hit or when used by comrades to bury the dead (see Chapter 3)[15].

It is a misconception that heavy shelling eradicated trenches, shelters or even any 'older' archaeological heritage. Once the top layer of soil has been mechanically removed, the shell craters can be clearly seen. While at first glance photos suggest almost complete destruction, excavations may reveal instantly that only a small part of the soil was disturbed by the craters, even in areas subject to the heaviest fighting and shelling

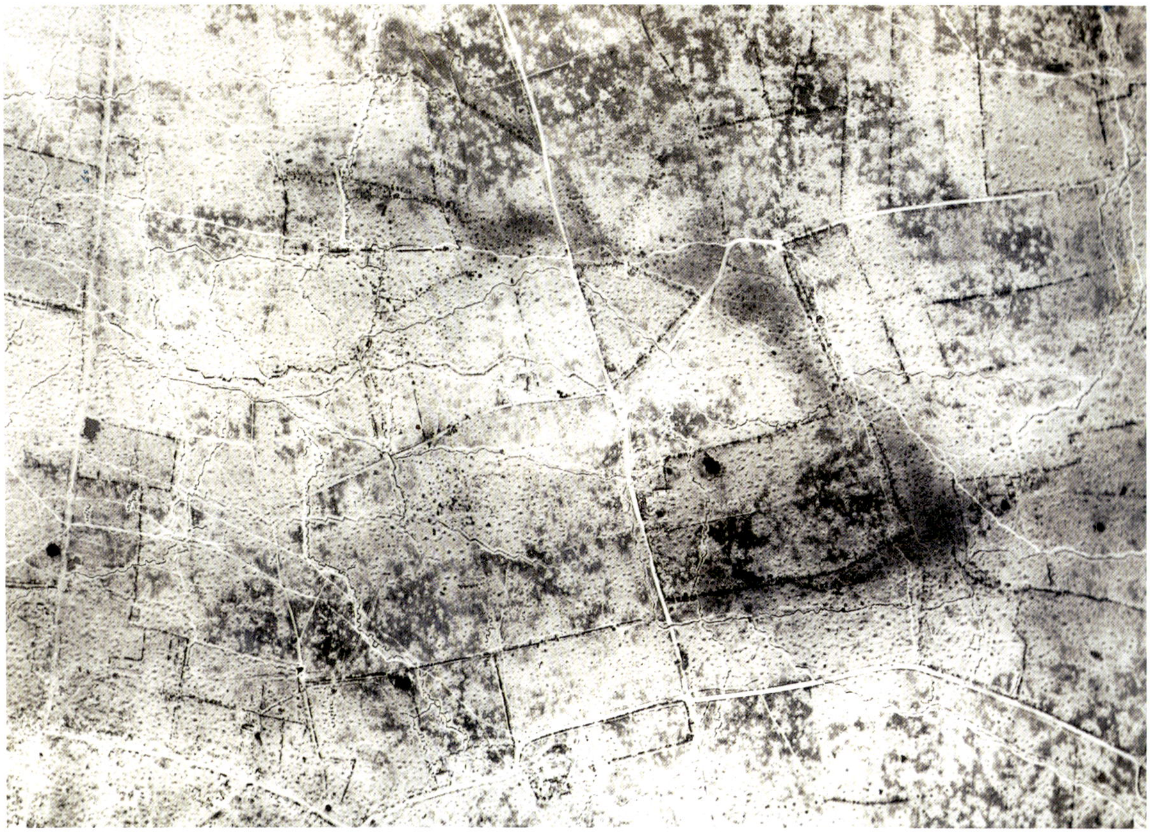

17A

17B

Metres

0 100 200 300 400

FIG. 17
British aerial photo dated 18 June 1917, showing hundreds of craters, together with a present-day aerial photo to the north of Messines.

FIG. 18
Excavation of a German tunnel near Messines.

FIG. 19 (pp. 26-27)
Extremely detailed French aerial photo of the destroyed German trenches and bunkers along the Ypres-Yser Canal, August 1917.

[16] Saunders 2007

(FIG. 17 & 19). This was possibly because the shells repeatedly threw up earth already churned up by earlier explosions. Only the largest-calibre artillery shells caused deep damage to the subsoil.

THE INSIGHTS GAINED FROM WASTE

According to leading British archaeologist Nicholas Saunders, war archaeology teaches us "what it means to be human in an industrially-waged trench war"[16]. War archaeology reconstructs daily life through the study of archaeological sites and artefacts. By far the largest proportion of the finds is waste: pottery shards, animal bones, building waste, and so on. An analysis of these artefacts can tell us a lot about daily life and the experiences of the soldiers in the trenches, military camps and hospitals behind the front (see Chapter 4). Or about the relationship between humans and animals under war conditions (see Chapter 5). In other words, the investigation of waste dumps often reveals new insights.

18

A TIME CAPSULE

A unique situation offering us many more details is when a context gets frozen in time, untouched by hand until accidentally unearthed by archaeologists. These time capsules are in most cases the result of accidents or disasters: a ship goes down and stays on the bottom, a house collapses and its entire contents get covered by rubble for centuries, a volcano erupts, covering a whole city in ash. Because nothing was intentionally saved or thrown away, we gain a very realistic view of daily life. In First World War archaeology, such finds are commonplace: exploding shells caused trenches to be buried, shelters were cut off from the outside world, underground tunnels and dugouts were abandoned and remained untouched for a hundred years. These are snapshots, time capsules left behind by the war. One splendid example is a German tunnel found in Messines, close to the front line (FIG. 13 & 18). When the tunnel was abandoned, it had not yet been finished. The tools were still standing against the wall, possibly after the last shift, ready to resume work. A few metres away, in an already completed storage space in the tunnel, crates full of cartridges and machine gun belts were stacked. For some unknown reason – possibly the explosion of mines on 7 June 1917? – work stopped and the tools stayed where they were, just like the thousands of rifle and machine gun bullets, only to be unearthed by archaeologists 95 years later.

NOT ALWAYS BY THE BOOK

Although each army provided its men with instruction manuals on how to construct trenches, archaeological research shows that soldiers very often improvised, especially in the first months of trench warfare. At the onset of winter, ways of combating the rising groundwater had to be found. Building materials were unavailable, as supplies produced on an industrial scale had not yet started arriving. The soldiers had to make do with what was available nearby, as seen in Noordschote, where an originally French back line has been excavated. The trench network ended up in the middle of no-mans-land in April 1915 during the Second Battle of Ypres, remaining virtually untouched. Its excavation yielded excellent results, showing how building methods were improvised. Almost everything that could be found in the neighbourhood was used. To keep their feet as dry

as possible, the soldiers covered the bottom of the trench with doors, shutters and bricks from nearby farms. Even more striking was the use of a harrow and a dog cart as a floor covering in the underground shelters. Near to Langemark and Bikschote, a deep layer of straw was found at the bottom of the German trenches dating back to the autumn of 1914. After all, the barns of the fleeing farmers were filled to the brim with winter supplies (**FIG. 20**).

The first trenches took account of a strategic battlefield 'layout' and had to be first and foremost easy to defend. Often, it is obvious that the soldiers did not expect to stay in the trenches for long. The ones dating back to the start of the war were often dug too deep. While offering protection against bullets, they quickly became full of groundwater and rainwater (see Chapter 2).

THE REMAINS OF SOLDIERS MISSING IN ACTION

Excavations in the Westhoek have unearthed many human remains. Conscientious archaeology is needed to recover these in a responsible manner. The field registration and association of the corpse with the artefacts surrounding it can, in certain cases, lead to identification, especially when thorough historical research is conducted. In this way, the fates of a small number of missing soldiers on the endless list of names have been clarified (**FIG. 21**)[17].

War remains are considered part of our archaeological heritage because the distance in time is now sufficiently wide. Yet the period can at times seem very close, making us adopt a different attitude towards the fallen. Human remains from the First World War are approached differently to bones from, for example, medieval burials[18]. This is partly because of the possibility of identifying them, allowing us to trace their family members – albeit from future generations. The recovery of 25 British and Australian soldiers in a mass grave in Fromelles in France was described by the physical anthropologists as a 'humanitarian project' rather than an archaeological excavation[19]. Giving a missing soldier his name back is not just a technical matter but also a form of

[17] Robertshaw & Kenyon 2008
[18] Scully & Woodward 2012
[19] Corfield 2010
[20] His Majesty's Stationery Office 1922

20

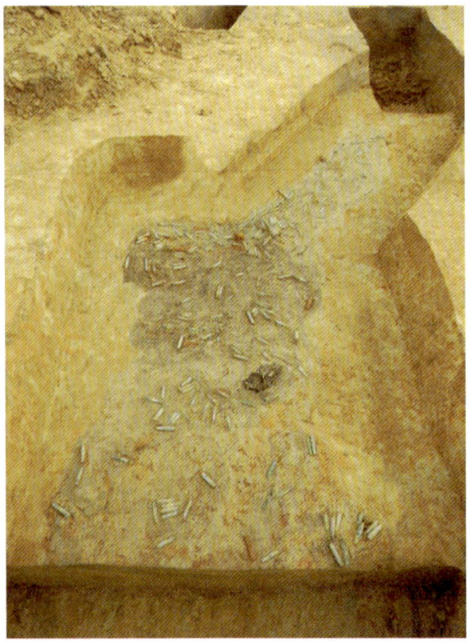

21

22

FIG. 20
The bottom of a German trench near Langemark, where the German advance ground to a halt in 1914. The bottom is littered with bullet shells and straw. The bullet shells have markings showing they were manufactured in October/November 1914.

FIG. 21
The Menin Gate in Ypres inscribed with the names of 54,900 British soldiers killed in the war without a known grave or still missing.

FIG. 22
The burial of 8 French soldiers in the French military cemetery Saint-Charles De Potyze in Ypres. The soldiers had been found by archaeologists working in Diksmuide.

respect and tribute. This is something special for field archaeologists – and something for which they are not prepared in their training (**FIG. 22**).

Naturally, interesting archaeological research questions can also be answered. There are few things more specific to human culture than the way we deal with the dead. Archaeological research provides insights into how this was dealt with on the battlefield and behind the lines. It also shows how the confrontation with death evolved as soldiers became increasingly used to the horror over the course of the war. The study of bone remains allows us to gain a picture of living conditions, disease, causes of death and injuries caused by the industrialised conduct of the war. Numerous excavations reveal a wide variety of ways in which bodies were buried, how burial places came into being and why so many missing soldiers are still found each year (see Chapter 3).

THE DANGER OF THE 'IRON HARVEST'

One constant danger specific to the excavations in the Westhoek is that of unexploded ordnance. The British alone fired some 190 million artillery shells and more than 12 million mortar shells in France and Belgium during the war[20]. In 1917 the shelling in Flanders reached an unprecedented scale, with 7.8 million projectiles being fired in just a few months to 'soften up' the enemy in preparation for the Battles of Messines and Ypres in 1917.

Belgium's Unexploded Ordnance Department (*Dienst voor Opruiming en Vernietiging van Ontploffingstuigen*, or DOVO for short) estimates that between 10 and 30 percent of all shells fired did not explode due to technical defects or to the soft, saturated and muddy soil in which they fell. Moreover, some of the ordnance is filled with poisonous chemicals or gas, which, over time, can start leaking. Every year local farmers plough up just a fraction of this 'iron harvest'. Due to the nature of their work, field archaeologists are the first to come into contact with buried projectiles. This leads to an ambiguous situation. On the one hand, the projectiles are part of the material heritage of the conflict, providing information that, for example, helps to date structures. But on the other hand, they are still life-threatening.

Increasingly, the safety of archaeologists is guaranteed by special ordnance disposal companies tasked with freeing the land from unexploded ordnance and also with assisting archaeologists in the field (**FIG. 23**). The ordnance uncovered is then collected in bulk by DOVO, which renders it harmless in its disposal plant in Houthulst (**FIG. 24**).

CONCLUSION

In recent decades, a lot of ground-breaking work has been done by amateur archaeologists, archaeological consultancies, government archaeologists, academics and museums. The archaeological traces and structures from the First World War have since been accorded their rightful place within the whole archaeological heritage. "What is the benefit of First World War Archaeology?" is a question no longer asked.

The 140-plus archaeological projects conducted over the last few years (**FIG. 25**) have only scratched the surface of what is still in the ground. All too often, the focus is on the front-line areas. Sites in the hinterland are often found by accident, in connection with excavations associated with other periods.

The challenge now is how to deal with the quantity of new data resulting from this research. Out of the mass of archaeological remains, those artefacts have to be selected that are unknown or only known in a different context, which fill in knowledge gaps or somehow stand out from the rest.

The battlefield archaeology of the 1980s and 1990s has evolved into an interdisciplinary conflict archaeology. New research methods and techniques are increasingly being used (see Chapters 9 and 10) to chart and interpret the remaining heritage. The results constitute the basis for protecting or safeguarding valuable zones. In this way, the discipline has evolved from a site-specific affair to an interdisciplinary and integrated study aimed at a more landscape-based approach to WW1 archaeology.

The multiplicity of excavations has revealed a mass of structures and finds to be studied, acting as a stimulus for more scientific research in studying the finds. Examples include the analyses of organic finds providing more information about dietary patterns, the study of animal remains or the origin of building materials found in the trenches.

Each of the following chapters deal with a particular aspect of this recent archaeological research.

The first chapters look at the results of archaeological excavations and the analysis of the finds and structures. Subjects addressed

23

24

FIG. 23
An archaeological excavation near Langemark was temporarily stopped after an unexploded British shell was found.

FIG. 24
The 'iron harvest' at the DOVO base in Poelkapelle, ready to be destroyed.

FIG. 25
Overview of the archaeological work in the Westhoek.

FIG. 26 (pp. 32-33)
German aerial photo showing Ypres in flames in April/May 1915.

include trench building, the underground war and the excavation of human remains and temporary burial places, with attention paid to the rich discoveries in the camps and hospitals close to the front line, but also to sites far behind the front. The results of scientific research on the skeletal remains of animals show that it was not only people who were affected by the war. Extensive research into food leftovers and waste pits allows us to gain insights into the nutrition of soldiers at the front.

Subsequent chapters look at new research methods, such as archaeological aerial photography and the use of innovative and high-tech research methods. These boost our understanding of the landscape as the last witness of the war, revealing a rich archaeological landscape much more extensive than previously thought. The final chapter looks to the future, taking a deeper look at our appreciation and protection of the war landscape and the relics contained therein.

25

Front line 1915-1917 **Archaeological excavations**

Kilometres
0 10 20

1 Bikschote 1914-1915: in the footsteps of the 23rd German Reserve Corps

Bert Heyvaert
Thomas Apers
Simon Verdegem
Maarten Bracke

27

13 m
3 m

French front line 22/11/1914
German front line 22/11/1914
Excavation zone

1 Grave containing 7 soldiers
2 Grave containing 5 soldiers
3 French foxholes
4 French foxholes
5 Trench resulting from joining foxholes together
6 Bunkers and the German front line

FIG. 27
Overview map.

[1] Gierath 1928
[2] Holste 1934

A straight line dissecting the front. This is probably the best way to describe one of the largest archaeological excavations in Flanders. A few years ago, a natural gas company submitted plans to construct a pipeline from Dunkirk to Maldegem. The consequences for the archaeological heritage were immediately clear. Halfway between Ypres and Diksmuide, the pipeline would cut right across the First World War front. A team of archaeologists was therefore given the chance to survey the pipeline's route in depth between Vleteren and Houthulst. For the 30-plus archaeologists working on the project, this was a journey back in time, a hundred years back into an unknown past.

Around the middle of its route, the gas pipeline followed a special route for somewhat more than 1.5 kilometres (**FIG. 27**). Between Diksmuidestraat in Langemark-Poelkapelle and the Ypres-Yser Canal, it followed exactly the same route taken by the German 23rd Reserve Corps in November 1914. Almost 35,000 Prussian soldiers from the 45th and 46th Reserve Division fought against their French opponents to gain a few metres, from the village of Bikschote to the canal. Another battle awaited them in 1915, this time in the trenches along the canal. Enemy artillery and water, wind and cold were equally fearsome enemies.

The excavation results revealed many specific details about the fate of these young men. Laying these results alongside the German regimental histories, we can take an in-depth look at the fortunes of the Prussian reservists during their fifteen-month stay north of Ypres.

KILLED ALONGSIDE THE LOBEEK

At the end of October 1914, German soldiers belonging to the 23rd Reserve Corps marched into the Westhoek between Ypres and Diksmuide. Everyone felt that something was about to happen. After advancing through Belgium without any major incidents, the time had come to confront the Allied troops. Along a line from Ypres via the Yser Canal to Diksmuide, they had reached the last defensible ground before the coast. The battles that awaited the Prussian reservists were part of what would go down in history as the First Battle of Ypres, lasting from 19 October to 22 November 1914.

The German troops were on the northern part of the battlefield, looking out not on to the towers of medieval Ypres, but on to the region's typically flat landscape. Before moving into the battlefield, several officers took the time to survey the site from a church tower: "In a landscape criss-crossed by drainage channels, the 2- to 3-metre-high banks of the Yser Canal rose up in front of us, a fortification canal filled with water. Here and there, trees relieved the monotony of the landscape, lining the straight roads, the lonely farms and the overfull channels bordering the extensive pastures."[1]

The 15-kilometre-long Ypres-Yser Canal linked the Yser with Ypres. Back in the seventeenth century, the famous French military architect Vauban had already recognised the canal's strategic importance and had had it reinforced as a line of defence. In 1914, the canal had not yet lost its importance. The advancing German troops approached the canal along what is now the Provincieweg, a road ending at the bridge over the canal at Steenstrate. But first, the village of Bikschote loomed up, overlooking the important crossing point from a small height. At the beginning of November 1914, the Germans began their attack on Bikschote, up until then still firmly in French hands. Leading a group of German infantrymen, Lieutenant Walter Holste soon discovered that the Flemish landscape, despite its flat nature, was full of obstacles: "This is set to be an outright woodland war here in this cluttered Flemish country with its innumerable fences, hedges, meadows and drainage channels! Through fences and enclosures, through fields and meadows, over and through the channels up to our bellies in water, we are advancing in jumps and bounds, in search of an invisible enemy."[2]

Near Bikschote, the archaeologists entered the terrain described by the young officer. Before long, the battlefield revealed its first secrets. Just north of the stream, the Lobeek, a shoe sole was found in the excavated soil. It quickly became clear this was no run-of-the-mill find: a large, rectangular pit could be discerned in the yellow, sticky earth. It soon turned out that these were human remains. The archaeologists carefully removed the earth from the grave, revealing the corpses of seven soldiers (**FIG. 28**). Six had been buried side by side, while the seventh had been laid alongside their feet. On their shoulders the embroidered regiment number 209 was found on the remains of the grey combat uniforms (**FIG. 29A**). Two of them were wearing the German *Pickelhaube*, the spiked helmet featuring the Prussian eagle. Scraps of clothing were uncovered, including buttons adorned with a Prussian crown and textile fragments with typical red piping. Personal artefacts were also found on

28

the corpses. One of them had a glass bottle in his breast pocket, once filled with schnapps (FIG. 29B). Another had a pencil in his pocket, and remains of paper, possibly a small German Bible (FIG. 30). After an in-depth investigation, it became obvious what had happened: these men had not died in a field hospital but had been killed in action. A study of the bones revealed that, apart from one forty-year-old, all were in their early twenties. The cause of death was also clear, given the presence of French bullets and lead shrapnel from artillery shells. Perhaps the bodies were gathered up from the battlefield by their comrades a few days after death and hastily buried together, not far from where they had been killed.

On the other side of the Provincieweg, the team made its next macabre discovery. Not even 250 metres to the west of the grave next to the Lobeek, they again came across human bones. Again, these were Germans, five soldiers buried on top of one another in a narrow pit in the same attack zone – probably other soldiers from the same regiment.

The regimental history of the 209th reserve infantry regiment (RIR 209) adds clarity to what happened. Most of the men in the regiment came from near the Hanseatic town of Stralsund. On 30 October, two of the regiment's battalions, some 750 soldiers, were ordered to advance to the western edge of Bikschote and the 't Smiske junction. Possibly, the Lobeek was a difficult obstacle to overcome. Even before they reached the stream, they came under French fire. The German soldiers who did manage to get over were no problem for the strong French defences. By evening, all the survivors were back in their original position. Losses were very high, with both battalions losing up to 60 percent of their men[3]. The 209th regiment ceased to be a fighting unit at the Lobeek.

We do not know exactly who the soldiers were. From historical sources and the regiment's list of those missing, some 20 soldiers are possible candidates, but unfortunately no conclusive identification was possible. The unearthed remains were given a military burial in 2014 at the German military cemetery in Langemark.

[3] Schulz et al. 1930

THE FIRST WINTER OF THE WAR

Ten days later, the German troops were more successful. On 10 November 1914, the 45th and 46th reserve divisions mounted their last major attack against the French troops, pushing them so far back that they now stood literally with their backs to the canal. The German front line now ran along Oostpoeselstraat and the Lobeek to just past the centre of Bikschote, and the 215th reserve infantry regiment (RIR 215) had the most ground to cover. After about 200 metres, the soldiers reached the 't Smiske junction, which was heavily defended by the French. After house-to-house fighting in the hamlet, they crossed to the other side of the Provincieweg. Out in the open fields, they advanced about 800 metres across a slope, under heavy fire from the French machine gunners. They ultimately managed to capture almost the entire

29A

29B

30

FIG. 28
German grave containing the bodies of 7 soldiers belonging to RIR 209.

FIG. 29
Uniform fragments bearing the regiment number 209 and a bottle of spirits.

FIG. 30
Fragments of paper, possibly from a German Bible.

area north of Steenstrate. Towards evening, they reached Westpoeselstraat[4], where they dug in, ready to storm the bridgehead. The French, however, turned out to be a tough nut, maintaining a firm hold over Steenstrate. Moreover, the effects of the flooding of the Yser plain were now clearly felt just north of Steenstrate, where the canal separated the two sides. At least for the moment, the German advance ground to a halt. The *Kanalstellung* was there to stay[5].

Arriving at Westpoeselstraat, the gas pipeline reached the place where RIR 215 dug in for the winter on 10 November 1914. From studying aerial photos taken during the war, the archaeologists knew that the Germans had dug well-constructed trenches on both sides of the road, and traces of them were soon found when they started excavations. Just to the east of the road, an erratically dug trench was revealed. The soil was literally strewn with German bullets (**FIG. 31**). The production dates, clearly stamped on the base of each bullet, made it clear that nearly all of them had been made in the first months of the war or in preceding years. This was the place where RIR 215 had dug in on the evening of 10 November 1914. Hundreds of empty shells bear witness to the various French attacks in the following days and weeks. As it was not immediately obvious exactly where the enemy was positioned, the Germans were very nervous. The alarm was frequently raised, with the soldiers opening fire across no-man's-land[6].

At the end of the year, the Germans began licking their wounds. Of the 3,000 men originally belonging to the 215th reserve infantry regiment at the beginning of the war, just 1,000 were left. Six hundred had been killed, and almost 1,500 were wounded or missing[7]. Fragments from the diary of the French 89th territorial infantry division, the division defending the lines on the other side of no-man's-land, paint a grim picture of a no-man's-land littered with hundreds of dead bodies (**FIG. 33**). It soon became evident that any thought of breaking through before winter was out of the question. The provisionally dug trench was completely unsuitable for the winter months and had to be adapted. A second trench was constructed with a slightly different orientation, dug in a more systematic pattern with gun emplacements and semi-circular traverses. But the soldiers were still of the opinion that their stay there would be

FIG. 31
Hundreds of German bullet shells were found scattered on the floor of the German trench.

FIG. 32
Chair and table in a German trench.

[4] Willers & Mangels 1926
[5] Willers & Mangels 1926
[6] Willers & Mangels 1926
[7] Willers & Mangels 1926

31

32

only temporary. Paying no attention to drainage, they probably sank deeper and deeper into the mud. Various finds indicate that the occupiers did their best in the circumstances to make their conditions at least bearable. From the farms immediately behind the front, the soldiers had, for instance, taken a small chair and a box top to serve as a table (**FIG. 32**). A century later, these were still standing in a corner of the trench, admittedly in a somewhat decayed condition. Near the furniture, the archaeologists also found a complete German overcoat. A tarpaulin perhaps served as a roof. Such a context appeals to the imagination and brings the war to life: a soldier sheltering from the war, sitting at a table or playing cards with his comrades.

CONSOLIDATION FOLLOWING A GAS ATTACK

In the spring of 1915, the line east of Westpoeselstraat was consolidated. The *Pioniere*, the German engineering corps, came to help the infantrymen, with a new trench appearing on the archaeological site a few metres behind the one dug in the winter of 1914-15. The new one was shallower, thereby avoiding the possibility of groundwater seeping in. The new position was made up of 8-metre stretches of trench in a zigzag, linked by short, semi-circular traverses. The floor was covered by long planks. At regular intervals, small wooden shelters (1.8 x 2 metres) were built, offering at least a minimum of comfort and protection against the rain and wind. The archaeologists found four of them (**FIG. 34**). The 4-square metre shelters (the size of a small two-man tent) were home to four or five soldiers.

Writing in 1926, Hans Willers, at that time a young lieutenant, remembered well life in the trench in spring 1915. "The trenches got better and better. (...) Planks or wooden platforms have been laid everywhere, and the floor now has a drainage channel. The walls have been reinforced with wattle and equipped with loopholes.

FIG. 33

A fragment from the diary of the French 89th territorial infantry division describes the front sector on 18 December 1914.

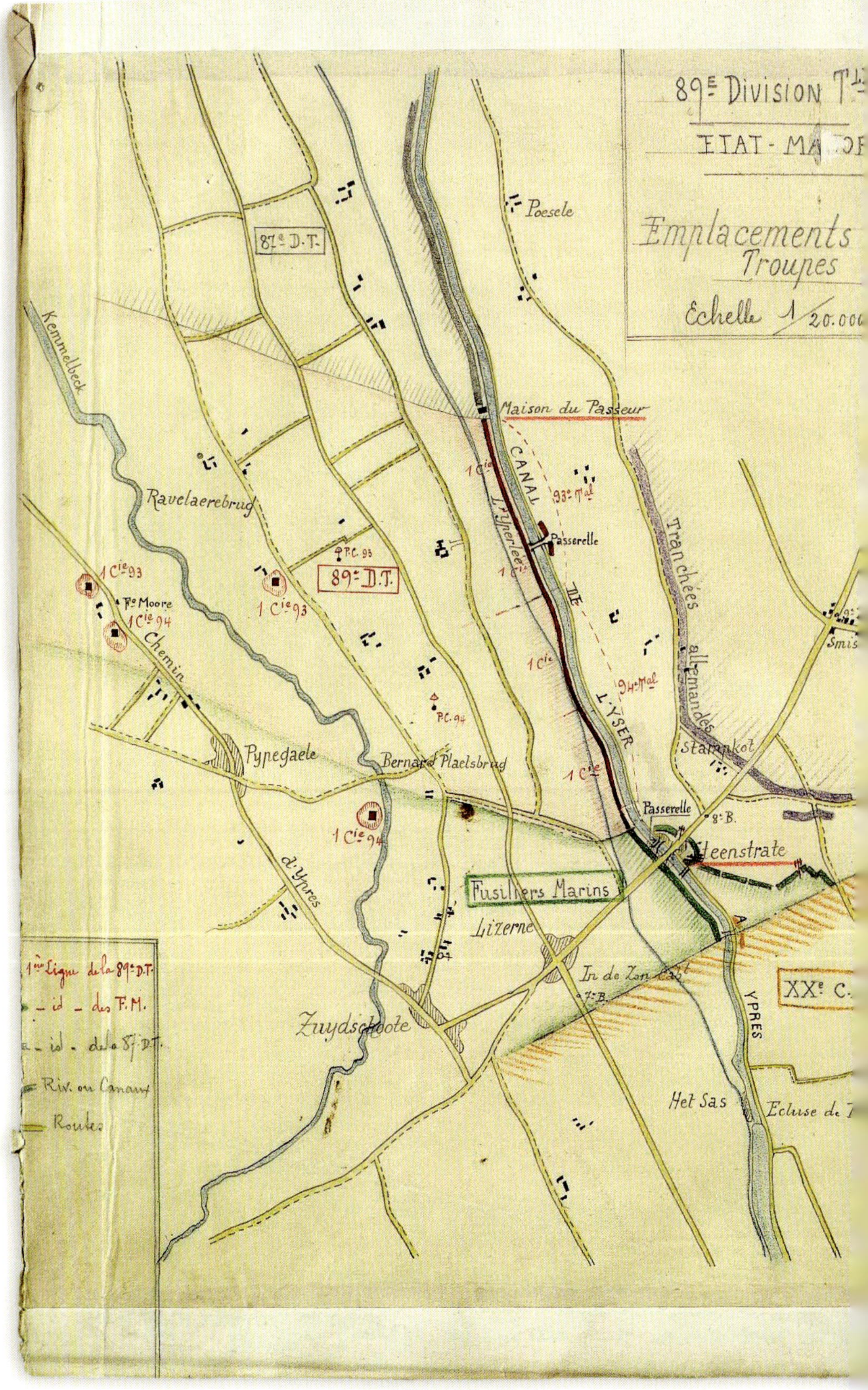

p. n° 50

Q. G. Oostvleteren, 18 Décembre 1914

Conformément à l'ordre donné la 89e D. T. appuie par son artie et par des feux d'infie l'offensive des marins dans la direction de Bixschoote où plusieurs tranchées allemandes sont enlevées et ont fait une centaine de prisonniers.

Le séjour dans les tranchées devient de plus en plus pénible, tant en raison des difficultés d'accès (on enfonce dans la boue jusqu'au genou pour y aller) que de l'eau qui augmente dans l'intérieur des tranchées. De plus en avant des parapets, il y a environ 1500 cadavres non enterrés qui pourissent depuis un mois. Certains parapets seraient même constitués avec des cadavres recouverts de terre.

Au moment de la relève un homme a été blessé par une balle de mitrailleuse. Il parait que les allemands profitant des couverts qui se trouvents sur leur rive amènent des mitrailleuses qu'ils dissimulent à une quarantaine de mètres du ~~cadavres~~ canal et ouvrent le feu au moment présumé de la relève.

Pièce n° 51

Q. G. Oostvleteren, 19 Décembre 1914

Rien à signaler

Pièce n° 52

Q. G. Oostvleteren, 20 Décembre 1914

Continuation des travaux. Améliorations des travaux au moyen de fascines et de ponts jetés sur les fossés et canaux. Amélioration des tranchées au moyen de clayonages.

Deux aéroplanes allemands ont évolué au-dessus d'Oostvleteren ~~ayant~~ et ont jeté des bombes sans résultat.

Pièce n° 53

Q. G. Oostvleteren 21 Décembre 1914

Rien à signaler.

Pièce n° 54

Q. G. Oostvleteren, 22 Décembre 1914

Rien à signaler

Pièce n° 55

Q. G. Oostvleteren, 23 Décembre 1914

Conformément à l'ordre annexé, la 178e Brigade a glissé plus au Sud et a occupé aujourd'hui les tranchées comprises entre la "maison du Passeur" et les premières maisons de Steenstraat.

Our rifles lie there, with the bullets next to them. (...) There are sufficient well-built shelters roofed with thick beams and half a metre of earth on top. The walls are made of wooden planks, which is why we call them 'our wooden huts'. The floor as well is made of wood, again helping to keep out the damp. (...) But the bad air in the shelters is quite a problem. The small charcoal fires make the air unbearable, leaving their marks in our eyes and on our faces. The trenches are subdivided into sections, and each unit decides for itself who takes which watch. Each section has its own shelter, in which four to five soldiers sit. Two men stay outside, keeping watch over no-man's-land, maintaining order in the trench, cleaning their rifles and eating."[8]

Though primitive, the shelters were the centre of a soldier's life during his three-day stint in the foremost trench. When not keeping watch, he would spend his time sleeping, eating or playing cards in the small shelter. In the remains of the shelters, the archaeologists also found many artefacts of daily life: cutlery, water bottles, preserves, even a perfume bottle – which does not even seem that amazing after reading Lieutenant Willers' account. Remains of a mustard pot indicate attempts to add some taste to the rations.

On 22 April 1915, the German Fourth Army restarted its operations, with the Second Battle of Ypres heralding a new phase of the war. Whether work on the new German position had already begun is not quite clear. Following the infamous gas attack between Steenstrate and Langemark on 22 April 1915, the trenches on the archaeological site would seem to have served as a staging post for the offensive. Steenstrate fell to the Germans, and for the first time the German soldiers saw the other side of the canal. But fierce opposition drove them back to their starting position. The German army command now woke up to the fact that the front in Flanders was stalemated. In their planning for new offensives, they now turned their eyes to France, while the German troops in the Westhoek resolutely opted to defend their positions.

This also necessitated changes to the positions along Westpoeselstraat. The corps command redeployed its troops at the front, so that the junction next to our later archaeological site became the new border between two army divisions. The trenches were now taken over by Prussian soldiers belonging to the 212th reserve infantry regiment (RIR 212), mainly from Hamburg and Bremen. They formed the left flank of the 45th reserve division. The garrison was not exactly in an enviable situation. Where their position crossed the road, there was a big gap in the German defences. They had no link to their neighbours from the 46th reserve division on the left, making them extremely vulnerable to a French-Belgian attack. And prospects did not improve. At the end of May 1915, they were given an extremely dangerous task. On the other side of the road, some 40 metres from the safety of their parapet, they had to build a 450-metre-long trench in the muddy no-man's-land littered with craters, to connect up with the trench network of their neighbours to the left.

The archaeologists were able to investigate in detail the work some 40 metres away from the position. Digging down half a metre, they came across the trench floor, indicating that it had been built almost completely above ground. The regimental history of RIR 212 reports that about 100 sandbags were needed for 1 metre of trench[9]. To construct just the short stretch of trench investigated by the archaeologists, the soldiers had to fill 4,000 sandbags in 1915, all done at night. They frequently had to drop tools and duck down to avoid the red glow of Belgian flares that regularly illuminated the front. Any movement in no-man's-land immediately came under fire, often destroying the work completed so far.

As work progressed, the soldiers probably gradually decamped to the other side of Westpoeselstraat in the second half of 1915. Their new accommodation must initially have looked very much the same, with small wooden shelters worked into the sides of the trench at regular intervals. Despite the drier weather, circumstances were not much better. In July 1915, the regiment command received an urgent report from Lieutenant Thurmeyer, the leader of the 3rd company, requesting fresh straw for his shelters, as his men were plagued with lice. Chlorine lime was supplied as a disinfectant[10]. Meanwhile, the front line along the canal was being increasingly bombarded by French and Belgian heavy trench mortars.

CONCRETE

To avoid the destruction of their *Kanalstellung*, the Germans started replacing the wooden shelters along the front line with concrete bunkers at the end of August 1915. The work was again carried out by the *Pioniere*, supported by a battalion from the 209th reserve infantry

FIG. 34
Remains of a concrete bunker with abandoned ammunition boxes on the wooden floor.

[8] Willers & Mangels 1926
[9] Makoben 1933
[10] Makoben 1933
[11] Makoben 1933:183, Vancoillie & Blieck 2016

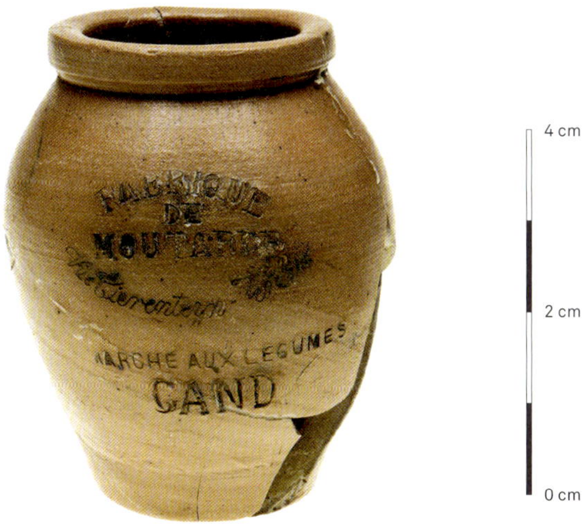

It doesn't always have to be bullets, shells or rifles. On the wooden floor of a German shelter, the archaeologists found several earthenware shards. After completing what seemed like a jigsaw puzzle, the text on the pot can now be read: 'Tierenteyn-Verlent'. Above are the French words *Fabrique de Moutarde* and beneath them *Marché aux Legumes* in *Gand*. This is the well-known Tierenteyn mustard from the Groentenmarkt (vegetable market) in Ghent. We can't trace exactly how a mustard pot managed to find its way to the front, but what is clear is that at least one German soldier must have purchased a pot of local mustard when passing through Ghent.

D

division. After their ranks had been replenished following the disastrous October of 1914, they were given responsibility for the front sector along Westpoeselstraat in September 1915. Via a narrow-gauge railway, supplies were brought as close to the front as possible: rails, corrugated iron sheets, strip steel, timber, roofing, nails, sacks of cement and thousands of prefabricated concrete bricks[11]. Pouring reinforced concrete in the foremost trenches was much too conspicuous. Though structures made with concrete bricks were not as strong, building them was less conspicuous and quite fast.

The excavations along Westpoeselstraat provided a good picture of the results of their work. After fighting their way through an obstinate layer of concrete remains, the archaeologists came across three bunkers on a 30-metre stretch of the front (**FIG. 35A**). The Germans clearly wanted to offer each front-line soldier the relative safety of a concrete roof over his head. The shelters measured 4.2 x 3.5 metres, with walls almost 1 metre thick. This left about 4.5 square metres of wooden floorspace for the occupants. Though not much bigger, the new accommodation was a lot safer. Safety was further improved by a thick layer of sandbags along the sides and on top of the bunkers. The soldiers were, however, regularly exposed to enemy fire when

34

35A

35B

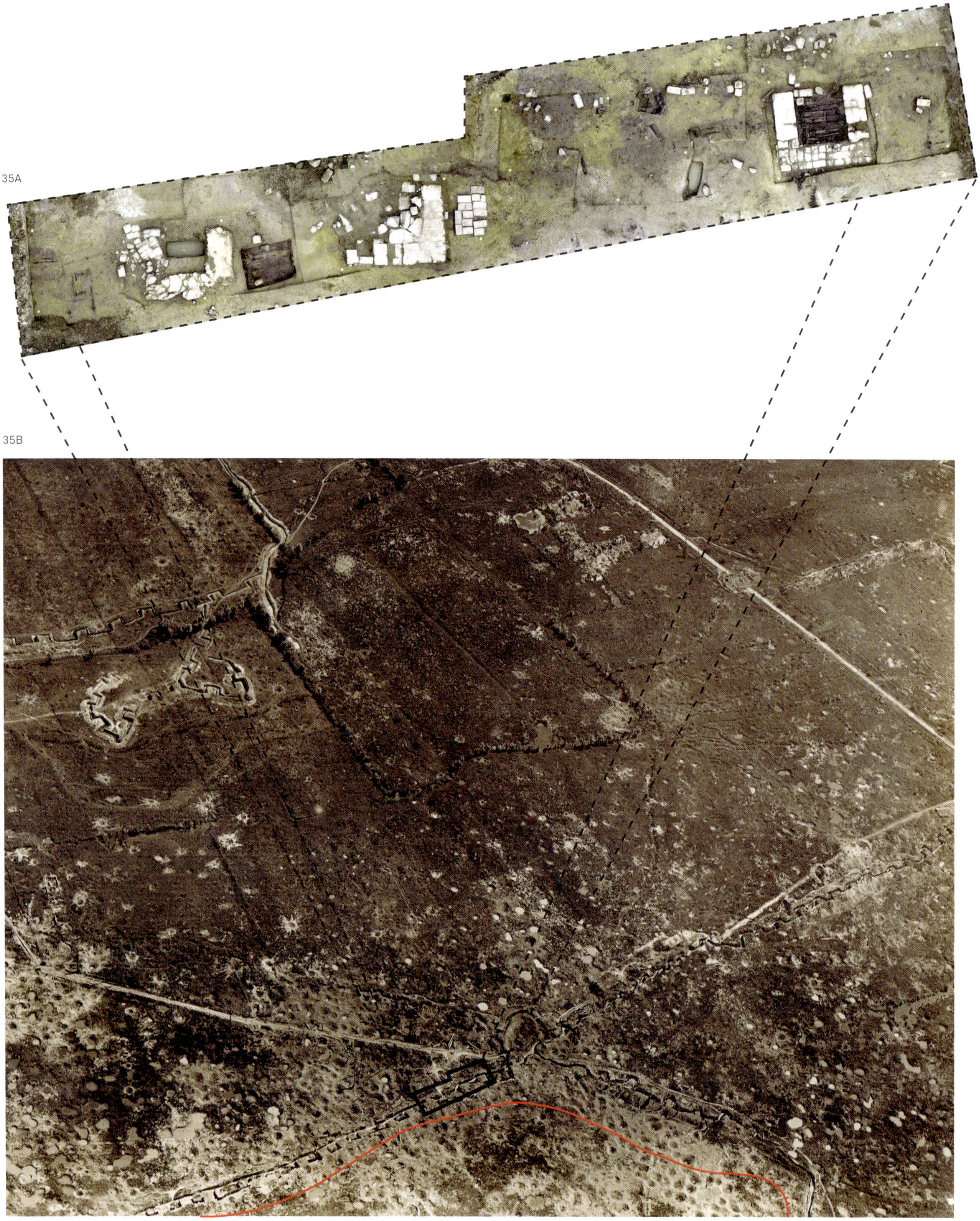

German front line

[12] Schulz et al. 1930

repairing items in front of their trenches. In one of the uncovered bunkers, three crates of ammunition for a Maxim machine gun were found. The wooden or concrete platforms next to the bunkers were possibly used as emplacements for trench mortars or machine guns trained on no-man's-land. Here and there, steel sniper shields were also found. A good sniper posted along Westpoeselstraat would have been able to shoot at Belgian and French troops up to 500 metres away. At the end of 1915, the soldiers of the 209th regiment could view their work with satisfaction. According to the regimental reports, concrete bunkers were available nearly everywhere, providing protection against the murderous French-Belgian trench mortars. In one of the bunkers, the archaeologists came across a concrete brick marked with the German Iron Cross and the years 1915 and 1916, a souvenir carefully inscribed by the manufacturer. This also indicates that, even in the third year of the war, the troops were still busy working on fortifying their positions.

DEPARTURE FROM THE *KANALSTELLUNG*

In early 1916, the regiments of the 23rd reserve corps said goodbye to their positions along the canal, which had become their second home. Just a few days before they left, however, they were subjected to one of the heaviest bombardments of their whole time by the canal. In the detailed regimental history, several young officers noted their impressions of the battlefield. Their description matches the numerous traces of shelling found by the archaeologists: "The position was littered with craters. Deep holes gaped in our parapets. In many places, the concrete walls of our bunkers were exposed. Our old wooden shelters were torn to pieces. Between the ruins lay broken mortars and all sorts of building material. Craters 6 metres wide and 3 metres deep surrounded us. One ammunition depot had exploded, and another had been completely destroyed. The big question was: why? And then we picked up our shovels and started digging again."[12]

Fig. 35A & 35B
Aerial photo taken in 1917 and drone photos of the same spot showing three excavated bunkers.

FIG. 36
A Belgian trench mortar on the other side of the canal.

36

2 A cross-section of the northern Ypres Salient

Simon Verdegem
Marc Dewilde
Bert Heyvaert
Franky Wyffels

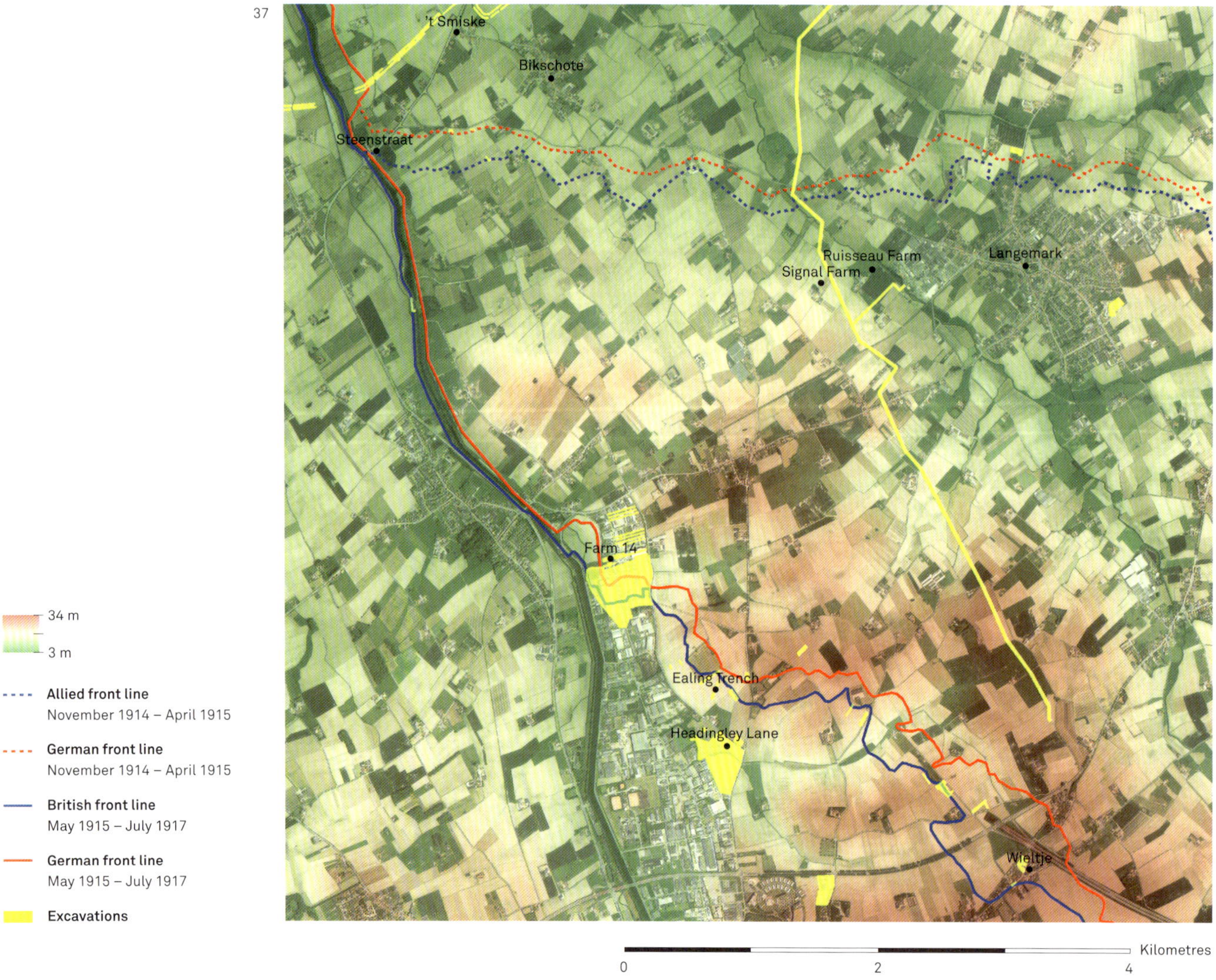

37

FIG. 37
Map of the excavations.

FIG. 38
Sketch drawn by the French 87th Territorial Division showing the fighting around Bikschote on 23 October 1914.

After the First Battle of Ypres, waged between 19 October and 22 November 1914, troop mobility ground to a standstill, with both sides resorting to trench warfare. The landscape became criss-crossed with trenches and other military infrastructure elements. Never before had the Westhoek been transformed within such a short period and on such a large scale. During the post-WW1 period of reconstruction, the vast war-torn landscape was cleared up, with many of the above-ground traces of the war wiped away. But much remained under the ground. Systematic archaeological research is now unearthing a lot of this material.

Over the last fifteen years, archaeologists have excavated trenches in dozens of places in the Ypres Salient (**FIG. 37**)[1]. The results of the excavations are gathered here for the first time. They represent an archaeological cross-section of the Ypres Salient, painting a poignant picture of life in the trenches and the evolution of trench warfare.

[1] Dewilde 2006, Dewilde et al. 2007, Van Hollebeke et al. 2014
[2] Nel 1922

STALEMATE IN THE TRENCHES

Some two months after the war began, the fighting approached the Westhoek. In a final attempt to reach the Channel ports in France, the German army threw everything into the battle. In the north, it tried to cross the Yser between Nieuwpoort and Diksmuide. In the south, Ypres was the last obstacle in the way of reaching Dunkirk and Calais. The Battle of the Yser and the First Battle of Ypres commenced on 18 and 19 October 1914, respectively. The Allied forces – the French and British in Ypres, the Belgians further north – were forced to yield ground inch by inch. But the Germans did not achieve the desired breakthrough.

In its early phase, the war was still mobile. Battle theatres and positions changed so fast that detailed historical maps or sketches found in regimental diaries or field reports are rare. And yet the battle left its marks. Along the route of a gas pipeline, archaeologists working at the 't Smiske junction, to the north of Bikschote, discovered field graves and foxholes in a place where, according to historical sources, heavy fighting had occurred at the end of October 1914 (**FIG. 38**)[2]. The exact location of the subtle traces in the ground tells us a lot about the course of the battle. These were the earliest defences constructed during the war in the Westhoek. A shallow foxhole provided a minimum of protection to a soldier lying in it, much less than the

38 •••••• 't Smiske

deeper trenches that were constructed when the two sides dug in at the end of the mobile phase of the war. The discovery of these French foxholes bears witness to the attempts to hastily construct a final line of defence (see also Chapter 1). After pounding the tough Allied defences for weeks, the Germans stopped their attacks, especially as winter was setting in. On 22 November 1914, the offensive ground to a halt, and both sides started to dig in where the fighting had stopped. This often involved little more than interconnecting the hundreds of shallow foxholes. At the end of the day, two lines of trenches emerged, with a no-man's-land in between.

IMPROVISATION IN THE EARLY LINES

The archaeological excavations show that the trench occupants tried to make their accommodation as comfortable as possible once the offensive had ended. Winter brought rain, and the straw that had initially helped keep the bottom of the trenches relatively dry was no longer sufficient. Greater adaptations were called for. The armies were not, however, prepared for large-scale trench warfare. There was not sufficient building material for hundreds of kilometres of trenches, and the troops were forced to improvise. They took what they needed from the abandoned farms and ruins surrounding their positions. Anything of use was taken in an attempt to keep the often-desolate trenches more or less dry and navigable.

In Noordschote, Zuidschote, Bikschote and Langemark, trenches have been found with straw (FIG. 40), rubble (FIG. 42), or roof tiles, planks and doors serving as flooring. To keep their feet dry, the soldiers placed doors on bricks. Or they took bricks from the ruins of nearby farms and used them to construct a floor. Literally everything could be used to make the stay in the trenches as comfortable as possible. Despite all these 'home comforts', the trenches remained unmistakably part of the battlefield. Traces of the battle were to

FIG. 39
A typical early British or French trench in the Ypres Salient. The Germans captured this position during the Second Battle of Ypres.

FIG. 40
Straw and ammunition remains on the bottom of an early German trench in Bikschote.

FIG. 41
A German *Pickelhaube*, left behind in an early trench near Kitchener's Wood.

FIG. 42
Brick flooring in a German front-line trench. Fragments of wood were found in what had been the walls.

39

40

41

42

be seen everywhere. The ground was strewn with large numbers of bullets and shells under and between the straw, with the occasional abandoned weapon or piece of equipment here and there.

TRACES OF THE SECOND BATTLE OF YPRES

In spring 1915, the German army command attempted to overcome the stalemate in the trenches in the Ypres Salient using a new weapon: chlorine gas. On 22 April 1915, German troops in the trenches between Steenstraat and Langemark opened the valves of almost 6,000 gas cylinders, beginning the Second Battle of Ypres. It was to last until 25 May.

The effect was greater than the Germans had dared hope for. Practically without opposition, they were able to advance 3.5 kilometres, creating a 6-kilometre gap in the Allied lines. Due to the chaos and panic caused by the gas, it took some time before the French divisions were able to regroup. British reinforcements were hastily sent to the north. The road to the Channel ports lay open to the Germans. But instead of making the most of the opportunity, they stopped and began to dig in. Dusk, their limited belief in the success of the gas and their shortage of reserves are possible explanations for the decision.

In the following hours and days, thousands of French and above all British, Indian and Canadian soldiers counter-attacked, in many cases without either knowledge of the ground or preparation. The human toll was very high, whereas the results were hardly worth mentioning. Nowhere were the Allied forces able to push back the Germans.

Although such attacks and counter-attacks had only a limited impact, the archaeological survey managed to reveal several results. On the German side, trenches were found here and there where the troops had spent their first evening. They are little more than a few shallow slit ditches without gangways, but with small, semi-circular crossings. The finds consist of hastily discarded material, such as a typical German *Pickelhaube* (**FIG. 41**), testifying to heavy fighting and chaos.

ALL QUIET ON THE WESTERN FRONT

After weeks of attacks and counter-attacks, which cost the lives of 40,000 soldiers, the German offensive ground to a halt on 25 May 1915. Both sides again dug in, constructing a network

FIG. 43

Troops from the Saxony 245th Reserve Infantry Regiment in rudimentary trenches at the start of the war.

FIG. 44
German troops in trenches along the Ypres Salient.

of trenches in a large arch around Ypres (the Ypres Salient), some 3 kilometres away from the town. A period of stable trench warfare ensued, without any major offensives. This phase was to last until 31 July 1917, the day the Third Battle of Ypres broke out.

After the Second Battle, both sides seem to have understood that a breakthrough was practically impossible. Attempts were still being made on other fronts, but in Flanders the armies were content to just defend their lines. They did this by systematically extending, adapting and improving their trench networks, turning them into virtually impregnable strongholds. A trench network was no longer just a system for warding off an attack. It also became a 'home' for the soldiers, a first-aid station, a headquarters for the officers and a storage facility for ammunition. To make all this possible, a lot more construction material than was available locally was needed. This led to the industrial production of building materials for trench construction, using techniques which were constantly developed and adapted.

On the ground too there was always work to be done. Due to shelling, waterlogging and other problems, the trenches were in constant need of repairs and other building work. The troops carrying out this massive building and entrenchment programme had to follow specific instructions and regulations (**FIG. 46**). Archaeological research shows a more nuanced picture, however. It seems that they were often unable to follow the instructions to the letter, as conditions on the ground did not allow this. In most cases, they found a solution through innovative use of the available materials.

The shape of the trenches also gradually became standardised. Whereas in the first year of the war, they were often built haphazardly, after the Second Battle they were dug in accordance to standard patterns. The most common were the front-line trenches with their regular gun emplacements. Backward-facing traverses offered protection against the effects of exploding shells. The pattern of such a trench closely resembled the battlements of a castle. At right angles to the front line, communication trenches were used to bring soldiers up to the front in safety. These were shaped mainly in zigzags or waves. Standardisation was to be found on both side of the no-man's-land, though the German and British armies each had their own approach.

45

46

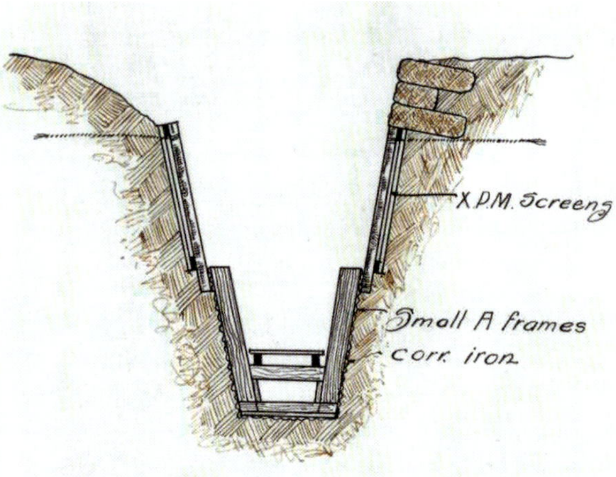

This trench warfare phase had a much greater impact on the ground than all previous phases. Aerial photography (**FIG. 45**) has revealed thousands of kilometres of trenches in Belgium (see Chapter 8) and remains from this phase are what archaeologists find most often.

DUCKBOARDS AND FLOOR PLANKS

A trench first had to be reinforced with floor and wall coverings. But even a small shower of rain could leave the bottom waterlogged, with the soldiers often having to wade through water. In response to this problem, the British introduced 'duckboards': sections of planks made of prefabricated joists upon which short crossing slats were nailed. Excavations show us that the duckboards in the early trenches were usually placed on the ground as closely together as possible to form a continuous pathway. It would seem that this system was no good at all. There are many examples of several duckboards being placed on top of each other to keep the floor out of the water. A temporary remedy, but again inadequate.

The solution was the A-frame (an inverted A), found in most excavations of British trenches. But even this system had its defects, and the search for solutions continued, as excavations of a British line showed. In the Ealing Trench to the

47

FIG. 45
British aerial photo taken on 1 May 1917 showing the extent of the trench networks in the northern Ypres Salient. The dark stretch in the middle is no-man's-land. The road from Ypres to Zonnebeke runs straight across the photo.

FIG. 46
Cross-section of a British trench with A-frames and corrugated iron walling.

FIG. 47
Excavation of a British trench in Wieltje, with duckboards resting on A-frames.

48

FIG. 48
Robust German trench with floor planks and wooden walling.

FIG. 49
German trench with A-frames under construction.

FIG. 50
Excavation of a German trench with floor planks and wattle walling.

FIG. 51
German trench with cast-iron guttering near Iron Cross in Langemark.

49

north of the Kleine Poezelstraat, the cross-beams were made higher by adding one or more beams. In Wieltje too, the A-frames seem to have been inadequate (**FIG. 47**). There, the old method of using several layers of duckboards was applied. What was new, however, was that they were not just placed on top of each other. Additional cross-beams between the duckboards ensured that they were even further out of the water.

The method used by the Germans was far less advanced. In most cases, they simply laid long planks on the ground (**FIG. 48 & 50**), sometimes with a primitive drainage channel underneath or just next to them. As the German trenches were on somewhat higher ground, they did not have so many problems with water. In cases where it was a problem, the Germans opted for more permanent drainage channels. These were often semi-circular cast-iron gutters which ran under the plank floor (**FIG. 51**).

The German constructions and building methods appear to have been less standardised, with more varieties used. The excavations show that wooden drainage gutters, brick rubble to make the soil less swampy and even street gutters were used. As in the British trenches, they sometimes constructed raised floors. Archaeological excavations and a few historical photos (**FIG. 49**) show that they also copied the British A-frames.

CHICKEN WIRE, CORRUGATED IRON SHEETS AND WATTLE AS WALL COVERINGS

The walls of the trenches also needed to be reinforced. The sandy-clay soil found in the Westhoek was not sufficiently stable, and there was a constant threat of trench walls collapsing. The threat was compounded by water and shelling.

The walls are difficult to study via archaeological fieldwork, as most of them have disappeared. In many cases in Belgium, only the lowest part of the trenches was buried. Nearly everywhere, the high groundwater level made it impossible to dig deep without having one's feet permanently in water. In most cases, the bottom of a trench was barely 0.5 to 1 metre below ground level. On both sides of a trench, at least 1 metre of raised earth and sandbags protruded above the surface. All above-ground traces were destroyed after the war, leaving only the deepest sections of the trenches for the archaeologists.

50

51

The British reinforced their trench walls first with chicken wire, held in place by iron stakes or horizontal planks (**FIG. 52**). Upon the introduction of the A-frames, they also started using sheets of corrugated iron (**FIG. 53**).

German trenches were for the most part on strategic high points, meaning that they didn't have to be so deep. Moreover, they were more often equipped with wide and high above-ground parapets. As a result, archaeological excavations are unable to provide much information about wall-reinforcing methods. Still, in a few places deep trenches have been found with traces of wall coverings. It would seem that wattle walls were the German standard. However, twigs rot quickly and in many cases all that remains are soil discolourations requiring meticulous excavation to even be able to see them.

SHELTERS

The trenches were equipped with shelters and dugouts to protect the soldiers against the weather and enemy fire. Shelters were mainly built into the front parapet, and sometimes into the rear one as well. In most cases, they were above ground to prevent water from the trench entering. For this reason, archaeologists mainly discover only the floors, made of duckboards (British) or wooden planks (British and German). Occasionally, the base of a wall can also be found. During an excavation along the Kleine Poezelstraat in Ypres, 23 shelters were investigated. They turned out to be rectangular shelters dug under the parapet of the British Headingley Lane trench (**FIG. 54**). They had a duckboard floor, sandbag walls supported by wooden poles and cross slats, and a roof of corrugated iron sheets topped by sandbags and earth.

German shelters close to Farm 14 in Boezinge turned out to be constructed differently. They were made of wood, had a plank floor, load-bearing poles, walls covered with planking and a wooden roof (**FIG. 55**). The construction was surrounded on three sides by a small wall of piled-up concrete blocks. The latter were prefabricated behind the front and transported to the trenches by mules or narrow-gauge railways.

E

F

Twelve metres below the hamlet of Wieltje, the 177th Tunnelling Company established a network of tunnels and underground chambers. Finished in 1917, the shelter was aptly named 'Hades Dugout' after the Greek god of the underworld. Although the dugout offered protection from enemy fire, descent into the tunnels was no fun, according to one eye-witness report: "Enter that hole in this trench and mind the step. There are about thirty of them, covered with wet slime continually drip, drip, dripping. There is a repulsive-looking rope on one side. At first you decline to touch it; but a warning slip and you seize it readily in spite of the dirt. (...) At last you reach the bottom and stand in a black and slimy river, slowly moving onwards and disappearing in the darkness, revealed by some weary-looking electric lights. Is it the Styx, you ask? Anyway, it stinks. Is it the portal of the infernal regions?" Colonel W.J.K. Kettie, 175th Brigade, Royal Field Artillery[3].

[3] Steel & Hart 2014

Metres 0 25 50 100

FIG. 52
British trench with walling made of corrugated iron sheets and chicken wire.

FIG. 53
British trench excavated near Cross Roads Farm in Ypres, with corrugated iron walling.

FIG. 54
Diagram of a shelter in the Headingley Lane trench.

FIG. 55
German shelter near Farm 14 in Boezinge, consisting of a wooden platform surrounded by a wall of stacked-up concrete blocks.

52

53

55

54

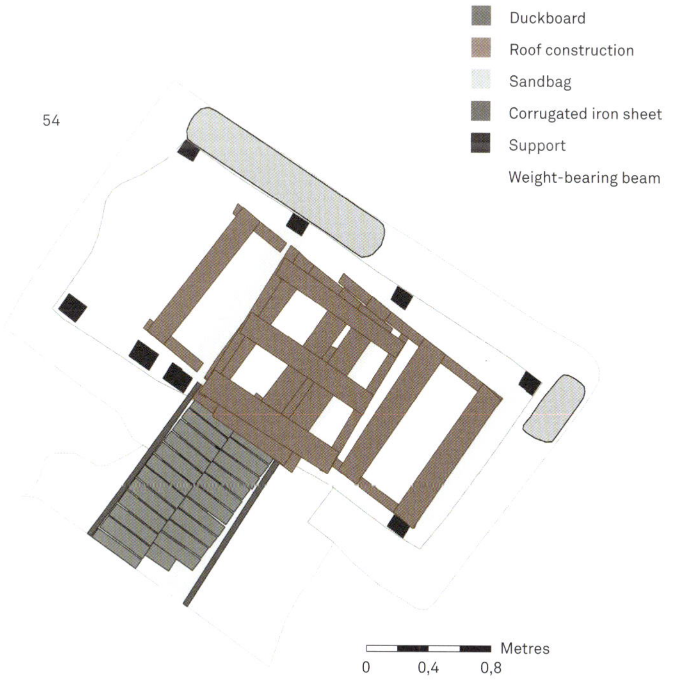

FIGHTING AGAINST THE WATER IN THE WIELTJE OUTPOST

In summer 2013, archaeologists investigated part of a British position in the hamlet of Wieltje (**FIG. 56**)[4]. The trenches found there seemed hardly to have changed since 1915. This was the first time archaeologists were able to study in detail a British position dating back to the first months after the Second Battle of Ypres.

In the end phase of the battle, in May 1915, British troops took shelter behind the hamlet. At the site later investigated by the archaeologists, a handful of soldiers had stayed behind to build an advanced outpost at night-time and under German fire. The outpost was linked to the main position by a long, narrow connecting trench. The British made strategic use of everything the terrain had to offer, including ruins and drainage channels. However, the strategic know-how of the British officers in 1915 contrasted sharply with their know-how in the field of trench construction, and the soldiers ended up having to improvise on the ground.

The duckboards in Wieltje were cobbled together out of all kinds of readily available timber, held in place with round poles that had to serve as walls at the same time. There was no drainage system. Apart from a shallow gutter to catch rainwater, the trenches were unprotected against the never-ending rain. The position was built in the dry summer of 1915, at a time when the groundwater level was low. The soldiers made the same mistake as at the beginning of the war: they dug out their trenches below the level that groundwater would rise to after the summer, overlooking the fact that the clay subsoil 1.5 metres deep would become almost completely saturated with water in the wettest months. They even dug part of the position below groundwater level.

FIG. 56
The Wieltje outpost in October 1915, just 200 metres away from the heavily fortified German front line.

FIG. 57
British waders found lying on the duckboards in Wieltje.

FIG. 58
Duckboards on the bottom of a trench in Wieltje. Behind them is the wooden floor of a small shelter.

[4] Apers & Heyvaert 2013

56

57

58

On 3 November 1915 the commander of the 2nd battalion of Sherwood Foresters described the situation in Wieltje as follows: “After last night’s rain the trenches are worse than any we have yet experienced in our 14 months of trench warfare. They are falling in every few yards and are full of water. The headquarters match the trenches. There is not one watertight dugout. A truly cheerful start to the winter campaign.”

Luckily, the British Empire provided a steady supply of rubber from Africa. This was used to produce trench waders, for which the British soldiers were envied by friend and foe alike (**FIG. 57**). Producing directly for the army, the rubber companies did great business. Though the soldiers in the trenches also had pumps at their disposal, the fact that more trench waders than standard soldiers’ boots were found in Wieltje is testimony to their efficiency. Keeping their feet dry was a top concern for the soldiers. For those who stomped through the mud for days on end in normal wet soldiers’ boots, the dreaded ‘trench foot’ lurked, a painful condition in which the feet first swell and then the tissue gradually dies.

After the misery of the winter, the commanders on the ground no longer considered it worthwhile to maintain the outpost. They abandoned it, building a completely new trench on higher ground, this time with proper drainage (**FIG. 58**). The old outpost quickly fell into disrepair and disappeared for a hundred years underground, together with the silent witnesses of a winter at war in which water was the worst enemy.

G

To keep soldiers’ feet dry in the trenches, the British started using A-frames, wooden constructions in the shape of an inverted A. Wooden planks or duckboards were then laid on the crossbar. The space under the planks was used to drain off water. A-frames with duckboards were found during roadworks in Wieltje, a front-line hamlet in the Ypres Salient. Located just beneath the asphalted road surface, the finds were in a very good condition.

THE DEVASTATING THIRD BATTLE

In summer 1917, Allied troops again took the initiative, planning a major offensive in Ypres in an attempt to break out of the Ypres Salient and fight their way through to Ostend and Zeebrugge, where the Germans had submarine bases. The battle started with a barrage of fire, meant to 'soften up' the enemy and prepare the way for the advancing troops. The effects can be seen everywhere, with the whole area scattered with craters. Excavations show us what effect the bombardment had on the German lines. Many trenches in the attack zone of the Third Battle show signs of damage, and in some cases it is no longer even possible to recognise a trench.

Traces of the offensive are also noticeable in the form of extensions to the British trench network, with new communication trenches ensuring that supplies of fresh troops could make their way to the front line (**FIG. 60**). Archaeological excavations point to a less permanent character, with trenches built without their walls reinforced by A-frames. They served just one goal: to bring troops to the front.

The offensive started on 31 July 1917. During the battle, even more use was made of temporary structures such as foxholes or reinforced shell craters, comparable to what we observed earlier at Bikschote during the First Battle of Ypres. The small sections of trench and the foxholes are very difficult to spot on the terrain amid the tangle of shell craters.

On the ridge near Pilkem, within the attack zone of the British Guards Division near Ypres at the start of the Third Battle, archaeologists

59

FIG. 59
German positions in 1917, devastated by British shellfire.

FIG. 60
British communication trench near the Kleine Poezelstraat in Ypres, dug just before 31 July 1917 to bring troops up to the front line quickly.

FIG. 61
British equipment found in a shell crater near Signal Farm: clips with .303-bullets for a Lee Enfield rifle, buckles and a spoon.

FIG. 62
British gas mask found near Signal Farm.

have excavated two fortified farms. Signal Farm and Ruisseau Farm had been converted into strongholds by the Germans (**FIG. 61 & 62**). Historical sources describe how the Guards were held up there. The archaeologists found foxholes attributable to the battle for the farms. In one pit, a soldier had left part of his equipment behind: a few grenades and associated launcher, ammunition bags full of cartridges, his drinking bottle and his gas mask.

After three months fighting the enemy and the mud, the Third Battle eventually also ended in a stalemate, without the objectives being achieved. The toll – 150,000 soldiers killed – was staggeringly high. In addition, the incessant shelling together with the very wet weather had turned the battlefield into a sea of mud. In most places where the front ground to a halt, there were more shell craters than solid ground. Furthermore, a large part of the existing infrastructure was destroyed, and it was impossible to construct any new trenches in the ooze. Shell craters and the network of bunkers were the only things able to withstand the shelling and still provide cover.

THE ADDED VALUE OF ARCHAEOLOGY

There can be no doubt: archaeology is indispensable for our knowledge about the First World War. Excavations have unearthed traces of what was buried in the ground of the Ypres Salient for a hundred years: the countless shell craters, a massive network of trenches, thousands of shelters and other structures.

Thanks to these material remains, we have gained an insight into the lives of the soldiers, showing how they had to improvise in building the infrastructure and how creative they must have been in their battle against the water. The circumstances on the ground were often quite different from what was laid down in regulations and standards as found in historical sources and in the literature. Archaeology has played a key role in allowing us to find out how the soldiers came to terms with these adversities.

Many of the smaller finds have a tale to tell, in certain cases quite personal, letting us get to know the soldiers as individuals. And although we can only reconstruct just a tiny fraction of their fates, without archaeology their story – no matter how fragmentary – would never make it into the history books.

60

61

62

NADIAN INF.
PRIVATE
WESTON H.V
WESTON W.W
WESTROPE G.
WHITE J.
WHITE W.
WIBBERLEY E.
WILBRAHAM
-TAYLOR H.
WILLIAMS D.E
WILLIAMS W
WINTER W.J.
WOOD W.J
WYLIE R.
YOUNG R.S.
YOUNG T.A.W.
YOUSE B.A.
NADIAN INF.
SAWTELL E.J.
STETHEM H.A.
TAPSELL R.
WALLIS W.
WILLIAMS G.
WILSON T.E.
PRIVATE
ADAMS E.
AITKEN W.
8TH BN. CANADIAN INF.
PRIVATE
CRACKSTON T.
CRAIG C.A.
CRAWFORD W.E.
CROOK H.J.
CURLEY W.
CUTHBERTSON W.
DAVIS W.H.
DE COURCY T.J.
PRIVATE
LAMB J.W.
LANGENBACH G.E.
SERVED AS
LEACH G.E.
LAWRENCE S.R.
LAWSON J.
LEADEN A.E.
LE BEAU O.
LIDDELL G.K.
LINKLATER F.
8TH BN. CANADIAN
PRIVATE
SHERIFFS C.
SIMMS A.
SIMS W.
SKILLICORN D.
SMITH T.
SMITH T.H.
SMITH W.J.A.
SPARLING W.J.
SQUIRES J.
STEPHENS A.
STEVENSON A.C.A.
STOKES R.G.E.
STORY C.R.
SUDDABY G.H.
SWINDELL T.J.
TAYLER H.L.
TAYLOR T.T.
TOPHAM B.M.
TOWNSEND F.B.
TREWELLA F.L.
TRUEMAN J.H.
TUNBRIDGE
ULLYOT E.B.
VANCE S.G.
WALKER L.B.
WAMBOLT B.
WARD A.E.
WARD M.
WARREN J.
WATERHOUSE F.
WHITE T.
WHYTE D.R.
WIFFEN W.J.
WILLIAMS E.
WILSON D.G.
WILSON J.
WILSON J.G.
WINSTONE S.H.
WOOD A.R.E.
WRIGHT W.H.
YASKEVICH P.
10TH BN. CANADIAN INF.
LANCE CORPORAL
ALLAN G.W., D.C.M.
DEIR W.
LAWRENCE A.E.
LITTLE W.J.
MACDONALD N.
MATHESON J.
PEARSON G.W.R.
ROUGHTON C.G.
STEPHENS W.J.McL.
STEVENSON A.
PRIVATE
ADAM C.H.
ALLINGHAM H.C.
ALLINGHAM J.R.E.
ALLISON H.
ANTHONY D.
ARMSTRONG A.P.
ARMSTRONG C.
ARTHURS J.M.
ATWILL S.G.G.
BALD A.T.
BALFOUR W.
BARFORD F.C.
GUTHRIE & WELLS LTD
DECO
CANADIAN INF.
PRIVATE
McGREGOR P.
MACKAY A.E.H.H.
McPHERSON A.
MACVICAR J.
MANGAN J.
MANSFIELD T.
MANSON D.A.R.
MARSHALL H.
MINNS J.A.
MOCKRIDGE W.
MOFFAT R.J.
ROBINS
ROSS G.
ROY R.W.
RUMBOLD
SAMSON W.
SAUNDERS
10TH BN. CANADIAN INF.
PRIVATE
WILLOUGHBY W.
WILLS J.G.
WISDOM F.W.
WONNACOTT F.L.
PRIVATE
WOOD C.P.
WOODS D.
WOOLLEY W.
YUILL L.H.
13TH BN. CANADIAN INF.
CAPTAIN
LEES G.O.
WHITEHEAD L.W.
COY. S.J.T MAJOR
WATSON A.C.
SERJEANT
BROWN D.M.
BYARS H.
CARYER W.E.S.
CASLAKE A.J.
DUNLOP M.B.
IMRIE C.W.
JARRETT E.H.
MacLEOD P.
MILLAR G.
NEIL W.O.
PHILLIPS E.J.
SALMON D.
SCOTT W.G.
TOWNSHEND F.C.
LANCE SERJEANT
BUCHANAN W.E.
REID J.L.
CORPORAL
PRIVATE
BENNETT S.
BEST T.
BETTINSON H.W.
BINGHAM F.
BIRD T.
BLAIN J.
BOLAND G.
BOLT R.S.
BRENNAN A.
BROGDEN F.
BUCHANAN D.M.
BURKE J.
BURRITT E.M.
BURROWS J.
BUSWELL E.S.
BYRNE G.F.
CAHILL J.
CALVERT J.C.
CAMPBELL D.
CARLEY D.J.
CARRUTHERS J.
CHAPMAN R.H.
CHEESMAN W.
CHISHOLM C.
CHRISTIE W.
CLARKE T.W.
CONN G.D.
13TH BN. CANADIAN INF.
PRIVATE
GOODALL J.
GOODWIN A.
GOODWIN J.E.
14TH BN. CANADIAN INF.

14TH BN CANADIAN INF.
15TH BN. CANADIAN INF.
16TH BN. CANADIAN INF.
18TH BN. CANADIAN INF.
19TH BN. CANADIAN INF.
20TH BN. CANADIAN INF.
21ST BN. CANADIAN INF.
22ND BN. CANADIAN INF.
24TH BN. CANADIAN INF.
ANTONY
d'YPRES
230728-6

3 Missing in action

Simon Verdegem
Marc Dewilde
Maarten Bracke
Franky Wyffels
Jan Decorte
Birger Stichelbaut

64

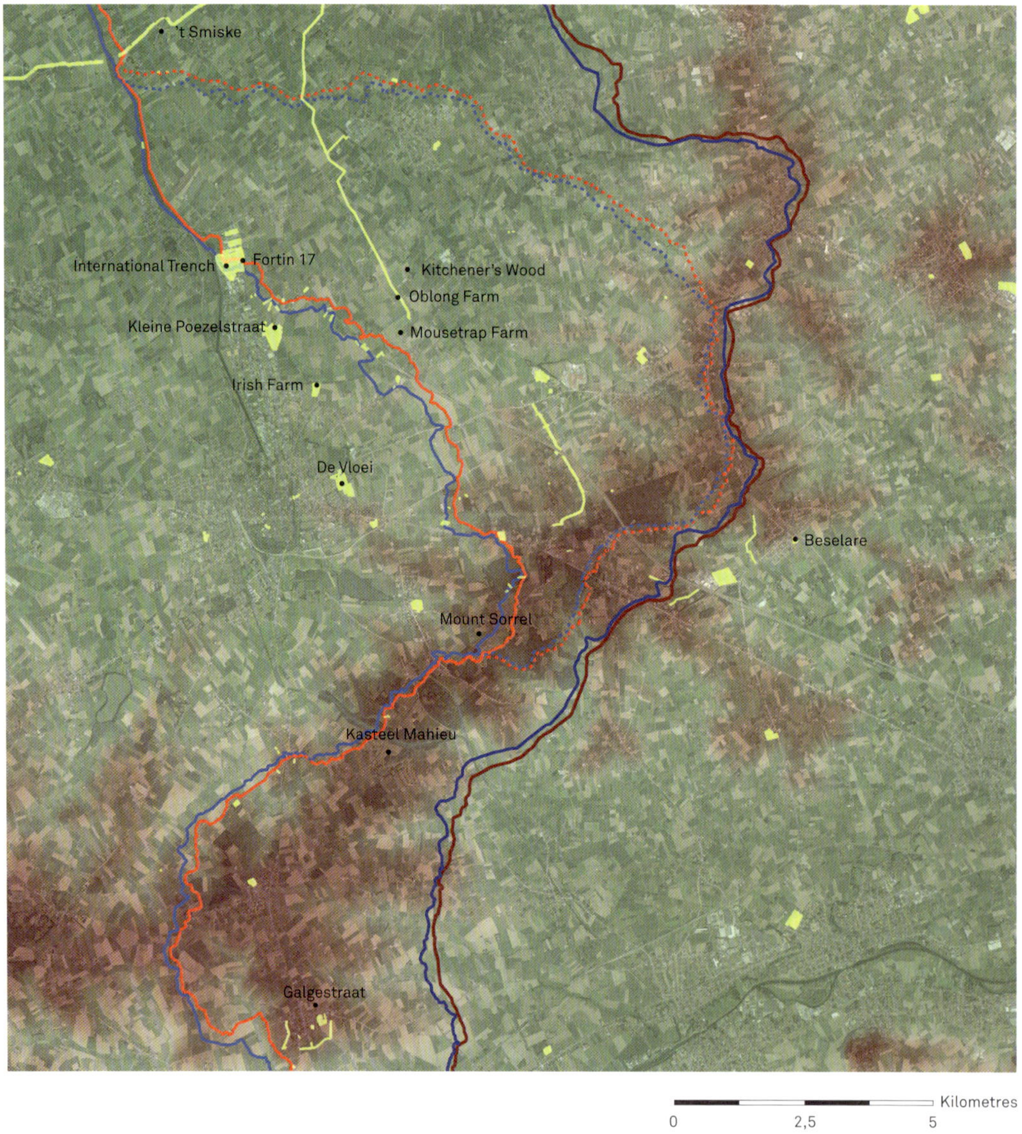

Allied front line
November 1914 – April 1915

German front line
November 1914 – April 1915

British front line
May 1915 – July 1917

German front line
May 1915 – July 1917

British front line
November 1917 – April 1918

German front line
November 1917 – April 1918

Excavations

FIG. 63 (pp. 62-63)
Colouring the names on the Menin Gate in Ypres, 1928.

FIG. 64
Overview map.

FIG. 65
The Memorial to the Missing at the Tyne Cot Cemetery lists the names of almost 35,000 missing soldiers.

65

Military cemeteries are an integral part of the Westhoek landscape. All of us have seen the endless rows of white headstones marking the graves of fallen Commonwealth soldiers. Many cemeteries were originally next to first-aid stations at the front or field hospitals behind the lines. Others were established on the battlefield where soldiers had been killed and where many graves were consolidated after the Armistice. But despite these extensive cemeteries, the ground below the former battlefields is still full of the remains of countless soldiers declared missing in action. Time after time, they are unearthed by chance while ploughing fields or during archaeological excavations.

How many fallen soldiers still lie under the fields of Flanders? The Menin Gate and other Memorials to the Missing list the names of some 103,000 Commonwealth soldiers missing in action (FIG. 63 & 65), while 47,500 unidentified bodies have anonymous graves in one of the many British cemeteries[1]. This means that some 55,000 dead from the British Commonwealth were never found. On the German, Belgian and French sides, the figures are more difficult to calculate due to a lack of comprehensive lists. But here as well, we are talking about tens of thousands, especially on the German side.

Similarly, the casualty figures for a number of battles speak volumes. After the First Battle of Ypres, the British Expeditionary Force alone had a death toll of 10,500. Fewer than 2,100 of them ended up with a known grave. The Second Battle of Ypres cost 15,500 British and Commonwealth lives, of whom just 3,735 ended up with a known grave. This means that some 75 percent of those killed in the early battles have no known grave. The Battle of Mount Sorrel, to the east of Ypres, was waged on 2-12 July 1916 and cost the lives of 1,765 Germans and 2,869 Canadians. Of the Canadian dead, 2,008 have no known grave and their names are inscribed on the Menin Gate. For every two fatalities buried in a known grave at the front, there are thus eight whose grave is unknown. While some of them undoubtedly lie in graves marked with an anonymous white headstone inscribed with the words 'Known unto God', most were probably left unrecovered on the battlefield.

These cynical calculations get people thinking. There are dozens of possible reasons why these missing soldiers have no known grave. Similarly, the circumstances under which their bodies are discovered by archaeologists differ greatly.

[1] Scott 1992

FIG. 66

British panorama photo taken near The Bluff.

KILLED ON THE BATTLEFIELD

Most of the dead soldiers found were killed in action, hit by bullets, shrapnel or artillery shells. And they remained where they fell. In the heat of a battle or in no-man's-land, it was too dangerous to recover the bodies.

A British panorama photo provides a penetrating illustration of the situation (**FIG. 66**). It was taken from the steep banks of Ypres-Comines Canal and shows the sector around Mahieu Castle in Hollebeke, today the grounds of De Palingbeek golf club. Where the trees start, we can see the high raised parapet of the German front line and in the distance the silhouette of the manor. In front of the German line lie the bodies of a dozen fallen soldiers, mown down in an attack. As they lay between the French and German lines in no-man's-land, they could not be recovered and buried. A German aerial photo taken one day earlier shows the same place from a different perspective (**FIG. 67**). On it, an aerial photo interpreter has marked the two front lines with dotted lines. The same corpses are to be seen as dark points in no-man's-land. We can only recognise them because we have the British panorama photo as a comparison.

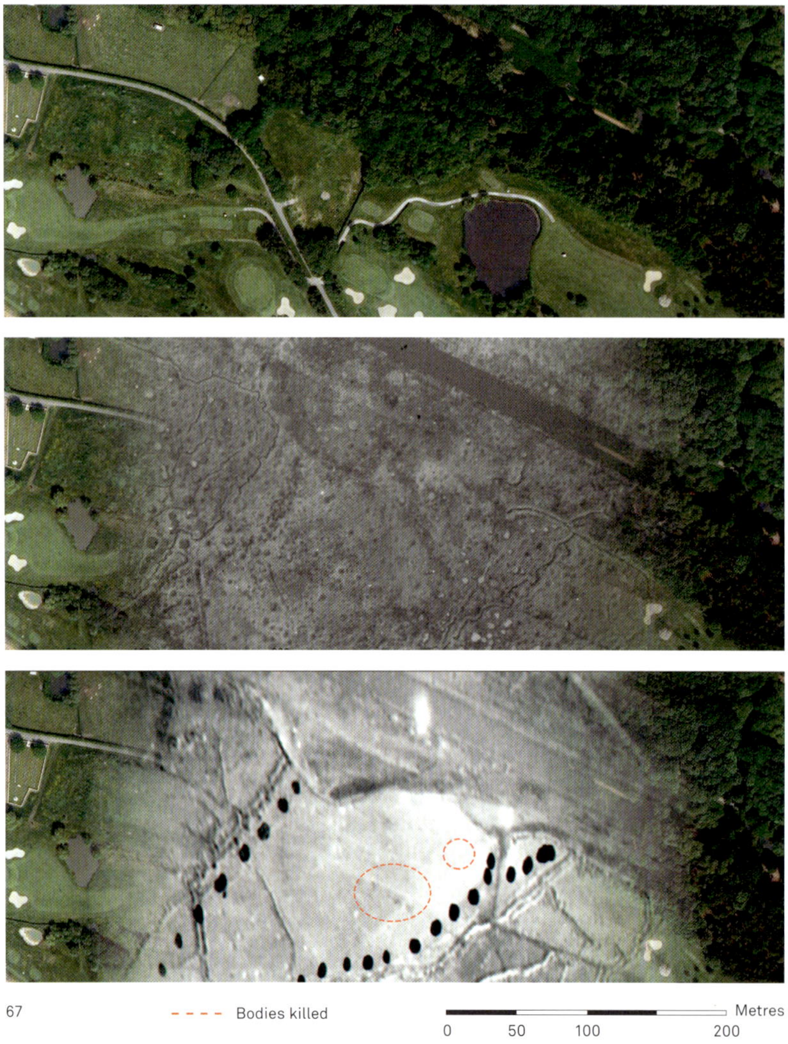

67

68

FIG. 67

Time series of historical aerial photos. From bottom to top, 1915, 1917, 2012.

FIG. 68

Dead Canadian soldiers on the battlefield of the Second Battle of Ypres.

FIG. 69

Fallen soldier.

FIG. 70 (pp. 70–71)

Inauguration of the Menin Gate on 24 July 1927.

After the First Battle of Ypres, waged between 19 October and 22 November 1914, the two sides dug in. For more than two and a half years, the front line was static. The never-ending shelling turned the no-man's-land into a desolate crater landscape. Both photos suggest that the bodies slowly sunk into the battlefield. Maybe they are lying there to this day, under the grass carpet of the golf course.

CORPSES ON THE SURFACE

Some corpses remained on the surface or came to rest in a rut, while others landed in a shell crater. The ones remaining on the surface gradually got covered by earth thrown up by later explosions (**FIG. 68 & 69**). After the war, the remains were not deep in the ground, making them very vulnerable to the ploughs working the fields. Every now and then they are still found, but usually so fragmented that their identity, or even their nationality, is impossible to tell. Along the route of the gas pipeline in Langemark, archaeologists found the remains of soldiers in 15 places within a stretch 8 kilometres long and 13 metres wide.

Not all fields are worked with the same intensity: some are used just for grazing, and others have been reforested. In terrain where the war is literally just a few centimetres below the surface, untouched remains are found more often. An area of grassland on a slope alongside the Kleine Poezelstraat in Ypres was unsuitable for agriculture as it was too marshy. During the war, the slope had served as protection for soldiers, keeping them out of the sight of the enemy who were dug in on the ridge a few hundred metres to the north. Leaving their cover on 23 April 1915 during the Second Battle of Ypres, infantrymen from the 2nd battalion King's Own Scottish Borderers joined their French comrades in a counter-attack. With the Pilkemseweg on its right flank, the unit advanced across the grassland. When the soldiers arrived at the Kleine Poezelstraat, they came into the gunsights of the German defenders and were mown down by bullets and shrapnel. They suffered very heavy losses, with the battalion losing 250 men, including 18 dead and 96 missing. The names of the 33 men whose bodies were never recovered are inscribed on the Menin Gate.

69

ANTONY
d'YPRES
240727-6

During the excavation, the archaeologists came across two soldiers possibly killed during this action. Both lay just 20 centimetres deep. One of them had probably been killed by an exploding grenade. His upper body was heavily mutilated and no longer in one piece. The cause of death of the other could not be determined. What was clear was that he had already been lying on the ground when a shell hit his body. The explosion tore the body apart, with the upper body pushed against the edge of the crater and the legs spread-eagled (**FIG. 71**). Such finds are sharp reminders of the horrors of the war.

BURIAL PITS AND SHELL CRATERS

One special category consists of the remains of soldiers collected during the war and (re)buried. This happened when the remains were (re-)exposed but were already in a completely decomposed state. Working near 't Smiske in Bikschote, the archaeologists came across a small rectangular pit full of human bones. Though no longer in skeleton form, they had been carefully stacked in the pit: first the legs, then the hips, the shoulders and the skull. A typical example of a burial pit (or ossuary). Between the bones a button belonging to a French uniform was found.

Many of those killed ended up in a shell crater during or after their death (**FIG. 72 & 73**). Some were killed by exploding shells and fell into the resulting crater. Just to the west of the Wijngaardstraat in Langemark, halfway between Mouse Trap Farm and Oblong Farm, the remains of some ten British soldiers were found. They probably all belonged to the 1st battalion Warwickshires and had taken part in the attack of 25 April 1915. As in most other unsuccessful counter-attacks during the Second Battle of Ypres, losses were high. One of the victims lay on his stomach in a shell crater. The upper body had been torn to pieces, with remains of the skull found separately. Investigation of the remains showed that this soldier had been hit by lead shrapnel. Some of his comrades fell in an existing crater and were gradually covered by earth during later barrages. Others again used a shell crater as cover or a shelter, only for it to become their grave.

CAPTAIN HENRY WALKER

The archaeological excavation along the route of the gas pipeline achieved fame through the TV series *Ten oorlog special: Onder Vlaamse velden*

71

72

FIG. 71
Body of a Scottish Borderer at the bottom of a shell crater to the south of the Kleine Poezelstraat in Ypres.

FIG. 72
Fallen British soldier in a shell crater near Oblong Farm.

FIG. 73
A water-filled shell crater containing the body of a German soldier killed in the attack on Broodseinde Ridge on 4 October 1917, photographed two weeks later by an Australian photographer.

(At War Special: Beneath Flanders Fields). In the fields between Mouse Trap Farm and Oblong Farm, the archaeologists found the remains of many soldiers. On a stretch 500 metres long and 13 metres wide, ten British corpses and one German one were dug up. The nationalities of four others could no longer be determined. At first, it was not clear how and when the soldiers had met their end. The pre-war production data of the bullets found with five of the British soldiers point to the beginning of the war. Given that nine of them lay within a 115-metre stretch, the archaeologists suspect that they were killed in the same action.

They found out more when excavating a large shell crater in the middle of the zone containing the bodies of two British soldiers. The skeletons were intact and were found with the soldiers' full equipment, including personal artefacts. Their cap badges indicated that they had belonged to the Royal Warwickshire Regiment, a feature that made targeted historical investigation possible.

The 1st battalion of the regiment mounted an attack against the German positions near Kitchener's Wood at dawn on 25 April 1915. At least, that's where they thought the Germans were. The British 10th Brigade commanded by General Hull had been rushed to the northern front to stop the German advance during the Second Battle of Ypres, with orders to drive out the German troops from Kitchener's Wood and Sint-Juliaan. The battalion formed the left flank of the counter-attack. On reaching Mouse Trap Farm via the Brugseweg, they closed ranks and advanced northwards towards Oblong Farm, where they fixed their bayonets and started attacking. Suddenly the German machine guns started rattling from the farm buildings ahead of them. The Germans had moved forward unnoticed under cover of night. Historical sources describe how the British foot soldiers were mown down. About 220 soldiers from the unit lost their lives that day. Of these, 192 have no known grave, and their names are inscribed on the Menin Gate.

73

The archaeologists soon suspected that they could identify one body. The uniform buttons and collar badges indicated that the soldier had been an officer, meaning that the list of possible victims could be cut down to nine. Alongside his military equipment, he was also carrying personal items, such as a purse, a flute, a pocket knife and binoculars (**FIG. 74**). The purse contained a silver medallion bearing the initials 'H.J.I.W.' and the date 15 March 1911. There was only one officer the initials could belong to: Captain Henry John Innes Walker. This was confirmed on cleaning the finds, when the same initials appeared on the lid of his binoculars case. The study of the bones, which also determined the soldier's age and height, removed all doubt.

Henry John Innes Walker was born on 12 February 1890 in Remuera, New Zealand (**FIG. 75**). He went to school at King's College in Auckland. At the age of sixteen, he played rugby and took part in athletics competitions. Two years later, he left school and joined the army. When he was twenty, he became a second lieutenant and almost immediately – on 15 March 1911, the date on the medallion – left for India, where he joined the 1st Royal Warwickshire battalion. On 23 August 1914 he arrived in France. Walker's first taste of action was on the Belgian border, where he was reported missing on 26 August. The news reached his parents two weeks later. A few days later, another letter arrived, this time stating that he was safe and well with his unit.

A few months later, a further telegram reached Remuera. This time, no correction followed. Captain Walker was reported missed in action during the 25 April 1915 counter-attack on Kitchener's Wood. Eye-witness reports of the circumstances surrounding his death varied greatly, but one thing was certain: he had fearlessly led his men towards the German lines, urging them on with his revolver – "Come on, lads."

FIG. 74
Artefacts found on the body of Henry Walker.

FIG. 75
Captain Henry John Innes Walker.

FIG. 76
Map of bodies dug up near the International Trench and Fortin 17 (Boezinge, Ypres).

FIG. 77
Diagram showing the capture of the International Trench on 10 July 1915 by the Lancashire Fusiliers.

FIG. 78 (pp. 76-77)
Soldiers killed on the battlefield.

74

75

76

- - - - British front line
Front line 5 July 191

- - - - German front line
Front line 5 July 1915

—— British front line
Front line 10 July 1915

—— German front line
Front line 10 July 1915

● Excavated bodies of unknown nationality

● Excavated German soldiers

● Excavated British soldiers

● Excavated French soldiers

A: Fortin 17
B: International Trench

77

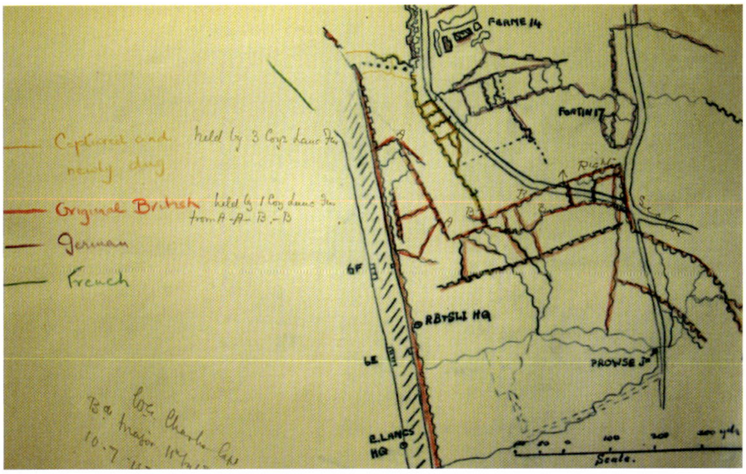

Walker was hit when jumping out of a shell crater, according to some, in the head, while others thought they had seen him mown down by bullets. What happened afterwards is unclear. What is, however, certain is that his body remained in the shell crater until it was discovered by the archaeologists. Some spoke of his being buried by his own men, while others thought he had simply remained lying there or had been buried by German soldiers.

Henry Walker, a New Zealander in the British army, died on 25 April 1915. That same day, his compatriots from the Australian and New Zealand Army Corps (ANZAC) landed on the beaches of Gallipoli in Turkey, an event commemorated each year in Australia and New Zealand on ANZAC Day.

BOEZINGE INTERNATIONAL TRENCH

Carrying out excavations in the industrial park in Boezinge, the Diggers, an association of amateur archaeologists, and the Instituut voor het Archeologisch Patrimonium (Institute for Archaeological Patrimony), a Flemish government scientific institution that has since merged into the Flanders Heritage Agency, dug up more than 200 French, British and German bodies. Historical research by the Diggers and the In Flanders Fields Museum has revealed how the men died.

After the Second Battle of Ypres, the British front line ran along the Ypres-Yser Canal. In an attempt to better position this line, on 6 July 1915 the British 4th Division launched an attack on the International Trench, a protruding trench that ran directly into no-man's-land (**FIG. 76 & 77**). Following heavy 'softening-up' shelling, the British captured the trench. But in the following days, the Germans counter-attacked ten times. Looking at a historical aerial photo and at a map showing where the excavated bodies had lain, we can recognise the International Trench as a cluster of German and British bodies, victims of the attack (**FIG. 76**). It was clear that the dead had been left where they fell. A second group of about 40 bodies came to light at Fortin 17, a solidly built fortification in the German front line. Two British soldiers were possibly killed in a raid on the German trenches. They were found just in front of the German trench. Similarly, the remains of two German soldiers were found just in front of the British front line. Dozens of other German bodies lay buried within the German lines.

79

FIG. 79
A German officer poses in French positions captured during the Second Battle of Ypres. Behind two dead French soldiers, a carefully built field grave can be seen.

80

FIG. 80
Exhumations of field graves after the war.

TEMPORARILY BURIED ON THE BATTLEFIELD

The missing also includes soldiers who were properly buried during the war, but whose graves got lost. Soldiers who had to bury their dead comrades on the battlefield often marked the graves. A mention in a diary or on a map ensured that the location remained known. After the end of the war, exhumation teams were able to dig up the bodies to give them a decent funeral elsewhere (FIG. 80). But shelling and other actions wiped out many of the markings, leaving the battlefield graves irretrievably lost.

On a photo taken near Sint-Juliaan, we can see a large shell crater with wooden crosses marking seven graves (FIG. 81). On one of them, we can read the name of Frank Barnard Bush Vickery from Bristol, a sapper belonging to the 478th Field Company of the Royal Engineers, who was killed on 16 August 1917 during the Battle of Langemark. Although his grave is clearly marked and historical sources list the coordinates, his body was never found after the war. His name is inscribed on the Tyne Cot Memorial to the Missing. These are the missing soldiers sometimes unearthed by the archaeologists.

In expectation of a proper burial in a cemetery, the soldiers buried their dead comrades with exceptional care. In such battlefield graves, archaeologists nearly always find remains of canvas in which the body was wrapped or

81

covered over (**FIG. 82**). The simplest form of burial was to place the bodies in a shell crater, an improvised battlefield grave. In nearly all such cases, the bodies are found lying on their backs, usually next to each other, although sometimes on top of each other.

Some of the dead even got a coffin. During soil remediation work in the Galgestraat in Wijtschate, a long-lost temporary grave of 21 German soldiers was discovered in 2015 (**FIG. 83**)[2]. At the bottom of an enormous shell crater lay 11 bodies, each covered with a coffin lid. A twelfth body lay alongside them. On top of them, an additional seven soldiers were buried, each in a coffin. The crater had then been enlarged to make room for another two coffins.

According to their badges, they belonged to the Königlich Sächsiches 15. Infanterie-Regiment Nr. 181 from Chemnitz. The unit had arrived at the Messines Ridge in March 1917. The war diary of the 48th Sanitäts-Kompagnie (stretcher bearers belonging to the 40th Infanterie-Division) reported that they had no longer been able to send the dead to the back lines due to heavy shelling from 1 June onwards. They had had to be buried on the spot, as shown by the excavations. During an offensive on 7 June 1917, when the British captured the ridge near Wijtschate and Messines, the burial place became lost.

Ten victims were found with identification plates on their chests giving their name, address, date of birth, registration number and regimental information. An investigation of the remains showed that two of the soldiers

[2] Dewilde & Wyffels 2015

FIG. 81
Temporary cross marking the grave of Frank Vickery.

FIG. 82
Remains of a German soldier near Kitchener's Wood. Canvas buttons indicate that the corpse was wrapped in canvas.

FIG. 83
Mass grave of 21 Germans in the Galgestraat in Wijtschate.

82

83

had been in their thirties. Most, however, were in their twenties, and some even younger than twenty. On 16 October 2015, they were given a proper burial in the German cemetery in Langemark.

MASS GRAVES

Graves with two or more bodies in one pit were often found. While in some the bodies are neatly arranged next to each other, in others they lie haphazardly (**FIG. 84**) – as found, for example, in the two mass graves in Bikschote dating back to the first months of the war (see Chapter 1).

On 23 April 1915, the North Riding Battery united with the East Riding Battery in the French Steenvoorde. They both belonged to the 2nd Northumbrian Brigade Royal Field Artillery from Hull and Scarborough in north-east England. In the coming weeks, they were involved in the Second Battle of Ypres. Their war diary records their action in detail.

On 25 May 1915, one of the two batteries was deployed along Zonnebeekseweg between Ypres and the hamlet of Potijze. The soldiers had been given the task of shelling the Bellewaarde Ridge, where a German attack was taking place. Their own positions were, however, hard pressed

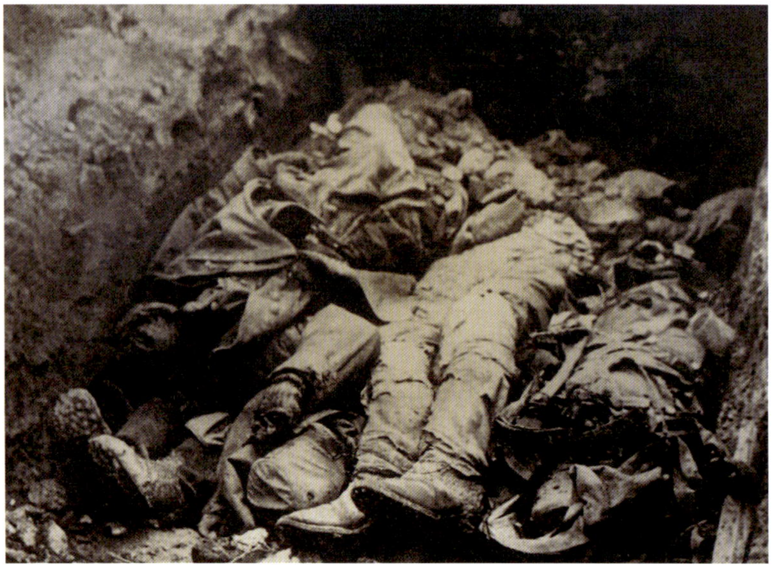

84

FIG. 84
Mass grave of at least five soldiers.

FIG. 85
Souvenir belt found on the body of Albert William Venus, with French and British buttons and badges.

85

Thanks to the personal artefacts found during the excavations, we are often able to gain a glimpse of the life of killed soldiers. One soldier buried in a mass grave near Wijtschate wore two silver medallions inscribed with the words *Gott Schütze Dich*. They were perhaps a talisman received from the home front. One of the medallions bears the date 14.4.1917. Therefore the man was buried after that date. On the back of the other one, the words *In Liebe v. Deiner treuen Grete 23.10.15* are engraved, a souvenir from a loved one back home. A bone whistle suggests that the person killed was an officer. There were no further artefacts to help identify the body.

throughout the morning. While loading one of their guns, three shells hit their position, with two direct hits on the gun. Five artillerymen were killed: T.A. Carr, J.W. Clarke, G. Robinson, J. Rowbottom and A.W. Venus. Sergeant G.P. Hill was severely wounded and later died of his injuries. An entry in the diary at 23:00 records the preliminary location of their grave: coordinate 28.I.9.a.99 on the British trench maps, under a hedge on the rear side of the farm. They were never found again.

This story and the record in the diary disappeared into oblivion for 98 years, until an archaeological survey was carried out in May 2013 in the new De Vloei industrial park along the Zonnebeekseweg in Ypres. The archaeologists came across a cramped burial pit with five bodies in it. The grave seemed to be a shell crater that had been extended. The soldiers had been lain close to each other. One body lay above the heads of the others (**FIG. 84**). Though the remains were not in a good state, the remaining pieces of uniform quickly put the archaeologists on the right track.

The first indications helping to identify them were the shoulder badges of the North and East Riding Batteries. Other artefacts were typical of an artilleryman, including two keys used to adjust the gun's range. The discovery of a rider's spur presumably indicated the soldier responsible for bringing up the ammunition.

This diary fragment from the archives of the In Flanders Fields Museum quickly helped identify the soldier. The excavation clearly indicated that this was a mass grave into which all the bodies had been put at the same time. A search of the archives and a DNA test by the British Ministry of Defence attributed the remains to Albert William Venus, 22 years old, and Joseph William Rowbottom, 27 years old. The other soldiers, upon whom no DNA tests were conducted, were given graves as unknown soldiers. On Wednesday, 20 April 2016, they were buried in the Ypres Town Cemetery Extension, just 500 metres away from where they had been found.

CLEARED BURIAL GROUNDS

Strangely enough, human remains and artefacts can still be found in the cleared cemeteries. On the British side, all burial grounds with fewer than 40 graves were cleared after the war, with the bodies exhumed and taken to central cemeteries, of which Tyne Cot Cemetery in Passchendaele is the best known. But the clearing was not always done carefully. Bodies were sometimes left behind, possibly because a grave was not marked. For instance, the Irish Farm Cemetery near the Ypres village of Sint-Jan was cleared in 1919, with the bodies taken over to the New Irish Farm Cemetery (**FIG. 86**). Apparently, some ten graves were overlooked, and were only discovered during later work on the site. On the basis of the artefacts found, some were identified as colonial troops, in this case Gurkhas serving in the Sirhind Brigade. They had taken part in the counter-attack at Irish Farm, after the Allies had been pushed back by the gas attack of 22 April 1915.

86

On the German side, all smaller burial grounds were cleared between the wars and in the 1950s. The graves are now part of the main German cemeteries in Langemark, Hooglede, Vladslo and Menin. These cleared burial grounds also contain archaeological traces and remains, telling us more about the burial grounds during and just after the war, and how they were cleared.

In Beselare, archaeologists studied part of the formal burial ground of the German 246th Reserve Infantry Regiment[3], wanting to find out how the clearing had taken place and whether such sites were of any archaeological interest. The clearance dated back to 1955-1956. The identified bodies were taken to Menin, while the unidentified ones went to Langemark.

FIG. 86
The Irish Farm Cemetery was cleared in 1919 without much care.

FIG. 87
Gravestone of Jakob Grau.

FIG. 88
Wartime grave of Jakob Grau.

[3] Dewilde et al. 2015
[4] Vancoillie 2013

87

88

What happens after the remains of a soldier are found?

What happens when an archaeologist finds the remains of a dead soldier? Until recently, the police had to be informed immediately to rule out a suspicious death. Once it had been determined that the body belonged to a war victim, the Instituut voor Veteranen – Nationaal Instituut voor Oorlogsinvaliden, Oudstrijders en Oorlogsslachtoffers (IV-NIOOO), the Belgian Ministry of Defence's department responsible for such cases, was informed. This in turn contacted the British Commonwealth War Graves Commission, the German Volksbund Deutsche Kriegsgräberfürsorge or the French consulate-general in Brussels, depending on the soldier's assumed nationality. In most cases, one then had the time to make the necessary investigations, together with a physical anthropologist or a forensic archaeologist on the ground: unearthing the skeleton, registering and, when time allowed, studying and inventorying the remains. Everything was then collected by the police. The procedure was totally impractical and hindered the scientific investigation of the finds and thus any chance of identifying the victim.

Following discussions with the police and the Ministry of Defence, a new procedure was recently agreed. War victims are now considered to be an archaeological find. Any archaeologist finding human remains immediately contacts the police. Once they have been brought up to date and have given the green light, the archaeological recovery can start. The archaeologists are given 30 days to investigate, after which they have to hand over the remains and any artefacts found to the police.

The archaeologists have the task of excavating the remains as best as possible and inventorying all available information. How did the context come about? What was the victim's nationality? Can the regiment be determined? Are there any elements allowing the victim to be identified? Do the artefacts found open the door to any other, additional interpretations?

The remains are meticulously uncovered and registered, before everything is carefully lifted. The remains are then transported to an archaeological lab where they are carefully washed and anthropologically investigated. Forensic archaeologists inventory and interpret the finds, two steps of crucial importance for possible identification of the body. The location of the find, the available historical data and any artefacts found on the body can lead to a shorter or longer list of possible names.

The physical anthropological investigation can pinpoint the age and height of the victim, two key criteria helping to eliminate names from the list of possibilities. At the end of this process, a few names usually remain – but in most cases, unfortunately, not just one name. Historical research and DNA analyses can help trace possible descendants.

Once the research is completed, the remains and any artefacts are handed over to the police and from there to the IV-NIOOO. The latter is responsible for transferring the remains to the war graves institution of the country of origin, with a military funeral conducted at a cemetery near the place where they were found.

Despite the clearance, the excavation revealed a large number of personal artefacts and a few wooden coffins. The few remaining bones indicate that the recovery of the bodies was done with care. One interesting find was the gravestone of non-commissioned officer Jakob Grau from the 11th company of the 3rd battalion (**FIG. 87**). In the weeks prior to his death, his unit had seen action on the Bellewaarde Ridge. Grau was wounded and died in a field hospital behind the front. His body was brought to Beselare so that he could be buried with other soldiers from his regiment. On a photo taken during the war, a simple wooden cross marked his grave (**FIG. 88**). After the war, the burial ground was upgraded, and his grave was given a gravestone. Jakob Grau now lies in the Deutscher Soldatenfriedhof Menen Wald[4].

PERSONAL SENTIMENT

Though archaeologists are used to dealing with skeletons, encountering human remains of soldiers from the First World War is a poignant experience, even for the most seasoned of them. The body will always belong to a person who has been missing since his death. Nobody from his family has been able to say a final farewell. Archaeologists thus often feel a certain attachment to the body, very much wanting to know who the soldier was.

The most important thing is for the soldier to no longer be left behind on the former battlefield, and instead be given a decent burial in a proper cemetery. That is a further privilege of archaeologists researching the First World War. In what other area of archaeology can you take part in the funeral of a person whose body you yourself have dug up?

4 Just behind the front line

Maarten Bracke
Wouter Gheyle
Birger Stichelbaut

89

90

FIG. 89
Present-day aerial photo of Lijssenthoek cemetery with a superimposed aerial photograph of the hospital in the First World War.

FIG. 90
Hospital huts in Casualty Clearing Station 3 in Lijssenthoek.

FIG. 91 (pp. 86-87)
German trench map of the hinterland between Ypres and Poperinge, 20 April 1918. Hundreds of British camps are shaded red.

The picture we have in our minds of the First World War is one of trenches, bunkers and muddy crater landscapes. The front line was the worst place to be, a place of so much suffering. But what happened behind the front? And what can archaeological excavations tell us about life behind the lines?

Both sides of the front were characterised by an extensive network of camps, roads, railways and logistic hubs feeding the war machine at the front. A few kilometres behind the front line, just out of the range of enemy fire, both sides built hundreds or even thousands of camps, equipped with tents, barracks and dozens of field hospitals. Historical maps and aerial photos show how the war took full hold of the hinterland, especially between Poperinge and Ypres (**FIG. 91**).

AN ALLIED HOSPITAL

To the south of Poperinge, archaeologists excavated a special site during the construction of the Lijssenthoek Visitors' Centre.

At a farm alongside the railway line between Hazebrouck and Poperinge, the Allied forces constructed a group of evacuation hospitals from 1915 onwards. It all started with a small French field hospital with a few huts and some tents. On taking over the hospital in June 1915, the British greatly expanded it. In its heyday, it consisted of four casualty clearing stations (**FIG. 89 & 90**). The hospital was located at the end of the medical evacuation route for front-line soldiers.

In his war diary, Achiel Van Walleghem, the parish priest of Dikkebus, described the place on 22 August 1916: "In the afternoon I walked over to the Gasthuismolen in Watou. (...) Between the Leene and the Boonaert, along the cobbled road from Boeschepe, I walked through the large, beautiful hospital of the English. What splendid tents! So many of them pitched on the grounds which have been converted into a lovely park with flowers, fine lawns and lovely trees. (...) And a whole army of stretcher bearers and nurses. I also visited the large English graveyard next to the Boonaert. No fewer than 2,500 English soldiers are buried there. All graves are in a very good shape. Alongside the English graveyard is a French graveyard where some 40 French soldiers are buried."[1]

We have plenty of information about the construction of the huts and tents from documents and photos. What additional information can archaeology offer? And what structures and artefacts were left in the ground?

During the excavations, it turned out that the huts were very simple wooden constructions that hardly left any traces. All that remained were traces of the corner posts and the foundation piles for the walls. Remains of the poles are revealed as grey, circular or square discolourations, the result of the decaying of the wooden building material. The patterns of the poles indicate four huts. The south-facing corner poles of one hut were in metal shoes for extra support. A glass bedpan, medicine bottles and ampoules from a waste pit tell us what medical material was used in the hospital[2].

Through combining historical documents, aerial photos, material found in the ground and the excavation plan, the archaeologists were able to accurately reconstruct the hospital site (**FIG. 92**). Wounded soldiers were taken by road to a

[1] Spillebeen 2014
[2] Bracke 2011

Zuidschote
Steenstraat
5950
5948
6053
6049
6152
6150
6148
6253
6249
6352
6350
6348
Oosthoek
6451
Brielen
6552
6550
6548
Pottenhoek
Vlamertingen
Brandhoek
6653
6651
6649

Langemark
Wijdendrift
Pilckem
St. Julien
Keerselare
Frezenberg
Potijze
IEPEREN
5944
5946
5942
6045
6146
6142
6344
6342
6446
6443
6546
6542
6643

reception area approximately 9 metres wide and 28 metres long, located right next to the road. The hut had its own sanitary facilities. There were seven large rectangular latrines about 130 centimetres wide and 290 centimetres long, with a thin layer of pitch at the bottom to make them watertight and help empty them. Above each pit, one or two toilets could have been fitted. Next to the reception area was a sickbay for officers. At right angles to the huts was an operating theatre, smaller in size (8 x 21 metres), of which only a few piles were found. Between the huts were waste pits containing corrugated iron sheets with traces of German shrapnel, fragments of metal hospital beds and light bulbs. Next to the sickbays for the severely wounded were pits with signs of burning, probably where surgical material was incinerated.

A CAMP OF UNUSUAL HUTS

A remarkable site was discovered by chance in 2016 during a geophysical survey (see Chapter 10) of the front line at Madelstede in Kemmel[3]. Just beneath the surface, the archaeologists discovered not just trenches, but also a strange rectangular area some 60 metres long and 40 metres wide. In it, 30 rectangles were easily distinguishable. What were they?

After years of preparation, a major British offensive was launched on 7 June 1917. It was to go down in history books as the Battle of Messines. The battle began with the detonation of 19 mines beneath the German front position, which devastated the German front-line defences and left 19 large craters. Barely a week later, the front line was again stabilised, with Madelstede now some 5 kilometres behind the front line. Aerial photos show that in autumn 1917, a noteworthy military camp had been constructed in the middle of what had been no-man's-land (**FIG. 93**). The structure was demarcated by a fence or a drainage channel, with different entrances. Within this enclosure, five rows of six rectangles, presumably huts or shelters, were found, with space to circulate in between.

Both the layout and position of the camp invite questions. Why was it surrounded by a drainage channel? Why were there so many huts so close to one another? Why at that location, just a few kilometres away from the front line, but within the range of the German artillery? What was its function, who had had it built, what still remained in the ground, and why did it show up so clearly in the geophysical survey?

To find answers to these questions, a minor excavation took place (**FIG. 94**). Removing the earth from a long 2-metre-wide strip revealed

FIG. 92

Plan of the archaeological excavations in Lijssenthoek:

1. Reception area
2. Sickbay for officers
3. Operating theatre
4. Sickbay for soldiers with minor wounds
5. Sickbay for soldiers with serious wounds
6. Nurses' quarters
7. Administration
8. Sickbay for soldiers with serious wounds
9. Storage room for stretchers and linen

FIG. 93

German aerial photo of the camp in 1918.

FIG. 94

Excavation of a hut at Madelstede.

FIG. 95 (pp. 90-91)

Results of the excavation of one of the huts at Madelstede.

[3] Gheyle et al. 2016

92

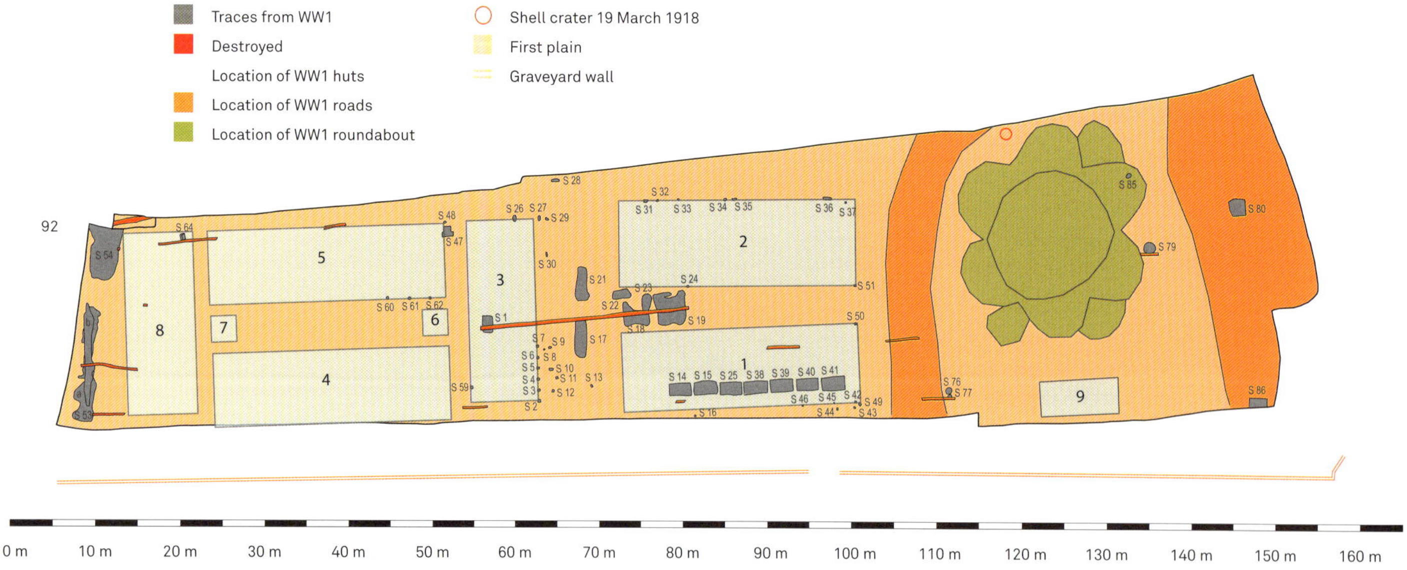

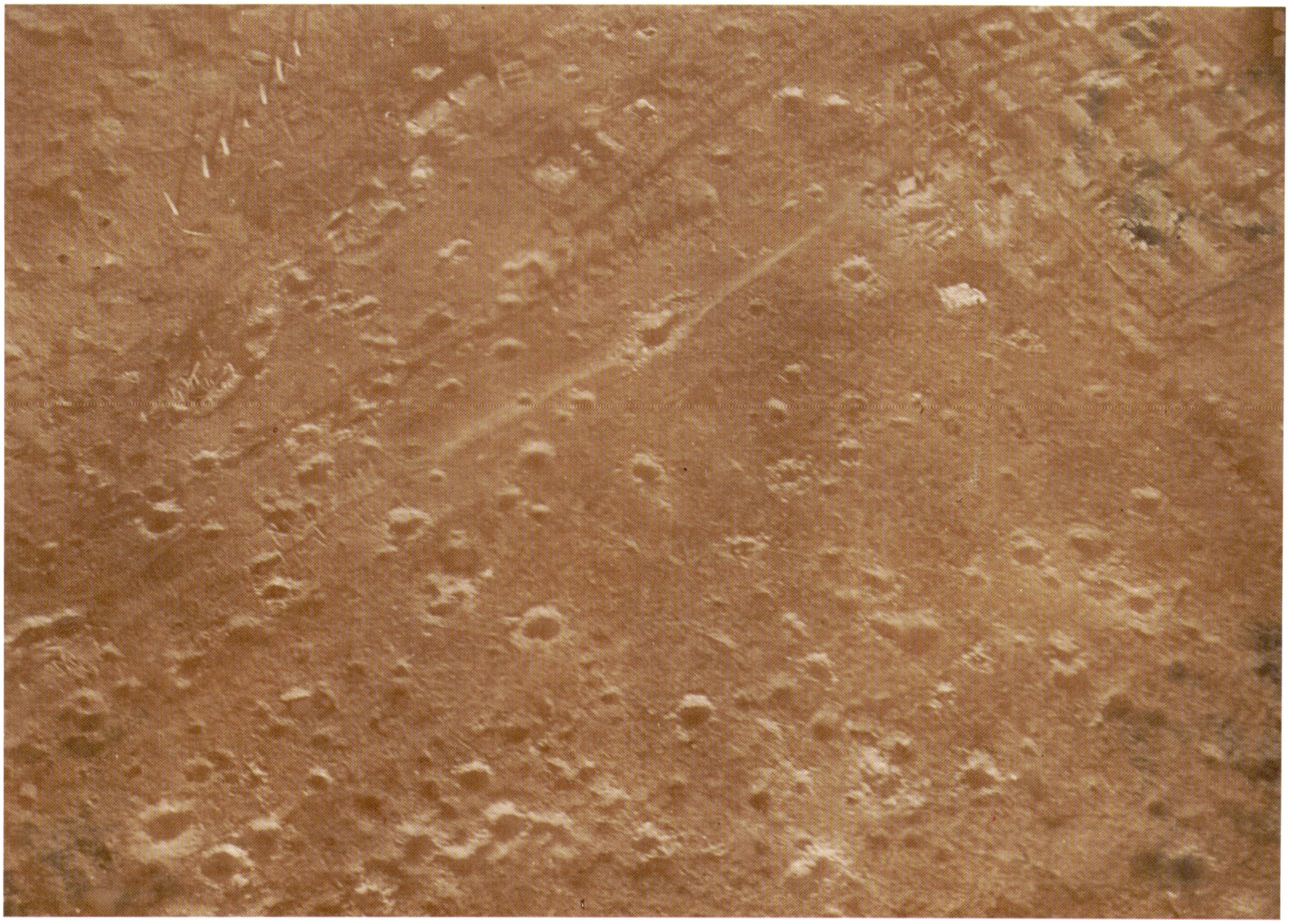

93

94

ten rectangular huts or shelters. They turned out to have been sunk at least 60 centimetres into the ground. Each had one entrance on the short side, with steps to get down. There were a total of five rows of six huts arranged in such a way that the entrances faced each other.

One hut was completely excavated. On the sides were remains of corrugated iron sheets that were used as a curved roof. The hut turned out to have a brick floor. The foundations consisted of a row of piles set in cement and covered with planks. The wooden frame of a bed stood on the floor. In the middle of the floor was a hole where a burner had probably stood (FIG. 95). To stop water getting in, a drainage pit with a grate over it had been dug.

96

FIG. 96

The huts at Madelstede must have looked like this British shelter with a stone floor, a corrugated iron roof and a bed in the corner.

FIG. 97

A typical waste pit, full to the brim with material.

The finds provide indications about who built the camp. As expected, most of the material was British (FIG. 98). A few artefacts, including a Rising Sun collar badge and a shoulder badge, indicate the presence of Australians. What was strange, however, was the presence of German gas masks and hand grenades. During the German 1918 spring offensive the site again became a front-line location, with German troops using parts of the drainage channel surrounding the site as a trench.

Historical research revealed that the camp had been extended in October 1917 as the winter quarters of the 5th battalion Australian Pioneers, an engineering unit that specialised in building roads and camps for other troops. The unit's diary shows that they were free to design their camp to their own needs: "It is quite a treat to have my own camp again and run it to my own way of thinking," wrote Lieutenant Charles Robert Duke. This probably explains the atypical form of the camp and its detailed arrangements: the men knew that they were going to have to spend the winter there. Charles Robert Duke

97

This German bakelite transport cap was found while excavating British-Australian barracks. Such caps were screwed over the detonators when shells were transported. At first sight it is just an ordinary item, found everywhere on the battlefield – until you decipher the incised words. On one side you can see the words 'Epres', on the other 'f[...]ck Stratfort'. Perhaps a British or Australian soldier staying in the camp wanted to refer to both the region of Ypres and his home area.

[4] Apers & Bracke (forthcoming), Bot et al. 2012, Bouckaert et al. 2009
[5] Apers & Bracke (forthcoming), Heyvaert & Bracke 2011

was to later write the following about his stay in the camp: "(...) tonight we are very snug – a good fire, a gramophone and a good dugout – it's funny to be here quiet and comfortable when not more than 7 miles away the S.O.S. has just gone up and the guns are roaring their hardest."

The excavation unearthed a previously unknown form of shelter, a cross between a light wooden shelter and a solid bunker. The finds also illustrate that many places along the Western Front have a very complex history, with front lines suddenly becoming hinterland and vice-versa.

NOSING AROUND IN SOLDIERS' TRASH

The waste pits in the hinterland are a treasure trove for archaeologists, telling us a lot about the consumption behaviour of the military and about the camp's function and period of use. They are time capsules, offering an insight into life at the time. Waste pits often show signs of fire: they might contain molten glass objects or the walls might have been reddened by the heat. In camps used for a long time, it was always more hygienic and practical to burn rubbish than to throw it away. In Madelstede, pits full of glass bottles were found outside the camp. In the turmoil of offensives and attacks the waste was simply chucked away, often in shell craters near temporary camps.

GLASS

Literally everything has been found in the waste pits (**FIG. 97**), including small charred seeds, fruit and large metal cooking pots, but especially glass. Studying the latter has revealed an enormous diversity, whether with regard to function, form, contents or origin.

Beer bottles were often found. They were either local (Hartmanns Proset, Brasserie de L'Ancre from Roesbrugge, Reninghelstsch *bruin bier*)[4] or from abroad. Quite a few of them had an etched inscription, a text embossed on the side, a stamped text on the bottom or a paper label. Most of the wine and champagne bottles had lost their labels, meaning it was no longer possible to find out where they came from.

Obviously, there was also stronger stuff. The well-known SRD rum jars had a capacity of no less than 1 English gallon (4.546 litres). The letters 'S.R.D.' stamped or printed in black on the side of each jar stood for Service Rum Distribution, though soldiers preferred the terms 'seldom reaches destination' or 'soon runs dry'. Rum was first distributed in the winter of 1914 as a means of fighting the cold. Other spirits found included Walker's Kilmarnock Whisky and Gordon's Dry Gin[5]. Spirits were generally imported from abroad. The SRD jars, Walker's Whisky and Gordon's Gin all came from England and Scotland. The most common were the SRD jars, as they arrived through military channels, while any whisky or gin had to be purchased personally.

Non-alcoholic beverages were mainly water, carbonated water or soda (**FIG. 99**). One of the most common types of bottled water found in British waste pits dating from the end of the war

FIG. 98

Some of the artefacts found during the Madelstede excavations: a transport cap, a comb with the word INVINCIBLE on it, a spoon, a King's Crown arm badge, an Australian Rising Sun collar badge, an ink bottle, a medicine bottle and two carved bullets.

Centimetres
0
1
2

were the dark-green bottles stamped *Ste Badoit* on the bottom, a French brand of carbonated water from the Auvergne–Rhône-Alpes region[6]. We can only guess why precisely this brand was common. Very typical were the decorated 'torpedo bottles' for soda, sporting the brand names Hill and Cammack[7].Torpedo-shaped, they could not be put down because they had no bottom. Therefore, after opening, they had to be emptied at once. Also typical of British waste pits are the Royal Warrant Idris bottles bearing the British coat of arms with the lion and the unicorn and inscribed at the bottom with the words *Dieu et mon droit*. The word 'Royal' meant that the company was a supplier to the court and therefore was also allowed to supply the military.

Many glass containers were for sauce or food. Square-shaped Garton's HP Sauce (aka brown sauce) bottles and hexagonal Pickles Glasgow bottles were frequently found. The sauces were used to add a bit of flavour to the monotonous rations. Sterilised pots for cured foods were common, whether in bottle form or as jars. Small cylindrical glass jars contained various sorts of paste.

[6] Bracke 2010, Bradt et al. 2012, Bracke 2014
[7] Bot et al. 2012

METAL, EARTHENWARE AND PIPES

Metal artefacts are often found in waste pits: buttons and buckles, ammunition and personal objects. Copper badges refer directly to a regiment and are often the starting point for further research.

The most noteworthy and illustrative metal finds are the identity tags, as they provide a direct link to an individual and what happened to him in the war. In the early months of the war, they were made of perishable material, and only later

99

FIG. 99
Selection of glass artefacts found in a waste pit in a French-Belgian camp on the banks of the Haringebeek (Roesbrugge-Haringe).

FIG. 100
Identity tag of Christopher Foley, found in the field hospital in Lijssenthoek.

FIG. 101
One soldier (Private Brett) made his own personal identity tag out of this silver French coin.

100

101

[8] Bracke 2013
[9] Bracke et al. 2012
[10] Bracke 2010

of metal. The excavation of the hospital site in Lijssenthoek unearthed five such identity tags[8], of which two have been identified. They belonged to British soldier Christopher Foley (**FIG. 100**) and French soldier Guiraud Jules Jacques. Both survived the war but must have been wounded at least once and nursed in Lijssenthoek.

Such finds are mirrors of personal fates and human tragedies, bearing witness to the fear of being buried anonymously somewhere on the battlefield. Sometimes soldiers even made their own identification plates (**FIG. 101**). Excavations regularly expose other personal artefacts, including pocket watches, religious pendants, pocket knives and objects with incised service numbers. Archaeological excavations are the only way of getting to know these kinds of artefacts.

In addition, a lot of earthenware is found, much of it consisting of cups, saucers and plates. Archaeologists refer to this as 'mass-produced white earthenware', as it was developed after the Industrial Revolution. It is often decorated, for instance with floral or geometric designs. Due to mass production, it was more affordable and of much better quality and more hygienic than the older red-glazed earthenware. In most cases, the producer's name was stamped on the bottom.

On the German side, earthenware mineral-water jugs were quite common. They always bore a seal with a brand name, such as Selters[9]. The jugs were brought from Germany to the front lines.

The waste pits also show how comfortably furnished some of the huts were. In several places, red flower pots and porcelain figurines were found.

In addition to the earthenware, fragments of white or red clay pipes were often found, or pipes made of Bakelite. Though usually quite simple, there were also some quite intricate ones. For instance, in Koksijde, three pipes decorated with faces (depicting a cavalryman, Lord Kitchener and Narcissus) came to light[10]. In the late nineteenth and early twentieth centuries, pipes with faces on them were a new trend, apparently also encompassing the military. Such pipes were more expensive than standard ones and probably only officers could afford them.

102

103

104

FIG. 102
Medical material (urinal, cylindrical bottles, an ampoule and the cobalt-blue fragment of a bottle with the words 'Not to be taken' on it) and several inkpots from the hospital in Lijssenthoek.

FIG. 103
A crucifix made out of a shell.

FIG. 104
Various hand-made artefacts (left to right): a miniature axe made from a flattened bullet point, bullets fashioned into chessmen (?), French Lebel bullet made into an arrowhead, possibly a tool used to make trench-art (?) and a bullet fashioned into a cross.

PERSONAL HYGIENE AND MEDICAL ARTEFACTS

Many objects found in waste pits are connected with personal hygiene, reflecting the personal side of life in a military camp. Toothbrushes made of hard plastic, ivory or even bone are the commonest finds. In many cases, the name of the producer is found on the handle. Some even sport slogans such as 'A clean tooth never decays – Prophylactic' or 'The Aero-Brush'. In some cases, the handles have been sharpened to form a toothpick.

Also found were plastic soap holders and simple containers with a lid. White porcelain jars contained ointments for the basic care of minor injuries or to prevent cracked feet and hands. Small blue, green or brown bottles of disinfectants are sometimes marked 'Not to be taken' or *Uitwendig gebruik – Usage externe*. Small ampoules contained iodine, used as a disinfectant. A lot of medical material was found in the Lijssenthoek field hospital (**FIG. 102**).

TRENCH ART

Far behind the front, the soldiers could rest and recuperate, as can be seen from the finds in the camp sites. Some of them spent their time making trench art – works of art made from military material (**FIG. 103 & 104**). Simple ashtrays made from the bottom of a copper shell casing were very common. More difficult to make were letter openers hammered out of the copper driving bands of shells. Other examples included decorated bullet heads, in most cases using French 8-mm bullets. These were cut and hammered into small crucifixes, toothpicks, arrowheads or even rings for fingers (**FIG. 104**). Objects used for games, such as chessmen, were made from scraps of clothing and bullets. Draughts were formed from bullet heads, tent rings and buttons hammered flat. The soldiers also did target practice, whether as a form of competition or a pastime, shooting at coins, as witnessed by two coins with bullet holes in them.

J

Soldiers were sometimes very creative, making use of anything found lying around the battlefield. The best-known examples of such trench art are decorated shell casings. These became very popular after the war as souvenirs. Among the large quantities of archaeological finds, there are often some quite unique pieces. These crude letter openers, possible toothpicks and additional unfinished material came from a pit in Roesbrugge-Haringe, a place behind the lines where soldiers could rest and recuperate.

5 Horses and mules at the front

Anton Ervynck
An Lentacker

105

106

FIG. 105
Artillery crossing the Ypres-Yser Canal.

FIG. 106
A dead stallion near the front in Ypres.

FIG. 107 (pp. 102-103)
Dead horses on the Ypres Salient battlefield.

Animals played an important role in the First World War[1]. Dogs pulled carts and pigeons carried messages, but the most important role was given to horses and mules. While also used for riding, they were mainly used for pulling and carrying purposes (**FIG. 105**)[2]. At the outbreak of the war, the armies were still not that motorised. And even in the later war years, motor vehicles were just not suitable for the war-torn terrain of the Western Front. With the permanent supply of food, building materials and especially ammunition to a static front line a top concern, the onus fell on horses and mules.

Statistics speak volumes about the importance of animals, whether for riding, pulling or carrying things. Figures illustrating their use in the British army are abundant. Immediately before the war, the British army had some 25,000 horses. Twelve days after mobilisation, there were six times that number, and around the middle of 1917 the figure reached nearly 600,000, alongside more than 250,000 other beasts of burden[3].This posed enormous logistical problems, with stabling, food and veterinary services needed. The army unit responsible was the Remount Department, and its strength grew from a few hundred men before the war to nearly 20,000 in mid 1917[4]. At any moment in time, the Army Veterinary Corps responsible for the health of the animals had 90,000 sick or recovering animals in its care throughout the world's war regions[5]. The German army gave horses a similarly important role[6]. It quickly requisitioned 615,000 horses on mobilisation in 1914[7].

The animals transporting items close to the front or in the hinterland were subject to great danger (**FIG. 106 & 107**). They were constantly fired at, as cutting off supply lines could have dire consequences. They also had to cope with disease, malnutrition, cold and other hardships. The animals were cared for in the camps behind the lines, but many died or had to be slaughtered. Although the British army's losses of riding and transport animals were not that high in percentage terms, losing about 15 percent a year, the French and British armies alone lost nearly 800,000 horses on the Western Front[8]. Another estimate reports that, of the 1,880,000 beasts of burden mobilised by the French army throughout the world, some 1,140,000 ultimately lost their lives in the war[9].This figure equates to 60 percent, corresponding to the estimated 15 percent lost in each of the four war years.

Their slaughter is therefore a historical fact. Though these non-human participants of the war are often forgotten, every now and then their carcasses, now just skeletons, are found during excavations in the former war zone.

[1] Cooper 2000
[2] Clarke 1917, Galtrey 1918, Singleton 1993, The War Office 1922
[3] The War Office 1922
[4] The War Office 1922
[5] Singleton 1993
[6] Van Creveld 1977
[7] Bucholz 1991
[8] The War Office 1922
[9] Bruneau 2005

BURIED, DUMPED, CUT UP

WW1 archaeology has only recently come into its own, a fact that's all the more true for the investigation of animal remains. For a long time, gathering this kind of material was not a priority – and had never been the case in classical Flemish archaeology. Above all, in rural areas, carcasses are to be found buried almost everywhere, and it is often not easy to determine which period they belonged to. It is very probable that thousands of animal war graves have been destroyed without them being documented or investigated. The recent efforts of several young archaeologists with a broader view of the meaning of heritage have ensured that animals now have their own place in WW1 archaeological excavations.

The examination of the remains of horses and other related animals shows that they died in very different ways, and that their remains were not always treated in the same way.

108

FIG. 108
Archaeologists at work on the route of a gas pipeline in Zuidschote at the end of 2014.

IN A NEAT ROW

During the development of the Sappenleen business park to the east of Poperinge, the remains of a British logistics hub were found in 2011[10]. The remains of trenches and bunkers were discovered, as were a place possibly used for preparing ammunition for use and a network of narrow-gauge tracks. The specially laid rails were suitable for the smaller wagons used for transporting ammunition, food and other supplies to the front line. The narrow-gauge tracks connected up to a standard-gauge rail network, in this case the railway running to the north of the surveyed terrain. British troops used this hub between 1914 and 1917[11].

The archaeological survey revealed three graves containing seven horses (**FIG. 109**). These were heavy draught horses with high withers (the highest part of the back at the base of the neck). The animals, both stallions and mares, were probably used for war transport, pulling wagons on the regular and narrow-gauge railways. Apart from one animal, all horses were adults – three and a half years or older.

The regular arrangement of the graves is significant. The pits were in a line at the edge of the camp, with the skeletons in a neat row. Two graves had two skeletons in them. A third pit was divided into three parts with a skeleton in each of them. All skulls had a bullet hole at the front, suggesting that the horses had been sick or wounded and had been systematically put down. The legs had been cut off so that they could be buried more compactly. The horseshoes had not been removed before the animals were buried. There were no indications that anything had happened to the carcasses. Whether the burials all took place at the same time cannot be discerned. What is clear is that the row of graves continued outside the excavation pit – in other words, additional animals had been buried there.

HEAVY STEEDS WITH PAINFUL LEGS

Close to a British-American camp in Watou, a pit was excavated in 2015 containing three slightly damaged horse skeletons (**FIG. 111**). Historical aerial photos show that the camp was set up between 8 March and 9 May 1918 and was abandoned before 20 May 1918. The remains found in the pit belonged to two adult stallions and one adult mare. The three animals were obviously draught horses, as could be seen from the size of their horseshoes. One of the horses had been buried with its harness. The signs of disease on their hooves are noteworthy, indicating that they suffered from laminitis, a painful inflammation between the hoof bone and the hoof, which ultimately immobilised the animals. Was that why they were put down?

[10] Demeyere 2010, Van Couwenberghe et al. 2011, Beke 2013
[11] Demeyere 2010

109

SKELETONS WITH MISSING BONES

The Zwijnlandstraat runs to the west of Poperinge, in the former war zone. A few barracks are marked on the trench maps, and in the north lies Agra Cross, a camp with a marshalling yard. In late 2013, a probe dig was conducted along the street, revealing a pit with the remains of horses from the First World War. The skeletons belonged to at least three adult draught horses, but parts of the skeletons were missing. Two of them were certainly stallions. There were no traces of violence, such as gunshot wounds to the skull. Nothing indicated that the dead horses had been used for food, but they might have been cut up to fit them into the pit, where the skeletons were disturbed at a later date.

KILLED BY FRIENDLY FIRE

During the war, Oostvleteren was at the northern end of the Ypres front. The village formed part of the Allied line of defence, with the front running along the Ypres-Yser Canal. A number of narrow-gauge railways served the front, transporting troops and supplies to and from the front. French units dominated, with Belgian units also present from 1915 onwards. British troops were there between June and November 1917.

110

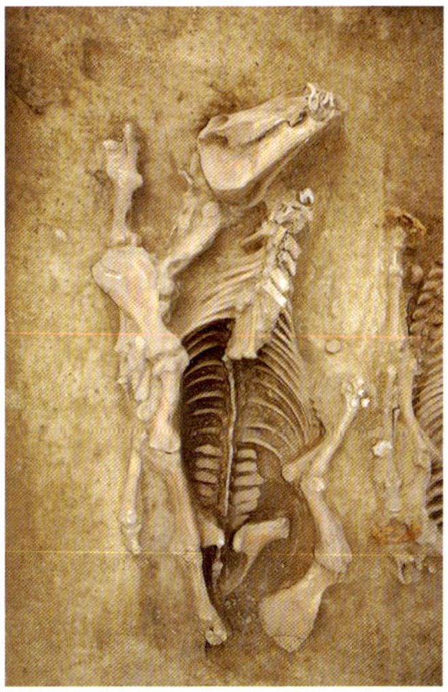

111

FIG. 109
Excavation of a row of horses' graves at the Sappenleen site in Poperinge.

FIG. 110
Horse grave at the Sappenleen site in Poperinge. The legs were cut away from the carcass to better fit the horse into the pit.

FIG. 111
Pit in Watou containing three horse skeletons. One animal was still wearing its bit and harness.

An excavation along the Kasteelweg in 2012 revealed a pit with the skeletons of two fully grown draught horses[12]. The skeletons were undisturbed, with each bone positioned as in a living animal. There was a hole right through the left shoulder of the largest horse (**FIG. 112**), and a bullet was found 15 centimetres away from the bone. Strangely enough, the bullet had been made in France[13]. It would therefore seem that the horse had been killed by friendly fire. This might have happened accidentally, but it is also possible that the horse was intentionally put down because it had become unmanageable. A shot in the left shoulder is very effective, being aimed at the heart. The skeletons of the two animals show no signs of the carcass having been put to use.

112

HEADLESS HORSES CLOSE TO THE MENIN GATE

Excavations close to the Menin Gate in 2012 unearthed the remains of horses used for riding or transport. They obviously dated back to the First World War[14]. Two skeletons were reported as found in an anatomically correct position but they had not been photographed or documented in any other way. Eight horseshoes, a bit and a halter were also found. A study of the bones revealed that the remains belonged to at least four fully grown horses. What was strange, however, was that all the skulls were missing. It seemed as if the horses had just been dumped after their death in a hole or depression next to the main road into the town. They might have been killed by shelling. Again, there are no signs that any further use had been made of the carcasses.

MULES FROM MISSOURI

Excavations along the route of a new gas pipeline in Zuidschote unearthed the grave of an adult animal (**FIG. 108**)[15]. The discovery was on the Belgian-French side of the front, along the first support line with small bunkers, just 500 metres behind the front line along the Ypres-Yser Canal. The skull had two, possibly three bullet holes in it, resulting from Belgian bullets, of which remains of the heads were found. It seems likely that the animal had been wounded and therefore had to be put down by the Belgians. The hooves were in a bad condition, possibly indicating laminitis.

An analysis of the bones showed that the skeleton did not belong to a horse but to a mule, a cross between a donkey and a female horse. Mules are sterile, so can't have any offspring. Therefore they have to be specifically bred from

FIG. 112
A bullet had gone right through the shoulder of a horse from Oostvleteren

FIG. 113
Photo of a soldier and his mule at the Western Front. On the back is written: 'She is very stupid but I am very fond of her'.

[12] Demey 2013
[13] Personal record, Dieter Demey
[14] Verdegem et al. 2013
[15] Bracke et al. 2015

[16] Clutton-Brock 1999
[17] The War Office 1922
[18] Hibbard 1919
[19] Hibbard 1919

horse and donkey populations. For thousands of years they have been used as beasts of burden due to their great strength and endurance. They are valued because they're stronger than a horse of similar size, inherit the endurance and disposition of the donkey sire, tend to require less food than a horse of similar size and are more disease-resistant[16]. Mules can be differentiated from horses by their short, wide heads, long ears, thin legs and small hooves.

The British were unable to import sufficient replacements from the United Kingdom to cover the daily loss of animals, without damaging the domestic economy. Therefore the decision was quickly taken to revive a supply line developed during the South African Boer War at the end of the nineteenth century: the purchase of animals from the New World, primarily from the United States. Alongside horses, farmers there made great use of mules, which, like horses, had proven their worth in the South African battles. A continual and large-scale supply of mules thus fuelled the Western Front. Up to the Armistice in 1918, a total of 428,608 horses and 275,097 mules were imported from North America[17]. As the US population of horses and mules at the time was enormous – the country had an estimated 21 million horses alone[18] – their sale, even on such a scale, was no problem for the US farming economy. Indeed, quite a few US farms made a fortune in this period. For instance, Guyton & Harrington, a company based in Lathrop, a small town in Clinton County, Missouri, supplied an estimated 350,000 horses and mules, about one half of all the animals imported from North America.[19]

113

FIG. 114

Skull of a horse found in Reningelst, with a bullet hole in its forehead.

K

Archaeologists are used to finding animal skeletons everywhere on the front. This mule skull came from Reningelst, a British logistics hub behind the front line during the war. An excavation there unearthed the remains of 27 carcasses dumped in pits. An analysis of the bones revealed a mix of horses and mules.

The horses and mules were transported by train to the US coast, where they were loaded on to ships. It seems that the mules coped better with the journey than the horses. In the first year of the war, two percent of horses died during transport due to disease or accidents, but a much lower percentage of mules. Later, the number of casualties grew as the German army increasingly tried to sink the ships or to kill their living cargo by shelling[20]. On arrival in England, the animals were quarantined for three weeks in the ports (Bristol, Liverpool and Southampton), allowing them to become acclimatised and to regain their strength. They were then transported to the Western Front. Between 1914 and 1918, some 500-1,000 animals left the USA every other day for Europe[21].

HORSES AS FOOD

Although Reningelst was located behind the front, it had to put up with a lot. French, British and Canadian troops were billeted there and it served as a hub through which food, ammunition and other supplies were transported to the front. Excavations in the village in 2009 revealed a large number of pits containing the remains of animals[22].These were not individual burials but parts of carcasses buried together with other waste material. The archaeologists collected parts belonging to at least 27 horses and mules.

The horses were 150-173 centimetres high. On the basis of the bone material, researchers can tell whether the animals were slender or robust[23]. In this particular case, the animals were robust, although there were two weaker horses among them, probably ridden by the men driving the draught horses. Generally speaking, the Reningelst horses were a mixed group, undoubtedly reflecting their varying origins: they had been requisitioned from many different places. This contrasts greatly with the remains of the mules, which showed much more uniform dimensions, as they all came from just a few American farms. They were all 150-161 centimetres high and had a much less robust skeleton than the group of draught horses. With the exception of one young animal, possibly a horse, all horses and mules found had reached adulthood. Both stallions and mares were present.

All skulls where the forehead was still present showed a bullet hole (**FIG. 114**). The animals had been shot to relieve them of their suffering. The skeletons of horses and mules tell us that, during their lives, they had much to endure. A unique feature of the Reningelst find is the cutting-up of the carcasses, with cutting and chopping marks suggesting that the meat was taken from the bones, perhaps as food for the soldiers. Another possibility is that civilians from the surrounding villages made use of the carcasses, but as mainly military waste was found in the pits, the first explanation seems more likely.

An invaluable source of information for this section of the front are the war diaries of Achiel Van Walleghem, the curate of Dikkebus, who was posted to Reningelst in 1916. He described life at the front in detail, for example the shelling in May 1917 during which several horses were killed along the transport lines from Reningelst: “Thursday, 31 May. Again, the transport lines have been pounded by heavy fire. (…) By the afternoon, 13 dead horses could be counted between Zorgfried and the Groene Jager (3 minutes down the road), and 30 up to the Café Français. This evening, the transport schedule is going to be changed to deceive the Germans. The ammunition will also be transported without wagons, with each horse carrying 8 shells. This way, things will not come to a halt if a horse is killed or wounded. And in the case of any shelling, smaller paths can be taken or the horses can cut across the fields.”[24]

MEN AND THEIR ANIMALS

The remains of a total of almost 50 different animals from seven Flemish sites were studied – obviously just a very small percentage of the animals buried along the front line. But we can see a certain pattern. There are significant differences in burial methods, reflecting the diverse war situations. Straight rows of graves and the fact that the animals were not used for food point to a different ‘war environment’ in Sappenleen in Poperinge than in the camp in Reningelst. In the first case, the animals had been put down, but had been given a ‘decent’ burial. In the second, the carcasses had been cut up and the meat removed before being dumped in the waste pits. While horses were true brothers-in-arms, their treatment in Reningelst was different to that in Poperinge. How did the Anglo-Saxon soldiers in Reningelst cope with eating horsemeat, something that was taboo in their home countries? The finds elsewhere indicate that the animals were probably killed by shelling. One of the horses buried in Oostvleteren may have been shot after getting out of control.

[20] The War Office 1922
[21] Lyddon 1938
[22] Bouckaert et al. 2009, Bracke et al. 2013
[23] Lepetz 1996
[24] Spillebeen 2014

[25] Van Emden 2010
[26] Brereton 1976
[27] Barata 2013
[28] Animals in War Memorial Fund 2016
[29] This contribution is a rework and update of an earlier report in Ervynck & Lentacker 2014

We can read in soldiers' diaries that close social contacts existed between the men and the horses or mules[25]. Many soldiers looked after the same horse or mule for months on end, with the trials endured bonding them together: "The soldier came to regard his horse almost as an extension of his being."[26] However, circumstances put great pressure on such bonds, and in many cases goodbyes had to be said. Killed animals had to be abandoned next to the road, in a shell crater or a hastily dug pit. Sick or wounded animals were put down and given a decent burial close to the camps behind the front. In other places, the hunger was so acute that the horsemeat was eaten.

Animals serving and dying in war have been honoured in publications and on war memorials[27]. One of the best-known ones is the Animals in War Memorial unveiled on 22 November 2004 in a corner of Hyde Park in London[28], inscribed with the words 'They had no choice'. Although that also applied to many soldiers, fortune smiled less on the animals. No horse ever volunteered to join the army![29]

115

FIG. 115
The Animals in War Memorial in London: 'They had no choice'.

FIG. 116
Requisitioning horses in Bousbecque, 1915.

6 Bread and soup: simple but nourishing food

Anton Ervynck
An Lentacker
Maarten Bracke

117

FIG. 117
German soldiers eating a meagre meal in a trench shelter in Zillebeke.

FIG. 118
Field kitchens belonging to a New Zealand regiment close to the front line.

118

Archaeologists want not only to reconstruct what existed in a certain place in the past, but also to find out what life was like, how people interacted, what they thought about life and death. WW1 archaeology is no exception here, with 'everyday life' on and behind the front line a fascinating field of research. For instance, what did the soldiers eat? For researchers this is an interesting question, but for soldiers at the front it was a daily concern. "An army marches on its stomach," the Roman doctor Claudius Galenus is supposed to have said in the second century AD. Soldiers suffering from hunger or given the same food day in, day out, are less likely to fight hard and more likely to pay less attention, lose their motivation and even mutiny. During the Great War, a good supply of food was essential, especially since the campaign lasted for years[1].

What did the cooking pots hold in store for the soldiers at the front (**FIG. 117**)? When WW1 archaeology started gaining pace, hopes were high that excavations would quickly find an answer to this question. At medieval or older archaeological sites, the archaeologists had almost literally stumbled across food remains, but in the excavated trenches this was never the case. It seems as if the soldiers kept their trenches clean and tidy, with a view to not making their stay there worse than it already was. While archaeologists have found cutlery, cans and bottles, no gnawed bones, fish bones or seeds have turned up. The same is true at sites behind the front, where again hardly anything has been found to indicate what was actually inside the cooking pots.

CORNED BEEF AND COLD STEW

For those with knowledge of what life at the front was like, the absence of animal or vegetable waste at the front lines comes as no surprise. The food brought in via the supply trenches was prepared behind the lines and consisted mainly of meals that leave practically no archaeological traces: soup, thin stew, porridge and, above all, plenty of bread or hardtack biscuits[2]. Warm meals came from mobile field kitchens (**FIG. 118**), but these had only limited possibilities and therefore produced just simple meals. In addition, the soldiers received canned food, but unfortunately any

[1] Arthur, 2014
[2] Lee 2014, Trueman 2016

remains of the cans themselves quickly degraded in the West Flemish soil. Moreover, the contents of such cans can only be guessed at, as no traces were left.

On the British side, neither the bully beef supplied in vast quantities nor the equally infamous Maconochie stew are of any archaeological interest. Bully beef, later popularised as corned beef, was nothing more than finely minced meat. Maconochie stew was a stew made of chopped turnips, carrots and potatoes, in a thin broth. Such meals left little waste of any interest to archaeologists[3].

The picture we get from historical documents about what the food was like in the trenches is that it was low-quality. This was not just the result of penny-pinching by army paymasters, but also of the sheer logistics of providing huge armies with high-quality meals. The result was little more than survival rations: *À la guerre comme à la guerre*. The British Empire employed 300,000 people to maintain food supplies. They were responsible for more than 3 million tons of food being shipped from the British Isles to the Western Front between 1914 and 1918. But even so, rations got smaller over the course of the war[4].Troops not posted to the front lines only got meat – or something resembling it – once every three days. The front lines were better off. However, as the kitchens were quite some distance from the trenches, the meals were delivered cold (**FIG. 119**). The soldiers sometimes used improvised fires to warm up the meals, but this had the disadvantage of the smoke attracting enemy attention.

119

SAWN BEEF

Archaeologists researching the subject of food made a breakthrough while excavating sites further away from the front. On the grounds of Hof ter Hille in Koksijde, where an Allied command post was stationed, a large pit was found in 2010. Apart from the usual glassware and ceramics, it also contained some bone material[5]. This has not yet been analysed. The same was true for a German site in Zonnebeke, where a small assortment of animal remains were recovered[6]. Furthermore, excavations on the site of the Allied hospital at Lijssenthoek in Poperinge in 2011 unearthed the bones of at least three chickens, curiously tucked away in a wooden box[7]. Also in the box were a bone from a rabbit and some grape seeds. It would be an exaggeration to consider the find an example of front

[3] Simkin 2015
[4] The War Office 1922
[5] Bracke 2010
[6] Bracke et al. 2012
[7] Bracke 2012

FIG. 119
Australian soldiers bringing warm soup to the reserve troops in Ploegsteert on 22 January 1918.

FIG. 120
Sawn beef bones found in Oostvleteren.

FIG. 121
A chicken leg with plastic rings indicating the owner (?), found in Oostvleteren.

supplies, but nevertheless it put the archaeologists on the right track. More bones were found at another hospital site, a little further away from the front.

In 2014, the archaeological team working in Oostvleteren came across waste in a place close to where a Belgian-French hospital had been located during the war[8]. In a series of pits that were almost in a straight line, they found thermometers, ampoules, medical bottles and glass syringes. An identity tag belonging to Sergeant Jean Wasson from Verviers, killed in Merkem on 12 December 1917 and originally buried in the Westvleteren military cemetery, provided a date. The pits also contained food waste, including the bones of chicken and rabbits. The find is significant because one of the chicken bones still had plastic rings around it (**FIG. 121**). Using a 0.5 mm sieve, the researchers sieved through the contents of the waste pits in search of minuscule food remains. One of the conclusions was that the hospital kitchens also cooked fish, in particular roach and tench, species found in the streams of the Yser basin[9]. The sieved remains also contained bones from brown rats – these were not an ingredient but rather uninvited guests. Between the vegetable remains, grains of barley and some charred beans were found[10].

The majority of the animal material found in the pits consisted of the bones of larger mammals, especially cattle, but also some sheep and pigs. The beef bones (**FIG. 120**) show signs not only of chopping with an axe or other sharp tool, but also of sawing with a thin (machine-driven?) saw. The bones had been cut into 10 centimetre sections, taking little account of the characteristic composition of the bovine skeleton, meaning it was not the work of a professional slaughterer.

[8] Bracke et al. 2015
[9] With thanks to Wim Wouters, Royal Belgian Institute of Natural Sciences, for the identification.
[10] With thanks to Brigitte Cooremans and Jan Bastiaens from the Belgian Heritage Agency for the identification

120

121

FIG. 122
German troops with bread.

123

This suggests that, once the meat had been removed from the bones, the latter had been boiled to extract the marrow or to make meat broth – 'bone broth' in this case. Bone marrow is very nutritious, while the bone fat released during boiling gives strength.

Most of the beef bones from Oostvleteren come from young animals, and not just from those parts of the carcass with the most meat on them. No skull fragments were found, suggesting that the animals were slaughtered elsewhere. Bones of the leg ends, also with little meat on them, were split longitudinally to get to the marrow. All this illustrates meat processing dictated by necessity. Nothing was wasted.

MORE SAWN BEEF

Another site where bone remains were found was in Zuidschote, among the French-Belgian trenches and bunkers. They came from a waste pit dating from 1916-1917[11]. The make-up of the animal remains is similar to that of Oostvleteren. Again, the bones come mainly from cattle, and to a lesser extent from sheep. Pig bones were not found. Smaller material was not present or not recovered. Again, the beef bones had been systematically sawn. Compared to Oostvleteren, there were fewer traces of chopping. Not only were no skulls found, but also no bones from the leg ends. Bones with little meat on them were therefore less used. It seems plausible that in Zuidschote, just 1.5 kilometres from the front line, there were fewer possibilities to process animal carcasses compared to Oostvleteren, located in a somewhat quieter setting 7 kilometres behind the front line. Or perhaps the supply chain from the slaughterhouse to the field kitchens was not always the same everywhere along the front, or maybe it changed over the course of the war.

GERMAN BREAD

During the construction of a gas pipeline on the border between Langemark and Houthulst in 2014, archaeologists unearthed a waste pit containing a range of rubbish, probably discarded by an army camp there in 1917[12]. It contained bottles, corks, bullets, some pieces of leather, a lot of textiles that looked like pieces of stockings, fragments of a kind of fibreboard, wood and fragments of pages from a book. These all clearly indicated that they were of German origin and had been set on fire at some time. Perhaps they were the remains of a clearing-up operation or a campfire.

The pit contained a few bones from pigs, a small assortment of plant remains with straw stalks, a few food remains such as the stones of

[11] Bracke & Verdegem 2015
[12] Bracke & Verdegem 2015
[13] With thanks to Jan Bastiaens from the Belgian Heritage Agency for the identification.

FIG. 123
Charred remains of *Kommissbrot*, found in Langemark-Houthulst.

FIG. 124 (pp. 122-123)
Bakers kneading *Kommissbrot* in a German bakery in Wervik, 1916.

peaches, plums and cherries, and charred cereal grains, among them rye and bread wheat (FIG. 123)[13]. Due to charring, the cereal grains had been preserved in the ground. While incineration causes considerable damage to archaeological plant material, at the same time changes occur in its chemistry and structural composition, as a result of which the plant remains suddenly become more likely to be preserved. This was also the case with a large number of objects first described as charcoal in the fieldwork. On closer inspection, it turned out that they were charred pieces of a sort of bread with a compact structure.

Not much research was needed to find out that this was the famous *Kommissbrot*, a dark type of German bread, baked from rye and other flours, historically used for military provisions. Sourdough and a little yeast caused the dough to rise slightly. After kneading, the dough was then pressed into blocks before being put in the oven. The result was a compact loaf that kept well and had a high nutritional value. *Kommissbrot* had been part of German soldiers' provisions well before the First World War and continued to be used until after the Second World War. It is still baked in certain non-military bakeries in Germany, albeit using a recipe less strict than that used in wartime[14]. There are accounts that, due to a shortage of flour during the war, sawdust was also mixed in, but archaeologists have so far found no evidence of this. Detailed investigations of the finds from Langemark-Houthulst may shed further light on this aspect.

The fact that pieces of bread have been found primarily on the German side of the front is perhaps not by chance, as bread played a more important role in the diet of German troops than in that of their Allied counterparts. British war statistics state that British soldiers were entitled to 16 ounces of bread, 16 ounces of meat and 4 ounces of bacon a day – an Anglo-Saxon culinary peculiarity, with bacon apparently not counted as meat. The British statistics also report the daily ration of their German counterparts: 26.4 ounces of bread and 10.5 ounces of meat[15].The preponderance of bread and the lower proportion of meat on the German side is striking. The German meat ration probably included bacon – or rather *Speck* – but this is not mentioned separately in these statistics: a subtle difference in culinary appreciation.

Sixteen English ounces make up one English pound (lb), approximately half a kilogramme, or 454 grammes to be precise. German soldiers were thus entitled to about 800 grammes of *Kommissbrot* a day. Its delivery was therefore crucial. Under normal circumstances, just a few slices are all that is needed to feel full, but no doubt that was completely different in war conditions.

[14] Wikipedia 2016
[15] The War Office 1922

A MEAGRE RECONSTRUCTION OF MEAGRE MEALS

Archaeological insights into soldiers' rations are still incomplete. Every opportunity to collect food remains must be grabbed at each new site. It would be interesting to better chart the share of cereals, vegetables and fruit, however little and however monotonous. It is equally fascinating to compare the meat supply in different parts of the front at different times in the war and between the two sides. For the time being, it would seem that beef was the most common meat ingredient in the field kitchens. Until now, no traces of the remains of dead horses and mules cut up for their meat (see Chapter 5) have been found in the waste pits. The 'scavenging' of dead animals was perhaps outside the normal food supply circumstances. More research is needed to support these findings – the cliché with which almost every archaeological report ends.

7 Archaeological finds in the hinterland: far from the front, but close to the war

Maarten Bracke
Wouter Gheyle
Johan Hoorne
Birger Stichelbaut

125

FIG. 125
Belgian troops in an improvised trench near Mechelen (Malines).

FIG. 126
Cross-section of a foxhole.

FIG. 127
Trench with shelters in Boortmeerbeek.

126

127

When speaking about the First World War in Belgium, we immediately think of the Westhoek, the westernmost part of Belgian along the French frontier and bordered by the North Sea. Less well known is the fact that the war also left its traces in the rest of the country. These include, for example, remains dating back to the first months of the war when the fight had not yet come to a standstill in the Westhoek (**FIG. 125**), and the remains of military infrastructures deep in the hinterland.

Archaeological remains in the rest of Flanders are discovered mainly by chance during excavations of sites from earlier periods. Not so long ago, archaeologists considered these war remains as 'recent disturbances', but now they are receiving the scientific attention they deserve. The density of trenches, bunkers and gun emplacements in the Westhoek is not repeated in the hinterland, which is characterised by a wide diversity of sites. In this chapter we would like to illustrate this diversity by looking at some of these sites.

FOXHOLES AND PERMANENT TRENCHES DATING BACK TO THE EARLY DAYS

Historical sources tell us that the war progressed very quickly to start with, as can be seen in the archaeological soil archive. Material witnesses of the first two months of the war are, in fact, quite rare. Foxholes are among the few archaeological traces of the short battles: very simple pits for one or more soldiers. They could be dug quickly and offered protection against an advancing enemy. Sometimes they were positioned in such a way that they formed a rudimentary line of defence.

Excavations conducted in the region south of Antwerp show how shallow the foxholes were (**FIG. 126**). Finds were limited to a few Belgian or German bullet shells, fragments of pipes, a few broken bottles and, occasionally, also parts of clothing such as buttons and buckles. The foxholes indicate where the German advance was resisted. Above all, they are important because they constitute the only material remains of a war that was still being conducted in a very mobile manner. They also constitute the oldest form of WW1 field defences. Within just a few months, they had evolved along the Western Front into extensive trench networks.

In the vicinity of Antwerp, Lier, Boortmeerbeek (**FIG. 127**) and Elewijt, a few sites dating back to the first days of the war have been excavated[1], revealing the first instances of fully

[1] Bax & Smeets 2014, Lefere 2014

128

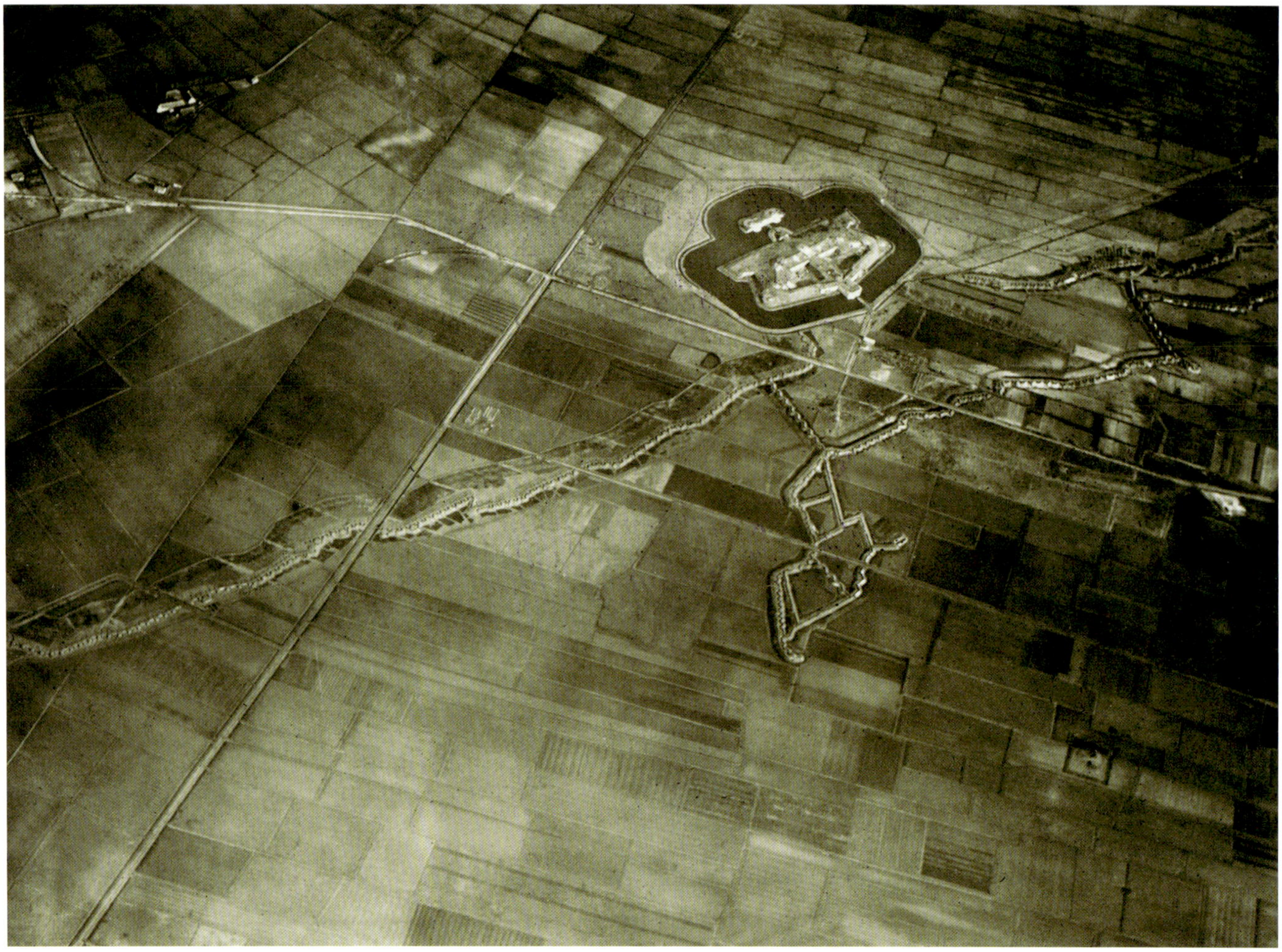

129

FIG. 128

German aerial photo of the fort of Stabroek and the German entrenchment.

FIG. 129

Excavation in Emblem. The brown discolouration in the soil indicates the course of the trench. The reinforced walls in the semi-circular traverse are clearly visible.

FIG. 130

German bunker in the Mastenbos in Kapellen.

130

fledged trenches found in Belgium. Along the Duwijck Canal northwest of Lier, archaeologists registered such a trench covering a distance of 90 metres[2]. Comparing subtle discolourations in the soil with historical pictures, the rectangular holes dug to a depth of 1.5-2 metres can be interpreted as shelters. Dug into the wall of a trench, they offered a minimum of protection against bullets, shrapnel and the weather.

Excavations were conducted in Emblem about 100 metres away from the fort of Broechem and not far from the Duwijck Canal (**FIG. 129**)[3]. Here again, a trench was discovered, this time 74 metres long. As in Lier, it was a linked-up system of fire bays with curved traverses branching off to the rear. One special feature were the man-made holes up to 1.3 metres below ground level. These indicate that a sizeable parapet must have existed above ground, probably with shelters incorporated into it.

GERMAN LINES IN THE HINTERLAND

After the fall of the belts of fortresses and the withdrawal of the Belgian army behind the Yser, the front line came to a halt in the Westhoek in October 1914, with both sides digging in. An extensive web of trenches then grew. During their occupation of Belgium, the German troops also constructed lines of trenches and bunkers further inland. The Belgian coast, from the front in Nieuwpoort up to Knokke, was fortified to ward off any seaborne attack. The occupiers also constructed a line of bunkers along the Belgian-Dutch border between the Zwin and Antwerp. The line, known as the *Hollandstellung*, was built as a defence against a possible Allied invasion from Zeeland in the case of the Netherlands renouncing its neutrality[4]. The Germans also reused a number of Belgian fortresses and defence lines, with the refurbishment of the defence ring around Antwerp the most striking example.

In 1914 the defences surrounding Antwerp consisted of several elements. Meant to stop the enemy, the outer ring was 94 kilometres long and consisted of 10 old and 11 recently built fortresses spaced at intervals of 5 kilometres. This ring formed the backbone of the Belgian defences. In between the fortresses was a line of fortifications, made up of barbed wire barriers, trenches and shelters which had been quickly constructed in the run-up to the impending siege.

After the city fell to the Germans in October 1914, the occupiers took over the Belgian defences, in some cases considerably extending them. Trenches were adapted to the German standard and during the course of the war hundreds of concrete bunkers were added. Dozens of them still exist. The northern part of the ring around Antwerp, from Stabroek to Schoten, was quite close to the Dutch border and constituted an extension of the *Hollandstellung*. From Schoten to Turnhout, the line followed the Dessel-Schoten Canal and was therefore referred to as the *Stellung Antwerpen-Turnhout*.

The German aerial photographer, Lieutenant Josef Zimmermann, took 53 impressive aerial photos during the war, showing the line of defence in great detail (**FIG. 128**). Commissioned by the Province of Antwerp, researchers from Ghent University recently studied the line's state of preservation, finding that, surprisingly, large sections still existed. The quality and diversity of this heritage are unique in Belgium. Above all, the well-preserved impressive German trench system dating back to 1917 is important. In particular in wooded areas, more than 10 kilometres of trenches and 399 bunkers have stood the test of time well (**FIG. 130**)[5].

[2] Laloo et al. 2013
[3] Dalle 2013
[4] Sakkers et al. 2011
[5] Gheyle & Bourgeois 2013

131

A complex system of trenches and bunkers was revealed in Beveren[6]. Originally a simple Belgian position dating back to 1914, it was considerably extended by the German army to form a stronghold with three parallel trenches. The development was guided by the experience gained at the front. The German soldiers gave up the fortification line of 1914 and replaced it with a continuous trench with semi-circular traverses and concrete bunkers. Communication trenches connected the trench with the rear lines. The bunkers served as shelters for troops, observers and gunmen. Apart from Belgian and German bullets, no artefacts were found.

[6] Van Campenhout & Alma 2014

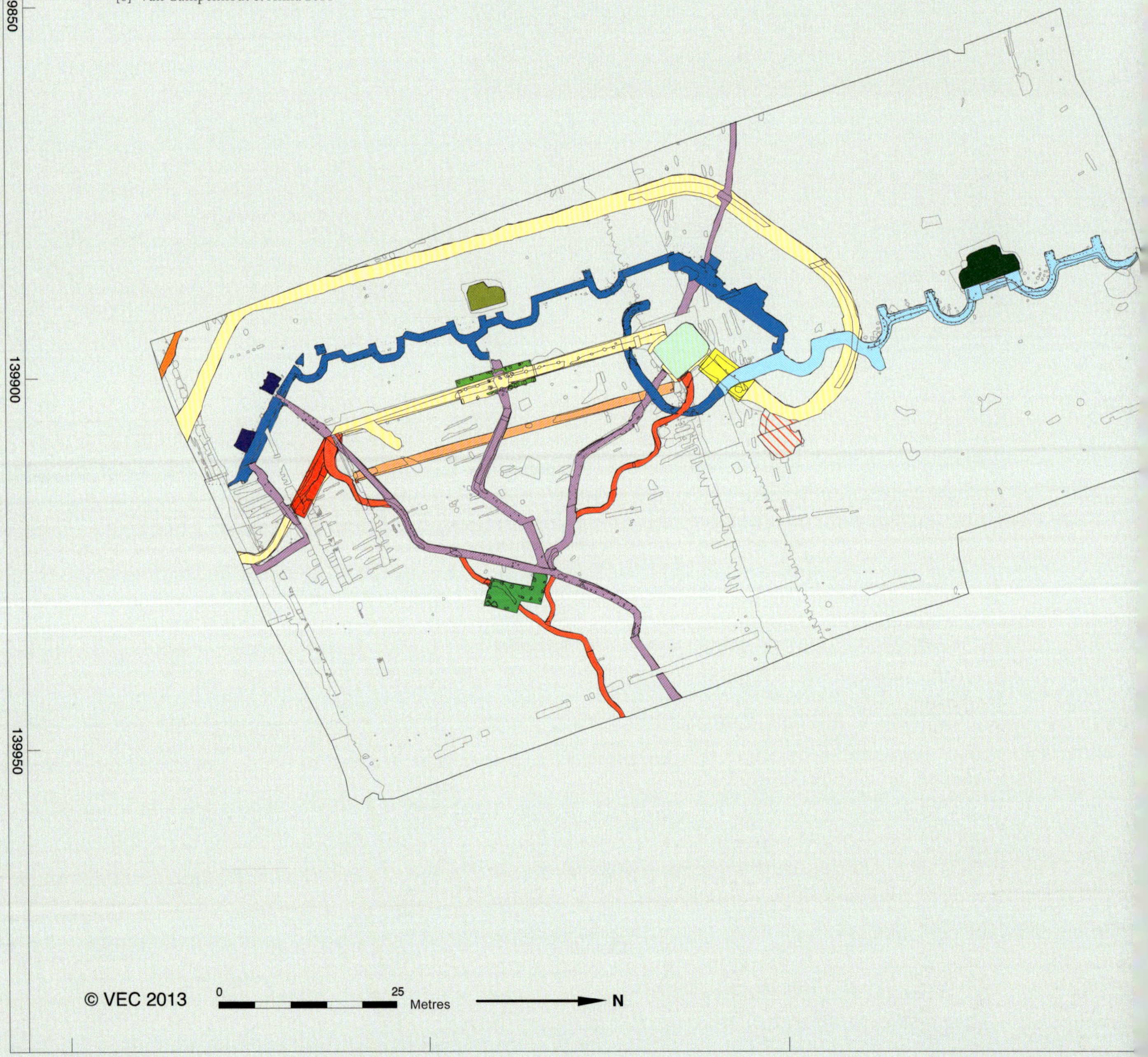

© VEC 2013

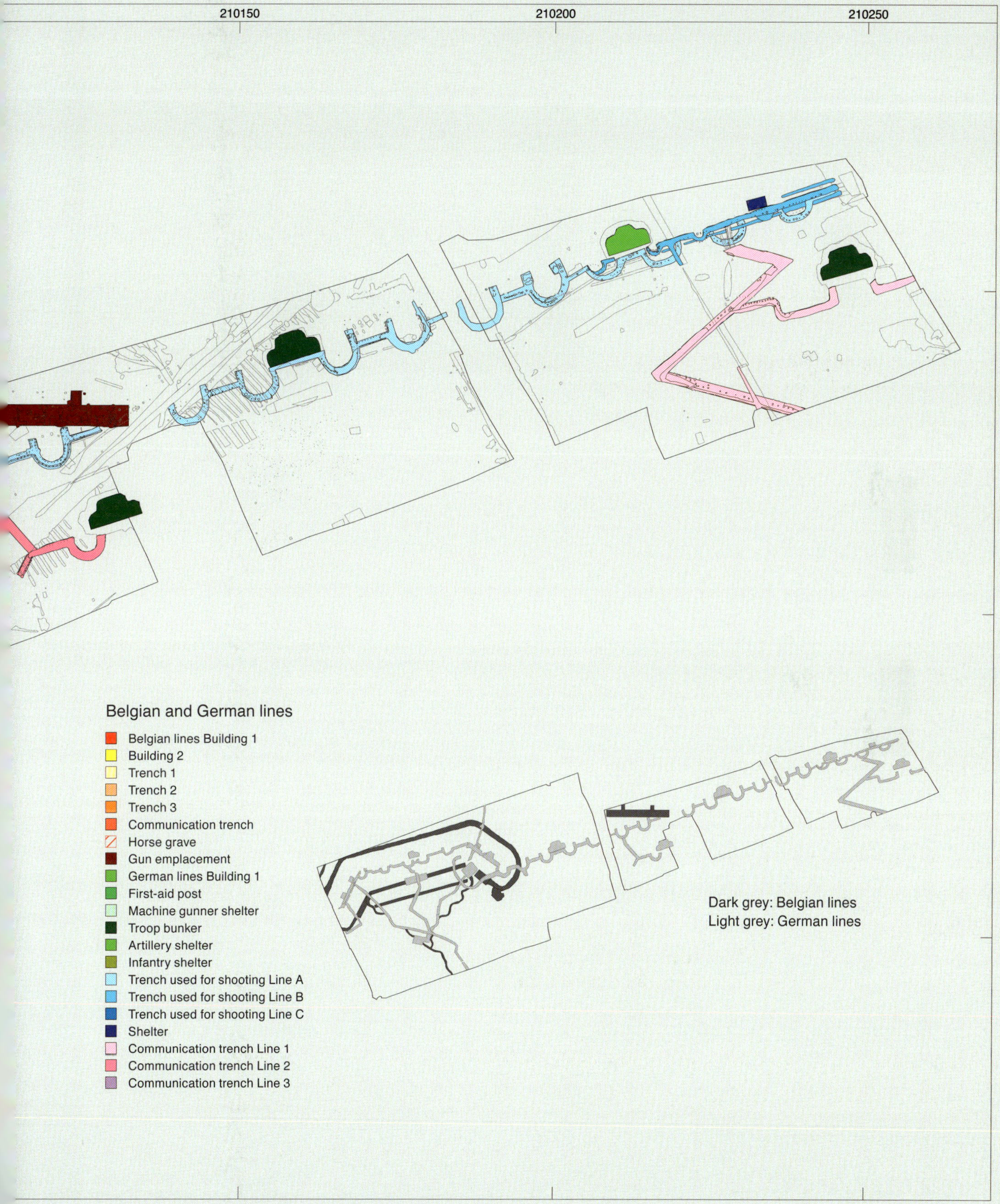
210150
210200
210250
Belgian and German lines
Belgian lines Building 1
Building 2
Trench 1
Trench 2
Trench 3
Communication trench
Horse grave
Gun emplacement
German lines Building 1
First-aid post
Machine gunner shelter
Troop bunker
Artillery shelter
Infantry shelter
Trench used for shooting Line A
Trench used for shooting Line B
Trench used for shooting Line C
Shelter
Communication trench Line 1
Communication trench Line 2
Communication trench Line 3
Dark grey: Belgian lines
Light grey: German lines

The trenches are so well preserved that visitors can get a very good idea of what they looked like at the front. They consist of a high bank of raised earth containing a 1.8-metre-deep trench (**FIG. 132**). The bottom and the walls were strengthened with wood. Every 6 to 10 metres, a square traverse branches out to the rear. Zigzag communication trenches connected the front trench with the rear second line. On the side facing the enemy, shelters were built into the walls and under the parapet, just like the early trenches of 1914. However, compared to the wooden shelters used in 1914, these were made of reinforced concrete, with walls up to 1 metre thick. Built to strict specifications, their function varied from a machine gun emplacement and company bunker to an observation post.

In the north of the Province of Antwerp, the German army built a line of fortifications between the occupied Belgian fortresses. In the Mastenbos in Kapellen one can still find hundreds of metres of remarkably well-preserved trenches and dozens of well-camouflaged bunkers.

M

132

In Puurs, close to the Fort of Liezele, archaeologists from the Flemish Heritage Centre excavated these remains of German trenches in 2016. Over a distance of more than 100 metres the ground was discoloured, showing where, more than a century ago, a trench had run. The semi-circular traverses offered protection against exploding shells. On the front side, small rectangular shelters had been dug out. The trench was part of the southern defence ring around Antwerp, the so-called *Südabschnitt*.

N

TRAINING BEHIND THE LINES

A study of historical aerial photos revealed that in almost all Belgian provinces, even far behind the front line, dozens of trench systems had been built for training purposes. They can be easily distinguished from the front-line trenches by their isolated location and the direction they faced (determined by the contours of the land rather than the position of the enemy) and because they are not connected to other trenches in the vicinity. The German army used them to train troops and teach them new infantry tactics. Other trenches were constructed for specific purposes. Copies of existing trenches were built to acquaint attackers with enemy trenches[7].

While some of the training grounds consisted of just one trench, in most cases there were two parallel trenches, with a no-man's-land in between, just like at the front. Rarer, and very special, were the extensive training areas: large swathes of the countryside redesigned to resemble the front. Above all, the training trench systems in the woods are very well preserved, as they were not levelled during the post-WW1 reconstruction phase. Thanks to digital detection techniques such as Lidar (see Chapter 9), dozens of these sites have been found in wooded areas, but also in dunes and heathlands. The most spectacular ones are to be found in Maasmechelen, De Haan and Koppenberg Woods in Oudenaarde **(FIG. 133 & 134)**.

[7] Grand Quartier Général des Armées 1916

FIG. 132
German trench with a high parapet in the Mastenbos.

FIG. 133
Deep German training trench in Koppenbergbos in Oudenaarde.

FIG. 134
Snapshot of manoeuvres of German storm-troopers belonging to Sturm-bataillon 4 in the vicinity of Koppenberg.

133

134

AMB_1849_3-7-17_3700m 12h.
S. POTTEBESEM
P: Cap. Jaumotte.
O: Lt Wouters.

FIG. 135

Aerial photo of German training trenches in Koekelare, 3 July 1917.

On an aerial photo taken on 3 July 1917, a Belgian photo interpreter marked the route of the trenches in a German training area with red ink (**FIG. 135**). The area was just to the north of Koekelare, 7 kilometres behind the German front along the Yser. We can see a typical training system reconstructing a situation at the front, with two networks of trenches opposite each other. A no-man's-land with simulated shell craters was meant to make the training as realistic as possible.

Archaeologists from the Flemish Heritage Agency excavated a small section of the area to study the construction and condition of such a site8. The study clearly showed that the craters had indeed not been caused by explosions, but had been dug out with spades (**FIG. 136**). The trenches were not very deep and were not equipped with any walling or flooring. We know from historical sources that soldiers in Koekelare were trained in the use of bayonets in man-to-man combat. The trench training also included the wearing of gas masks and reconnaissance at night.

136

FIG. 136
Excavation of German trenches in Koekelare.

FIG. 137
Zeppelin hangar in Gontrode.

FIG. 138
Airfield in Gontrode. Comparison between a present-day aerial photo showing archaeological traces and an aerial photo of the same place taken on 1 October 1917.

LUFTWAFFE AIR BASES

At the beginning of the war, aviation was still in its infancy. The first manned flight in an aircraft had taken place just eleven years earlier, in 1903. At the outbreak of the war, aircraft were used solely for observation purposes, sent up to find out where the enemy was. During the First World War, airborne weapons evolved at incredible speed. Specialist applications such as aerial photography were developed, artillery fire was now also directed from the air, fighter planes patrolled the front to shoot down enemy aircraft, and increasingly larger and heavier aircraft carried out strategic bombing raids for the first time in history.

On historical aerial photos we can make out several airfields just behind the front, far enough to be out of the range of enemy artillery but close enough to reach the front quickly. But there were also dozens of airfields further away, for example in Bruges, Roeselare, Kortrijk, Aalter and Ghent.

These consisted of little more than a levelled field on which aircraft could land and take off. Sometimes there was a paved runway for the heaviest bombers. Alongside the runway were hangars or special tents for the aircraft. Some also had short sections of trench alongside the barracks, offering shelter against air raids.

137

138A

138B

- - - - Paved runway — Foundations ☐ Bunker

0 50 100 200 Metres

139A

139B

Aircraft hangars

0 125 250 500 Metres

FIG. 139
Historical aerial photo taken during the First World War indicating the aircraft hangars.

FIG. 140
Excavation of the centre of the airfield in Sint-Denijs-Westrem featuring the remains of the German drainage system.

[8] Dewilde et al. 2015
[9] Dhanens 2008
[10] Delve 1997
[11] Dhanens 2008
[12] Dhanens 2008

Not much effort has yet been invested in studying the airfields in Flanders, and only a few sites have been looked at. One might think that, as most of the infrastructure (runway, barracks, tents and hangars) was above ground, there is little that archaeological excavation will reveal. Research at two airfields in Gontrode and Sint-Denijs-Westrem, close to Ghent, refutes this assumption, however.

In the dry August of 1999, aerial photographer Jacques Semey observed cropmarks while flying over Gontrode (**FIG. 138A**). Between two large concrete bunkers, a large rectangular area of discolouration can be seen, typical of buried foundations (see Chapter 8). In the right-hand corner of the photo we can also see long stretches of discolouration. By comparing them with historical aerial photos we can interpret the cropmarks.

During the war, Gontrode was a German Luftwaffe airbase. Starting in late 1914, it was extended to become a base for Zeppelins. Most of the bombing raids over Britain were intended to terrorise the civilian population[9]. The most striking structure was a huge Zeppelin hangar. The airbase was later extended with a view to carrying out bombing raids over Britain using heavy bombers. A new unit was set up for Operation Türkenkreuz[10]: Kagohl 3 (*Kampf-geschwader der Obersten Heeresleitung der Luftwaffe 3*), aka England Squadron, based in Gontrode and equipped with heavy Gotha G.IV bombers[11].

A comparison between the present-day and historical photos provides a lot of information about the archaeological remains of the airfield (**FIG. 138B**). The fact that the outlines of the enormous hangars are visible in the crops indicates that remains of the foundations still exist under the surface. Another noteworthy fact is that the runway can still be made out. This clearly shows that changes were necessary to allow the heavy bombers to land without them sinking into the marshy ground. Unlike most other airfields, parts of the runway were paved. Both sides of the runway were probably fitted with concrete drainage channels.

The aerial photos clearly indicate that the site has archaeological potential. Although the history of the airfield is well known, an archaeological excavation might possibly provide new insights into life on and around an airfield that played a crucial role in the development of military aviation.

Started in 2007, one of the biggest and longest archaeological surveys in Flanders is in Sint-Denijs-Westrem. Some 145 hectares on the grounds of the Flanders Expo are being developed into a new residential estate, The Loop. During the excavations, a site was found containing archaeological traces ranging from prehistoric to recent times.

Following the capture of Ghent, the German army quickly realised the potential of the terrain. Since the start of the century, the area had been used as an airfield by the Aéro Club des Flandres. Brought into service in October 1914, the airfield was extended from 1915 onwards to become the Armee Flugpark 4. Two units of the England Squadron were stationed there, taking part in bombing raids over the east coast of England[12].

Aerial photos show the airfield's structure, bordered by the Kortrijksesteenweg and the Ghent-Deinze railway line (**FIG. 139**). Around the runway, we can see large aircraft hangars, bunkers, barracks and anti-aircraft gun emplacements. Offering a glimpse of what is left of the airfield, the excavations focused on its central and northern sections. It quickly became clear that the runway was a levelled grass field, with the whole field used for taking off and landing. To prevent heavy bombers sinking into the mud, the field had to be kept dry. Therefore the German Luftwaffe invested a lot of effort in constructing a fishbone-shaped drainage system consisting of long ditches fitted with earthenware pipes, which quickly drained off any water (**FIG. 140**).

140

8 Archaeology from the air

Birger Stichelbaut
Piet Chielens
Jean Bourgeois

141

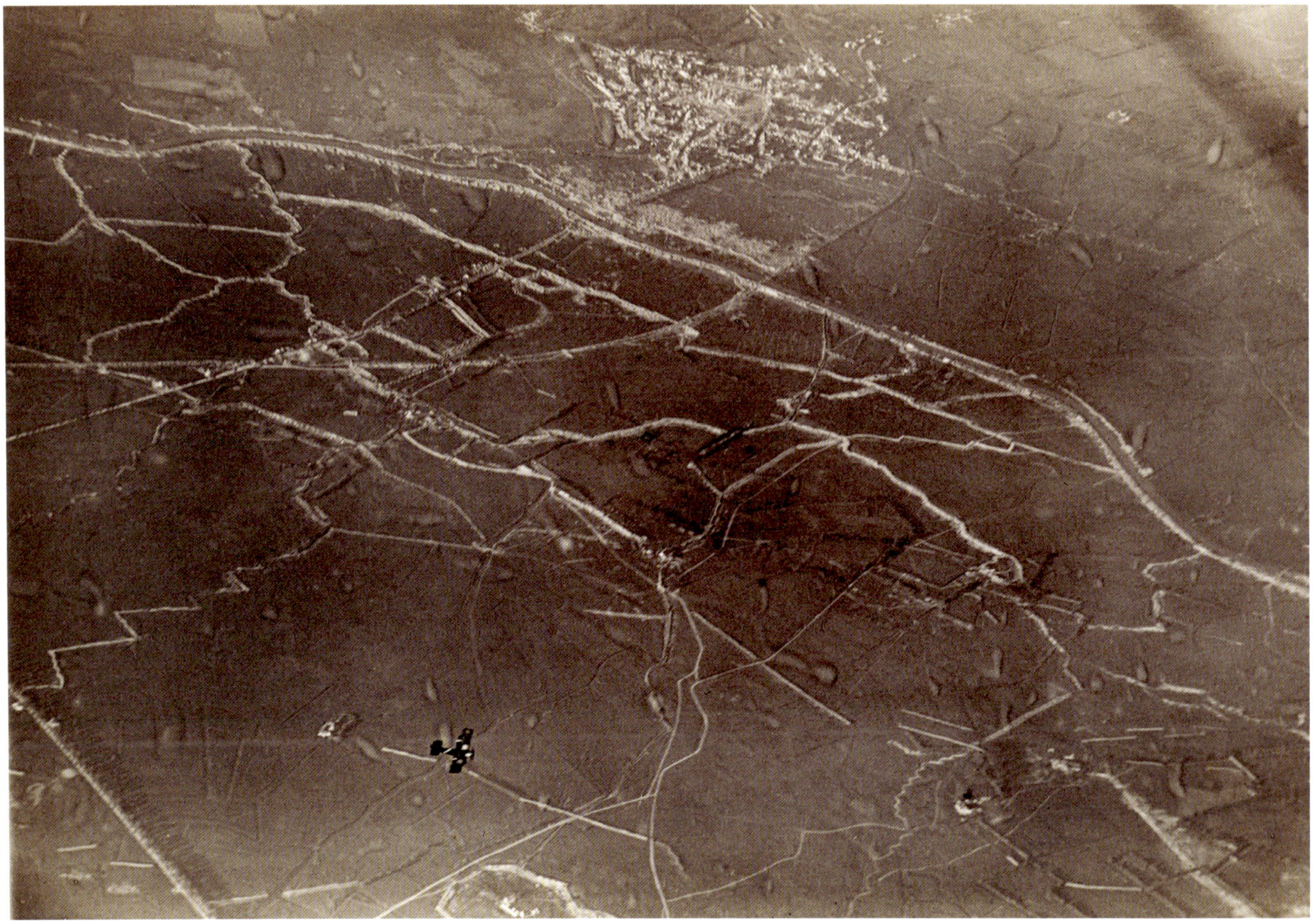

FIG. 141
Biplane over the Belgian trenches along the Yser. The ruins of Diksmuide can be seen at the top right.

These days an archaeologist's tool box contains a whole arsenal of digital tools to help trace, chart and analyse material remains from bygone times. Compared to traditional survey methods, they offer many advantages. They are non-invasive – the ground is left intact and they don't have a negative impact on the state of preservation of the artefacts.

Aerial photography is such a survey method and archaeology without it has become unimaginable. Over the last decade, it has become firmly rooted in WW1 archaeology. In contrast to other historical and map-based sources, aerial photos – whether taken today or a century ago – have the advantage of showing the Western Front in great detail. Moreover, as they are able to cover large surfaces, from several hectares to hundreds of square miles, archaeologists have been able to upscale the scope of their investigations from local to regional.

PIONEERS OF A BIRD'S-EYE VIEW

For aerial photography to be born, developments were needed in two totally different domains: photography and aviation.

Prior to the nineteenth century, experiments were made with optical and chemical processes. The development of the daguerreotype process in 1839 by Louis Daguerre and Joseph Nicéphore Niépce was an enormous step forward[1]. Around ten years later, glass negatives could be rendered light-sensitive using collodium, reducing shutter speeds to just a few seconds[2]. As regarded aviation, initial experiments were made with manned balloons in the late eighteenth century. Photography and aviation were first combined by the French photographer Gaspard-Félix Tournachon, better known under his pseudonym Félix Nadar. He took the first photos from a balloon over Paris in 1858[3]. Thanks to a new photographic process using dry glass plates developed by Richard Maddox in 1871, shutter speeds of under one second became possible. This process also meant that photos no longer had to be developed immediately[4]. Following the Wright brothers' first flight with an aircraft – the Wright Flyer – aircraft became another platform for taking photos, in addition to balloons.

Right from the beginning, there was great interest in using a bird's-eye view for archaeological purposes. In 1879, the archaeological excavations of Persepolis in Persia (now Iran) were recorded on a light-sensitive plate[5]. In Italy, the archaeologist Giacomo Boni photographed antique sites. In England, Lieutenant Philip Henry Sharpe took a famous photograph of Stonehenge in 1906[6]. But in the run-up to the First World War, aerial photography was still in its infancy.

On 4 August 1914, the First World War broke out in Belgium. What was initially planned as a quick sweep across Belgium ended up in a stalemate, with both sides entrenched for the winter. Both quickly realised the potential of a new weapon: airborne reconnaissance.

Pilots and observers became the all-seeing eyes of the army. What started as an initiative of a few enthusiastic pilots and observers quickly grew into a fully fledged and widely used discipline from mid 1915 onwards. Aerial photography became the most efficient way of gaining information about what the enemy was doing in his trenches, and for gaining an overview of one's own positions and the organisation of the hinterland. The armies took millions of aerial photos during the war; these were of key importance for compiling trench maps to give the infantry an idea of the location of enemy trenches. They also helped improve shelling accuracy and in spotting preparations for enemy offensives (**FIG. 142**).

Indirectly, the First World War and the deployment of airborne weapons were of great importance for the development of archaeology. On the German side there was plenty of experimentation with archaeological aerial photography. In 1918, German archaeologist Carl Schuchhardt photographed the *limes*, or Roman defensive system, in Romania using aerial photography[7]. The archaeologist Theodor Wiegand established the *Deutsch-Türkischen Denkmalschutz Kommando* within the Turkish army, an archaeological unit that documented numerous sites in the Negev, in the south of what is now Israel. In Mesopotamia, British officer George Adam Beazeley photographed archaeological sites such as Samarra in 1917 during photo reconnaissance flights intended to find German and Turkish positions[8]. In 1919, he wrote that archaeological surveys could in the future be greatly assisted by aerial photography[9].

On the Western Front as well, awareness grew that the method could be used for archaeological purposes after the war. The leading pioneer of archaeological aerial photography was Osbert Guy Stanhope Crawford, a British archaeologist who served with the 14th (London Scottish) battalion of the London Regiment near Givenchy in France during the war. His pre-war experience as a geographer and archaeologist was

[1] Leggat 2000
[2] Newhall 1982
[3] Deuel 1969
[4] Newhall 1982
[5] Chevallier 1971
[6] Deuel 1969
[7] Crawford 1954
[8] Bewley 1997
[9] Beazeley 1919

142

143

FIG. 142
Aerial photo of the severely shelled German front line in the Ypres Salient, 2 October 1917.

FIG. 143
German military aerial photo showing the Gizeh plateau, 1918.

FIG. 144
The different greens in the field indicate a zigzag communications trench in Loker.

144

put to good use in the army's mapping department. In this function he came into contact with the many aerial photos taken to map enemy positions. In 1917 he served as an observer and aerial photographer with the 23rd and 48th Squadron, carrying out reconnaissance flights over France and Belgium[10]. This wartime experience inspired him to use aerial photography after the war to study the prehistoric landscape of Great Britain. Thanks to his efforts, the interpretation of aerial photos became a standard tool in archaeological surveys[11].

[10] Hauser 2008
[11] Murray 2007
[12] Bewley 2002
[13] Bourgeois et al. 2010

WHAT PLANTS CAN TELL US

Under the right circumstances, artefacts and buildings buried in the ground can be discerned from the air through differences in the way crops grow. Drainage ditches dug into the ground, and also trenches, encourage plant growth, as the roots can grow deeper and therefore reach more nutrients. The crops are thus greener and taller. In periods of drought, they also stay greener longer. The opposite is true for the buried remains of walls and bunkers. Plants growing on top of them are unable to access so many nutrients, with the result that they do not grow so tall and are more likely to suffer in a drought.

After getting off the ground between the two world wars, archaeological photography in Britain was given a further boost during the Second World War. The war resulted in great steps forward not only in the technology used, but also in archaeologists being employed to interpret aerial photos[12]. The second half of the twentieth century saw further progress. Beginning in the 1960s in Wallonia, Charles Leva used the technique to track down Roman sites. In the late 1970s in Flanders, Jacques Semey began his magnum opus, taking more than 70,000 aerial photographs of thousands of sites in East and West Flanders[13].

In the Westhoek too, cropmarks reveal WW1 remains still buried in the ground, for instance at Lichtervelde, where, after a long period of drought, a remarkable photo was taken of an extensive German trench network clearly visible in the surrounding drought-stricken meadows. A second splendid example is a zigzag communication trench found near Loker (**FIG. 144**).

In July 2015, an uncommonly dry month, archaeologists took to the air for the specific purpose of finding WW1 traces. In the vicinity of Ypres and Zonnebeke they took a series of photos of cropmarks caused by trenches, buried bunkers and countless shell craters. One aerial photo, taken near Frezenberg in the municipality of Zonnebeke, shows a field with parched crops between the Ieperstraat and the Felix Nadarstraat (**FIG. 145**) (quite by chance the Felix Nadarstraat is named after the pioneering aerial photographer who flew in a balloon from Brussels to Ypres). In the foreground on the right, the concrete roof of a bunker can be seen protruding above ground. All over the field, dozens of dark green circular patches are visible, most probably deep shell craters. Three trenches can be seen, recognisable through their right-angled traverses or their zigzag form. Less evident is a drought-affected square shape indicating the underground remains of walls, very probably belonging to a bunker.

Using specialised software, any slanted photos can be 'straightened' in order to map the traces (**FIG. 146**). A detailed examination of the photo reveals two further buried bunkers. A comparison between the recent photo and an aerial photo taken on 24 September 1918 confirmed the assumption that the cropmarks originated in the First World War. But we can immediately see that not all the trenches and craters in the old photo are visible as

145

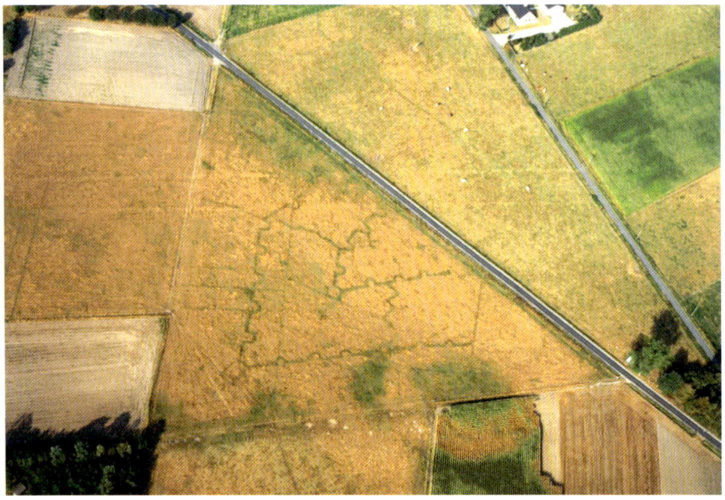

More than a century after the Armistice, many WW1 traces can still be seen in the landscape, though in many cases only with a trained eye. Some are only visible from the air, as a temporary discolouring of crops. Flying over Lichtervelde, an aerial photographer took this picture of the German trenches. The dark green lines provide a hint of what the soil has preserved.

FIG. 145
Traces of underground bunkers, trenches and shell craters can be seen in the crops.

FIG. 146
From top to bottom: aerial photo showing cropmarks; interpretation and mapping of the visible traces; the same area on a British aerial photo taken in 1918.

146A

146B

146C

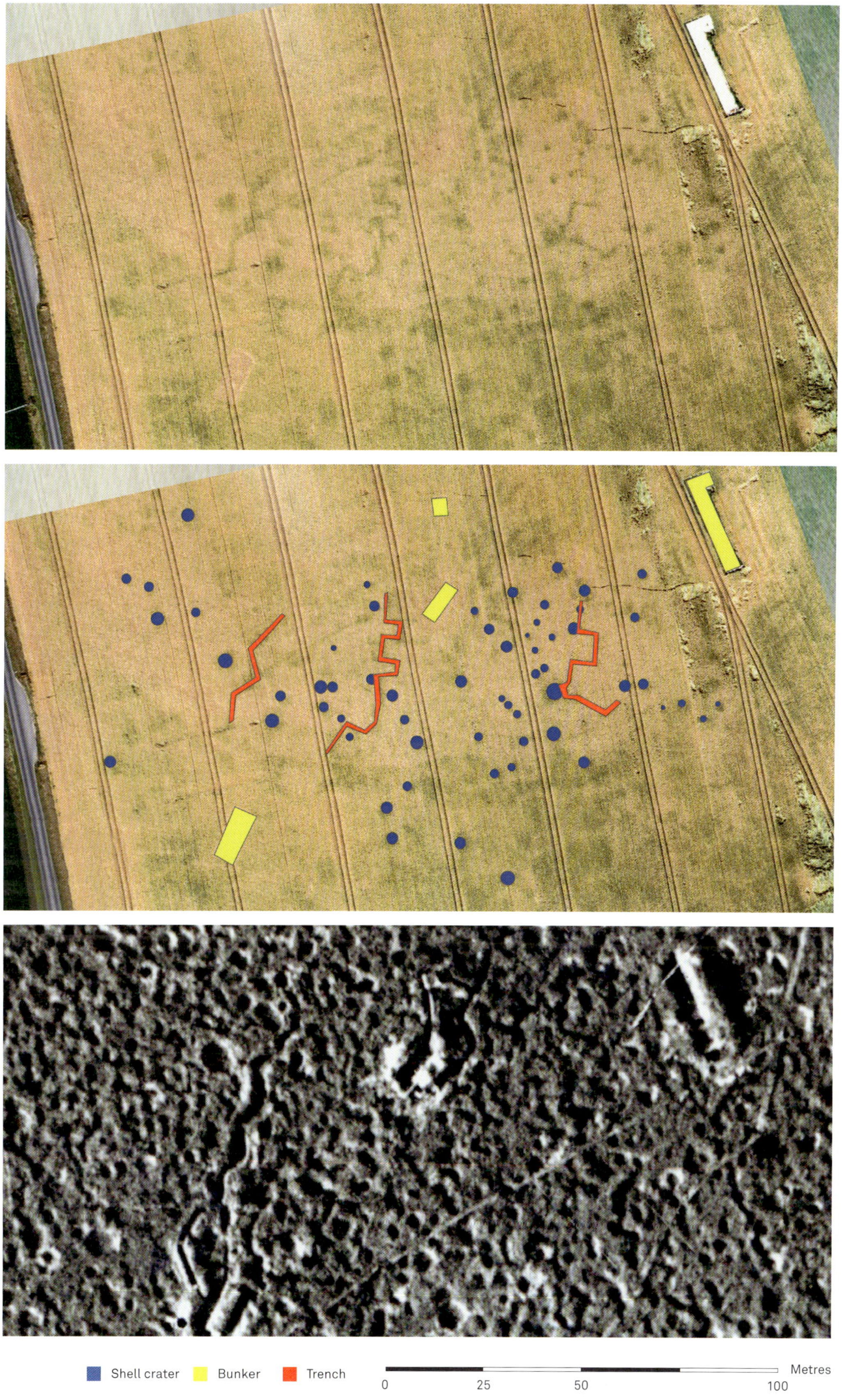

FIG. 147
Traces in the crops of dozens of shell craters in British and German trenches at Wijtschate.

cropmarkings. When using this method, the result is always dependent on the circumstances – in this case, the drought, the type of soil and an aerial photographer who spots the sites and takes a picture of traces that may only be visible for a few days.

HISTORICAL AERIAL PHOTOS

A second approach uses historical aerial photos as its starting point. During the First World War, aerial photos were used to gather military information and show up enemy positions. They can now help us gain an insight into possible war remains still under the ground. Incidentally, these are the oldest aerial photos available for these regions. Their bird's-eye view provides an overview of the landscape, showing how its various elements are linked together. Better than maps, aerial photos reveal the texture and fabric of this farmed landscape. The added value of such a bird's-eye view becomes clear when we compare a photo of the same place taken on the ground with one taken from the air at more or less the same time.

The *Ruiterstelling* was an impressive Belgian trench near Diksmuide. Consisting of several levels, it looked out over the notorious Trench of Death (in Dutch the *Dodengang*) on the Yser front. A photo **(FIG. 148)** shows the rear side of the position through the lens of René Glatigny, a Belgian stretcher bearer. A narrow-gauge railway can be seen just behind a wide wall of sandbags, with a small wagon on the spur branching off to the right. Replacement rail sections can also be seen, ready to carry out any necessary repair work. On 24 March 1917, a Belgian reconnaissance plane flew over the region **(FIG. 149)**. Flying at 1,400 metres, Lieutenant Lints took a series of aerial photos of this section of the front from his open cockpit. For the fraction of a second during which the landscape was recorded on the glass plate, the plane flew just over the spot where Glatigny had taken his photo.

Two photos of the same war landscape, yet totally different. On Glatigny's photo, the war is close at hand: the destruction and the mud are tangible and we can see a lot of battlefield details. By contrast, the aerial photo creates a distance between the murderous battlefield and the almost desolate, abstract-looking war-torn landscape, seemingly devoid of people. The details provide a glimpse of what lay on the other side of the metre-high wall of sandbags. Lieutenant Lints' photo shows the extent of the flooding, as

148

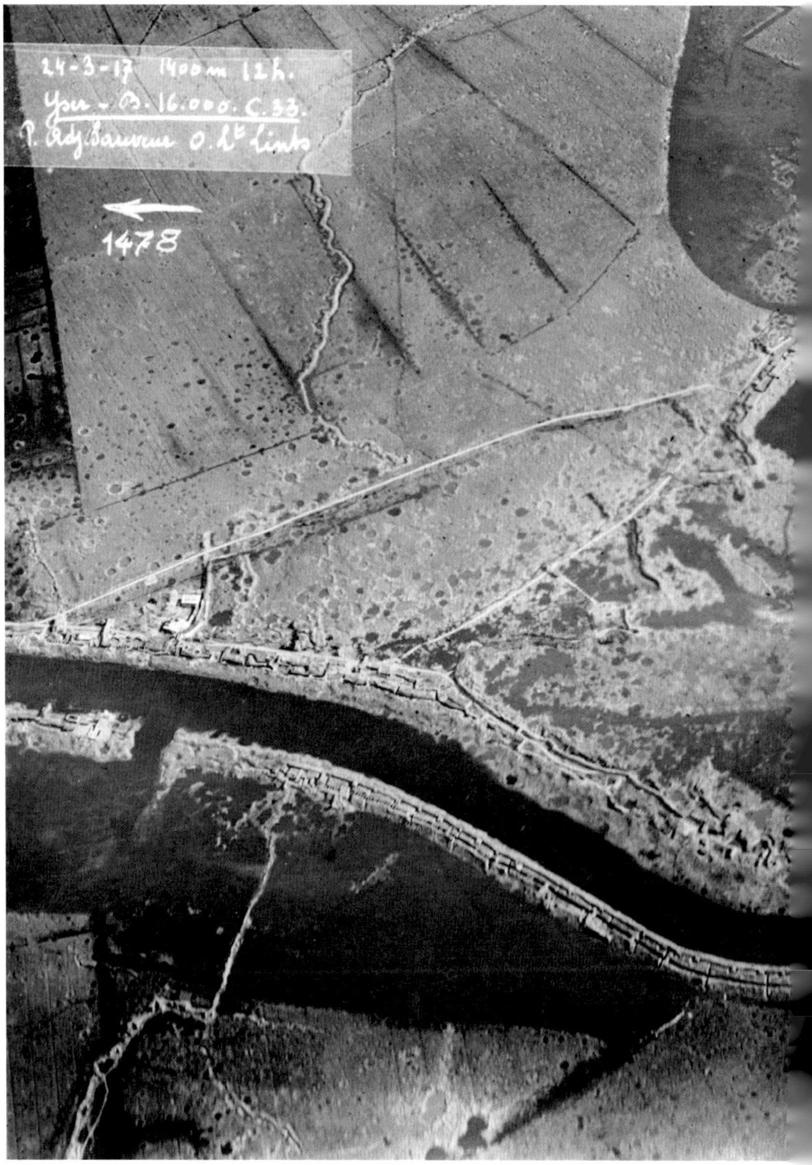

FIG. 148
The rear side of the Ruiterstelling alongside the *Dodengang*.

FIG. 149
Belgian aerial photo of the front alongside the *Dodengang*.

[14] Stichelbaut 2015
[15] Stichelbaut et al. 2017

149

seen by the darker colour of the flooded fields and meadows. It shows the exact position and the extent of both the Belgian and German trenches, illustrating at a glance how they were positioned with respect to the Yser. With closer examination, one can even see Belgian and German bunkers and countless small and large shell craters.

About half a million aerial photos taken during the war and covering the Western Front in Belgium and France are available in archives in Belgium, Germany, the United Kingdom, France, the United States and Australia[14]. Of these, some 23,000 have been digitised in recent years. The photos were taken between 30 December 1914 and 10 November 1918. Around 18,000 of them have since been localised and digitised for historical research in the In Flanders Fields Museum research centre in Ypres. The collection is a key source for research into the landscape and WW1 archaeology.

The historical pictures have been superimposed on modern aerial photos and digital maps[15].They cover the relatively quiet Yser front, the murderous Ypres Salient, the Messines Ridge and Wijtschate, and the hinterland on both sides of the front. Careful interpretation has allowed no fewer than 221,000 military traces to be identified (trench networks, gun emplacements, military camps, depots and other large-scale infrastructure elements), providing a detailed insight into the density, variety and spread of the wartime sites.

THE COMPLEX WARTIME LAYER

To gain a better understanding of the archaeological and landscape heritage of the First World War, the researchers are trying to draw as complete as possible a picture of the countryside's 'wartime layer'. Sequences of aerial photos taken over a certain period give an idea of what may be preserved. A small case study of a site near the hamlet of Reutel in Beselare illustrates the potential of such an approach. After the First Battle of Ypres, the German advance came to a standstill, with both sides digging in around the town, as well as at Polygon Wood and Beselare. The earliest aerial photos we have available of the site date back to 13 September 1915 **(FIG. 150A)**. The pictures show the abandoned German trenches about half a kilometre behind the former German front line which had been pushed back towards Ypres as a result of the Second Battle of Ypres. Hardly any damage can

150A

150B

FIG. 150
Successive aerial photos of the Reutel site:
A. 13 September 1915
B. 29 May 1916
C. 14 February 1917
D. 15 December 1917
E. Overview of visible traces

be seen. A picture typical of this phase of the war where the impact of shellfire on the landscape was still quite limited.

The subsequent picture shows the same place eight months later (**FIG. 150B**). On top of the German trenches, work has started on an extensive and beautifully designed cemetery with a geometrical layout and two commemorative monuments. The cemetery's original design seems to have been too small to accommodate all the dead German soldiers, and the cemetery was extended to the south towards the Oude Kortrijkstraat (**FIG. 150C**). Some 1,600 German soldiers were buried in this cemetery, the Korps-Friedhof[16].

During the Third Battle of Ypres, the landscape was transformed by incessant shellfire, causing widespread devastation. On aerial photos taken during this period, hardly anything can still be seen of the cemetery (**FIG. 150D**). During this offensive, the front again got closer. The Battle of Broodseinde on 4 October 1917 saw the British capturing the ridge. They took over the old German trenches built in 1915 and converted them into a new front line. Until the German spring offensive in 1918, the front remained quiet.

This depiction of how the wartime landscape evolved shows that there was no such thing as a permanent 'front line' or 'hinterland', with many places subject to a complex series of developments – that is, a complex layering of overlapping traces. Very little now exists to remind us of the turmoil the place went through a hundred years ago. Just the shape of a plot of grassland gives a vague hint of where the German cemetery used to be. Thanks to the analysis of aerial photos and the mapping of the interpreted traces (**FIG. 150E**), we now have an idea of what we might find beneath the surface.

VARIETY IN THE MILITARY LANDSCAPE

A second research focus covers the landscape. Combining information from thousands of aerial photos, researchers can gain an understanding of the structure, evolution and construction of the trench networks and the organisation of the hinterland infrastructure. The study area serving as an example in our case covers the Ypres Salient and the Messines-Wijtschate Ridge, as well as stretches of the British and German hinterland, an area of 620 square kilometres. The processing and interpretation of 9,000 aerial photos provided a digital map showing the positions of more than 162,400 wartime traces in this area alone[17]. Just restricting ourselves here to the categories of traces appealing most to the imagination, we can illustrate the extent of the trench war and the associated war heritage.

In the southern Westhoek, the trench war reached a tragic climax, with no other region in Belgium so completely transformed into a military landscape (**FIG. 151**). No fewer than 3,500 kilometres of trenches, but also planked paths, narrow-gauge railways and artillery emplacements, ran through the fields and meadows. We can distinguish a wide variety of earthworks on the aerial photos, ranging from the first

[16] Vancoillie 2002
[17] Stichelbaut et al. 2017
[18] Stichelbaut et al. 2016

150C

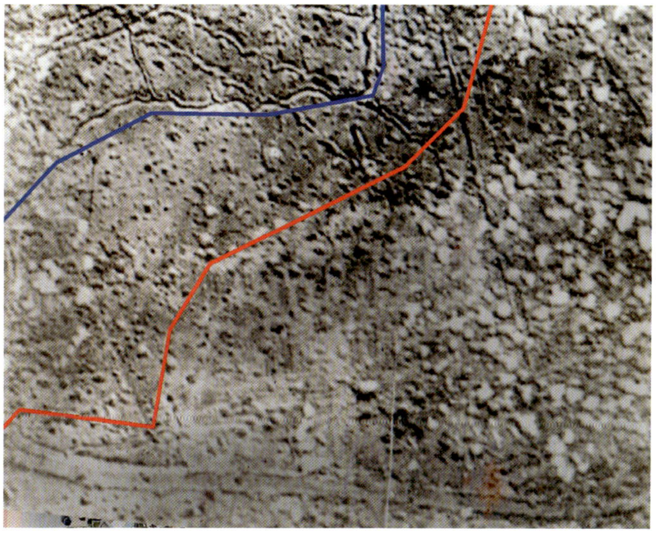

150D

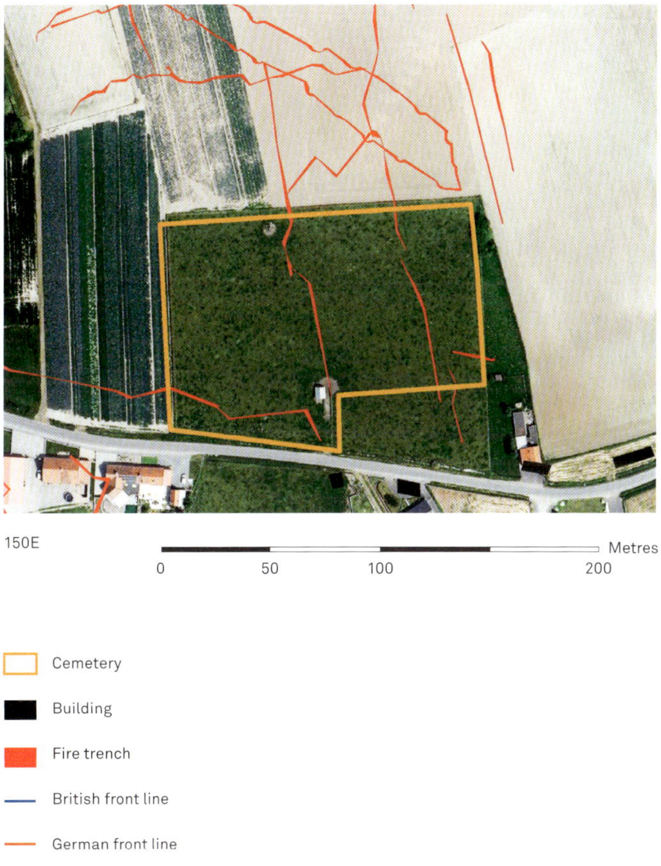

150E

foxholes and disordered trenches to the extensive and continuous trench networks in the period between the Second and the Third Battle of Ypres. Beginning in 1917, the lines of defence were extended in depth, ending up as well-organised groupings of fortified craters and bunkers. Visual domination over enemy positions became very important. The difference between seeing and being seen was always a question of life or death. Strategic heights (the Bellewaarde Ridge, 't Hoge, Hill 60, Mount Sorrel, The Bluff, St-Eloi and the Messines-Wijtschate Ridge) became the 'hotspots' of the underground mine war, leaving hundreds of deep scars in the landscape[18]. Close to the trenches or in many cases even part of them, more than 5,100 possible bunkers have been detected on aerial photos. The actual number is very probably much higher, as many bunkers were intentionally camouflaged to avoid them being detected from the air.

Further behind the front we come across a different sort of landscape, riddled with military camps, supply roads, ammunition depots and gun emplacements. No fewer than 29,200 huts and 27,200 tents were mapped. Some 1,700 kilometres of specially constructed military roads and 3,000 kilometres of narrow-gauge railways ensured the transport of troops, ammunition and supplies to the front.

Such figures bear witness to the unprecedented density of archaeological traces. Thanks to the aerial photos, the enormous extent of this wartime heritage is now visible. The research also highlights the necessity of considering individual sites within their landscape context.

FIG. 151

Map of wartime traces in the Ypres Salient for the period 1914-1918.

- Cemetery
- Gun emplacement
- Bunker
- Mine crater
- Shelter
- German trench
- Allied trench
- Narrow-gauge railway
- Hut
- Tent

0

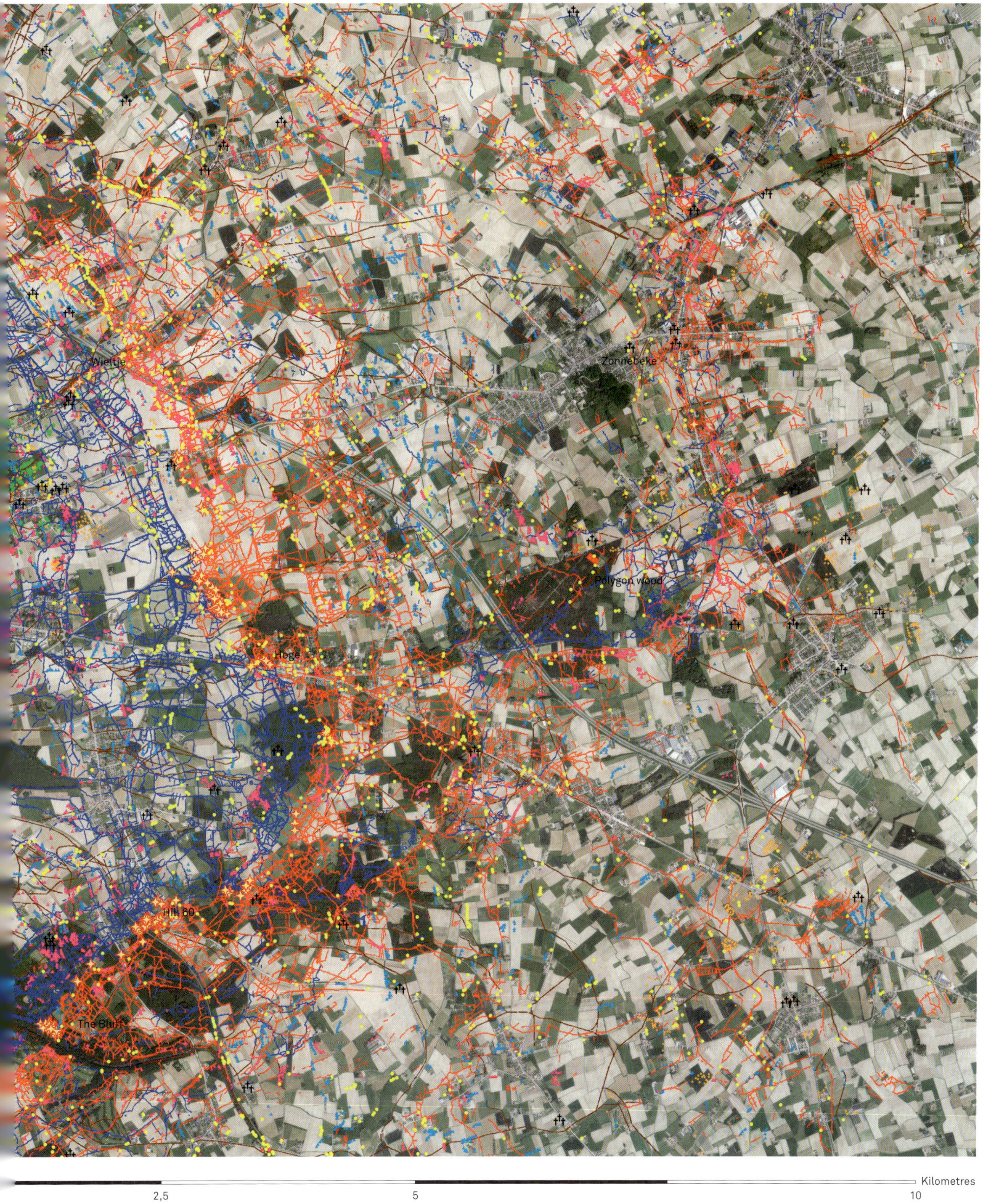
Wieltje
Zonnebeke
Polygon wood
Hooge
Hill 60
The Bluff
2,5
5
10
Kilometres

During the war, each side took spy photos from the air. These pictures are now invaluable for archaeologists and historians. They can tell us what happened in a certain place during the war and what possible remains are still under the ground. Through superimposing historical photos on present-day photos, we can gain a glimpse of the texture of the wartime landscape. At the IJzertoren in Diksmuide, the Belgian and German front lines, entrenched on opposite sides of the Yser, were just 50 metres apart. Today, nothing can be seen of the pockmarked landscape of 1917 (shaded grey), but much lies dormant beneath the surface.

Metres
0 50 100 200

152

153

FIG. 152
German bunker (dry rectangle) and shell craters, visible in the crops at Wijtschate in July 2017.

FIG. 153
Zigzag communications trenches and dozens of shell craters, visible in the crops at Comines-Warneton in July 2017.

FIG. 154

British aerial photo (June 1917) of the war-torn landscape near the hamlet of Hooge superimposed on a recent aerial photo of the same place.

9 Scanning the landscape with lasers

Wouter Gheyle
Birger Stichelbaut
Nicolas Note
Timothy Saey
Hanne Van den Berghe
Marc Van Meirvenne
Veerle Van Eetvelde
Jean Bourgeois

Archaeology is not just about underground traces. There are also many remains above ground, such as the mighty monuments of the past: moated castles dating back to the Middle Ages, forts, city walls, the remains of Roman aqueducts and tumuli. But there are also many more indications of past human activities, less evident among the modern constituents of today's landscape or removed from sight through trees and undergrowth. To map such elements, laser scanners are used to make digital elevation models (DEMs). The technique used is called 'Lidar', short for *light detection and ranging*.

During the last ten or so years, archaeologists have been using airborne laser scans. Aircraft are fitted with a Lidar system, which sends out laser pulses and picks up their reflections, bouncing off the bare soil, but also higher objects such as crops, trees and buildings. The elevation measurements thus gained are then transposed into three-dimensional images showing the form of the landscape. Through combining hundreds of thousands of measurements, experts can map large surfaces in a very short time. Special visualisation methods can even pick out minute differences in the elevation.

MISSING THE WOOD FOR THE TREES

The elevation measurements result in a digital map of the ground, a model showing the earth's surface with all its vegetation and buildings. Specialised filters can then 'weed out' the trees, undergrowth, houses and other unwanted objects, resulting in a digital model devoid of these intruding elements. One can even 'see through' the canopy of forest cover. Woods are

FIG. 155
Cross-section of a Lidar visualisation of the Bellewaarde Wood (**FIG. 156**). Green: trees and undergrowth. Brown: the ground. Orange: roofs of buildings. As a scale, the red silhouettes are fictional people.

FIG. 156
Aerial photo and digital elevation model of the woods covering the Bellewaarde Ridge.

[1] Kokalj et al. 2011, Kokalj et al. 2013

155

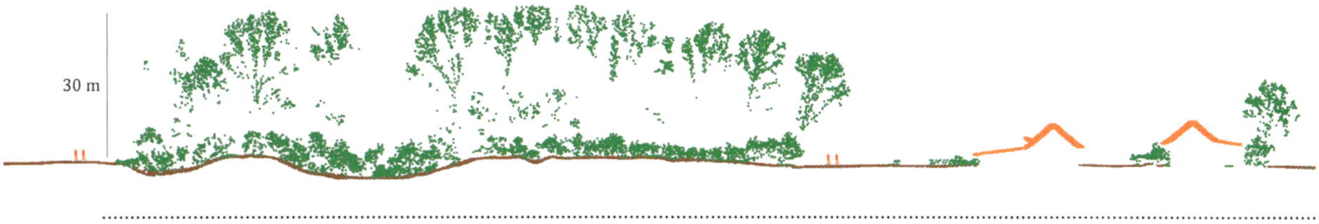

156

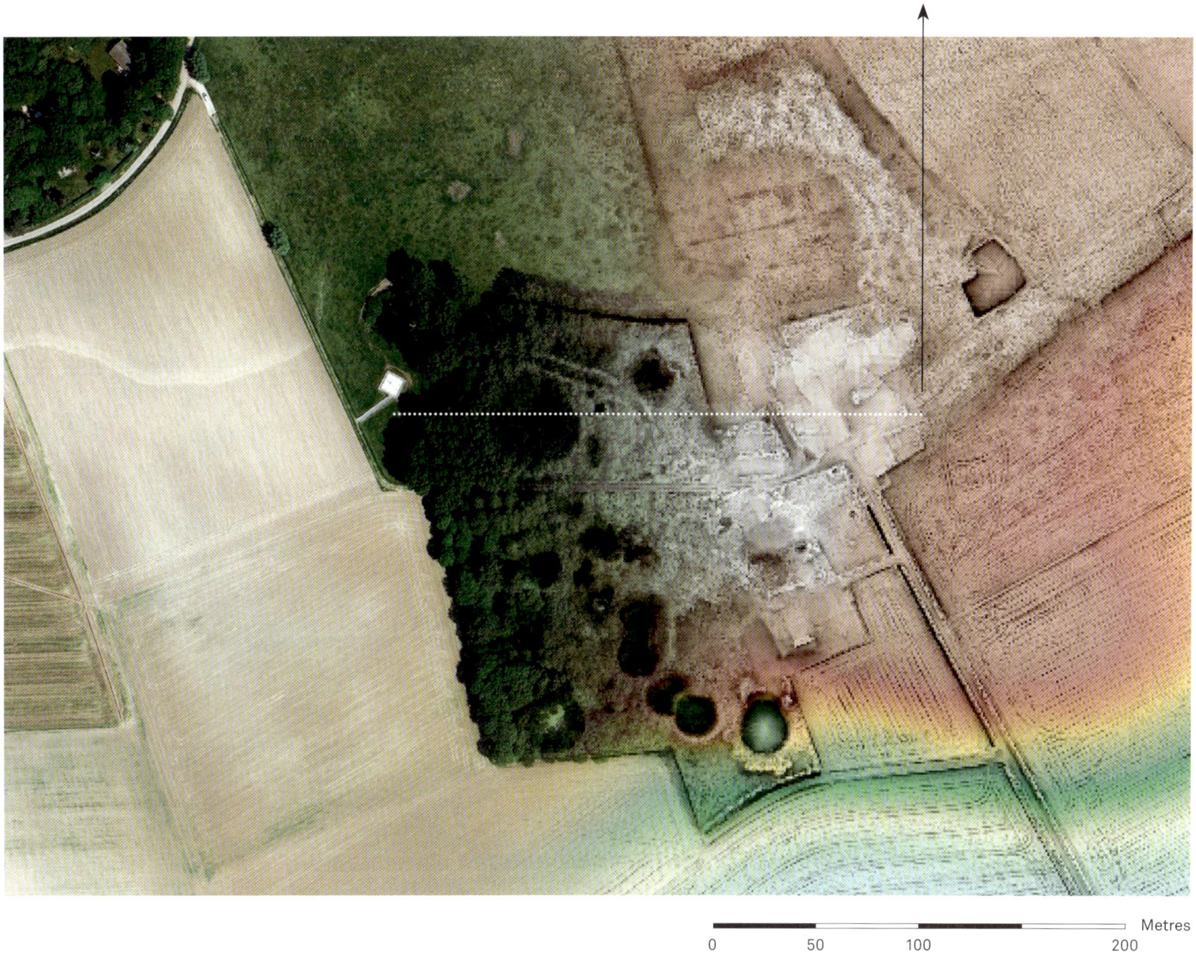

often *terra incognita* for archaeologists, as they can be difficult to access either from the ground or using aerial photography. This is where Lidar comes in, enabling archaeologists to look through the woods as if they weren't there.

A case study of the Bellewaarde Ridge to the east of Ypres illustrates the method's potential. During the war, the ridge was a hotspot of tunnel warfare, with British tunnellers and German *Mineure* attempting to undermine the front-line trenches through deep tunnels. Between September 1915 and July 1917, no fewer than 34 underground mines exploded, leaving deep craters in the landscape[2]. However, little of this can be seen on present-day aerial photos, as everything is obscured by the canopy of foliage. Even in the surrounding fields, nothing can be seen with the naked eye. Thanks to the digital elevation model, however, we can see through the tree cover, with a dozen large craters immediately becoming visible. A cross-section shows the trees and undergrowth as a mass of green dots. The ground itself is shown in brown. Some of the craters are a good 5 metres deep, caused by the enormous impact of the mine explosions (**FIG. 155 & 156**).

THE SCARS LEFT BEHIND BY TUNNEL WARFARE

Immediately after the war, villages were reconstructed and fields levelled and re-cultivated throughout the Westhoek, bringing the region back to normal life. It is generally assumed that this wave of reconstruction swept away any traces of the war. A few dozen bunkers and large mine craters, such as those on Hill 60 and at the Pool of Peace, still exist and are open to the public. A few authentic trenches and shell craters are also visible, but for the most part little seems to remain of the wartime landscape.

But the Lidar data tells a different story. Numerous traces are still visible as small differences in the topography, not only in places now covered with trees and undergrowth, but also in meadows and even ploughed fields. The rough and pockmarked landscape is scattered with the craters of literally millions of shells.

The Bluff in Zillebeke, a strategic ridge overlooking the Ypres-Comines Canal, still clearly bears the signs of that crater landscape (**FIG. 157**). Looking at the digital elevation model, we can see the traces of countless shell craters in and alongside the canal and to the north of it on what is now wooded land and meadows. Next to it, we can see the enormous scars left behind by the tunnel war. In late 1914, the two sides started tunnelling under each other's defences, packing the end of each tunnel with explosives and then detonating them, often as a prelude to an above-ground attack. Between 1915 and 1917, a veritable tunnel war was waged at five places in the Ypres Salient: Bellewaarde, 't Hoge, Hill 60, The Bluff and St-Eloi.[3] The Bluff was a ridge held by the Allies since the end of 1914, much to the annoyance of the Germans. On 21 January 1916, the explosion of German mines left a large crater in the side of the ridge. On 14 February, another mine-based attack took place, with the Germans managing to capture The Bluff, only to lose it on 3 March. In the middle of 1917, a dozen mines exploded. Thanks to Lidar, their craters have been identified, as enormous depressions in the ground (to the north of the canal in the photo). The scars these explosions left in the landscape are still clearly visible[4].

Apart from the typical crater landscapes, kilometres of trenches, narrow-gauge railways, shelters, roads and artillery emplacements are to be seen in the woods. Wooded areas were not cleared much after the war, and forestry has had little impact on what lies underground. As a result, the traces of the war are in much better shape. Lidar images of the Ploegsteert Woods in Comines-Warneton show them quite clearly. For most of the war, the woods belonged to the front-line area. The image shows a small section of the south-eastern corner of the woods, with the Rifle House Cemetery to be seen in the right-hand corner. In addition, we can clearly see two well-preserved winding trenches running towards the front (**FIG. 158**).

157A

157B

[2] Dewilde et al. 2014
[3] Barton et al. 2004, Stichelbaut et al. 2016
[4] Stichelbaut et al. 2016

FIG. 157

Present-day aerial photo and digital elevation model of the central part of the De Palingbeek and The Bluff estate, now, inter alia, part of a golf course. The vegetation – the trees and undergrowth – have helped conserve the war landscape. All darker points are craters and pits: easy to see in the wooded area, less distinguishable in the fields to the north. Centre: The Bluff, devastated by dozens of mine craters.

FIG. 158

Trenches, shell craters, shelters and other traces of military activity in Ploegsteert Wood.

158A

158B

159A

FIG. 159

German training ground in De Haan on a present-day aerial photo and the corresponding Lidar image showing traces of the war also found on old aerial photos. Red: trenches. Green: man-made craters. Green lines: firing ranges.

159B

BEHIND THE FRONT

Moving away from the front to the hinterland, we first reach a zone totally dedicated to the logistics infrastructure (see Chapter 4). With the war fought on an industrial scale, an enormous organisational effort was required. Both armies built ammunition depots, logistics centres, hospitals and camps. Here as well, Lidar has exposed several traces in the landscape.

Some 100 kilometres behind the front, the German Fourth Army constructed dozens of practice trenches. Some of them are remarkably well preserved and distinctly visible on the Lidar images, for example the ones in the Dune Woods in De Haan. During WW1, this area was used by the Germans as a training ground stretching to the fields behind the dunes. All typical constituents of a trench network are evident, with lines of fighting trenches linked together by communication trenches (**FIG. 159**). Hundreds of craters were dug to simulate the devastation at the front and get soldiers used to what awaited them. Firing ranges can be seen as long 'alleys' ending with a mound of earth to stop the bullets. Although large sections of this training ground still exist, it was unknown to archaeologists before the Lidar images were analysed.

An additional example is the training ground in Maasmechelen (**FIG. 160**)[5], where the Germans constructed an artillery practice range, a so-called *Minenwerferschule*, where recruits

[5] Flanders Heritage Agency 2016a

160

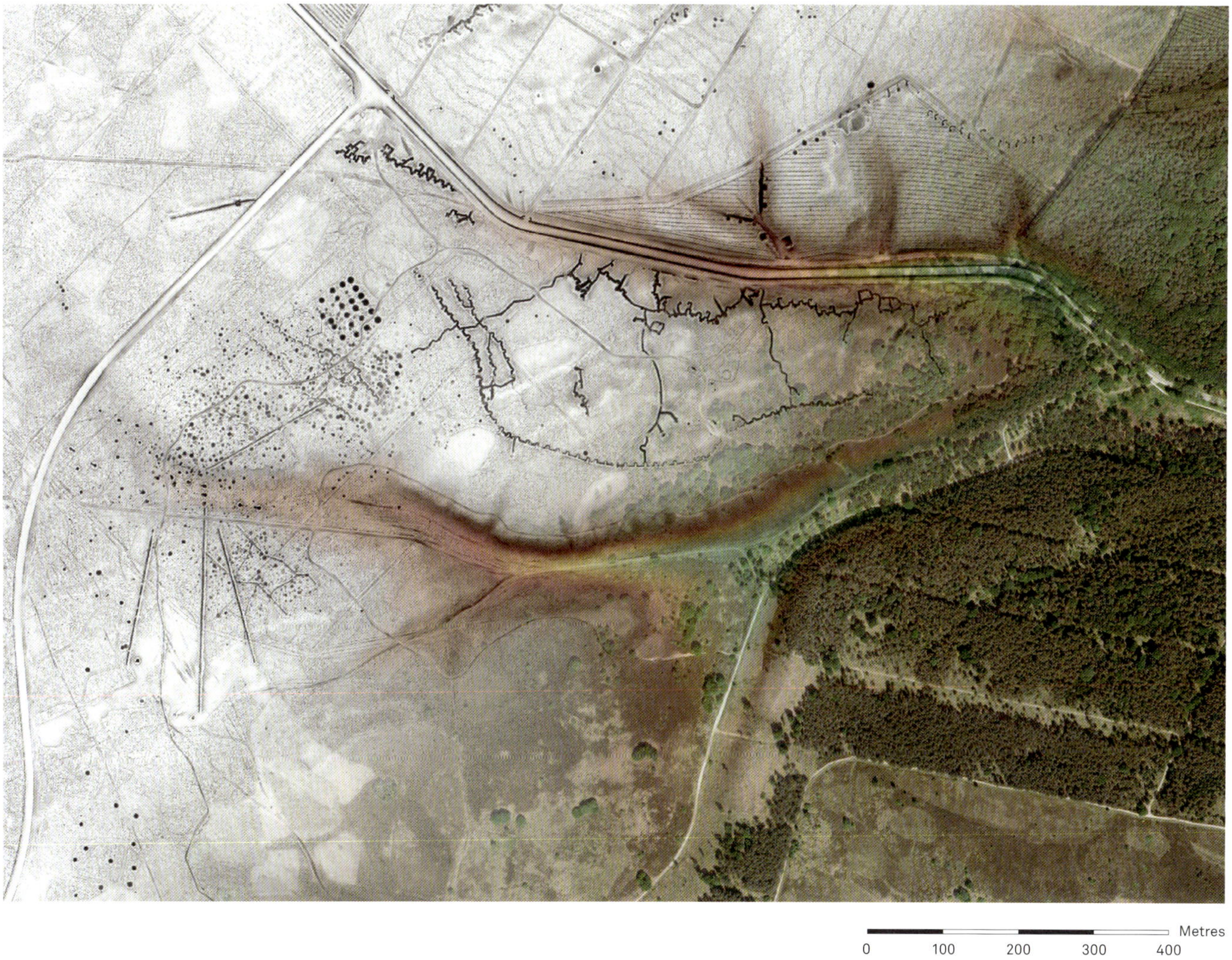

FIG. 160
Lidar image of the German training ground in Maasmechelen, with trenches and shell craters clearly visible.

were trained before being sent to the front. The training ground consisted of 4 kilometres of trenches with associated bunkers, barracks and firing ranges, as well as countless craters, which – other than in De Haan – were not always dug by hand, but were the result of practice shelling with mortars (the German *Minenwerfer*). The Lidar image reveals the site's extent and complexity, with many hitherto unknown details.

HUNDREDS OF NEW SITES

Exactly how much of the war landscape still exists? Although the current status of research does not allow us to provide an exact answer, until a short time ago we were aware of a dozen locations in Flanders with above-ground traces. Thanks to Lidar, we have now pinpointed hundreds of new ones, many of them in wooded areas but also in fields and meadows.

For a small stretch of the Western Front, between Kemmel and Wervik, we can now come up with a figure. Fourteen percent of the ground still shows traces of the war, well above what researchers expected. Thanks to historical aerial photos we know exactly what elements of the military infrastructure were constructed where, between 1914 and 1918. Lidar now shows us what remains above the ground, for instance at the Kemmelberg, where a zigzag trench can still be seen in the sloping eastern side of the ridge. Irregular differences in the topography point to shell craters. In the Flemish government's heritage inventory, this plot of land is registered as 'War landscape Kattekerkhofstraat 1' [6]. A larger-scale map of the site under investigation shows that the field should not be considered an isolated element but as part of an extensive area with remains in both the woods and the fields. Particularly notable are the large number of shell craters on the sides of the Kemmelberg and in the surrounding fields. Zooming in on the area around Heuvelland, we find more than 120 plots of land containing previously unknown remains of the war **(FIG. 161)**.

[6] Flanders Heritage Agency 2016b

Q

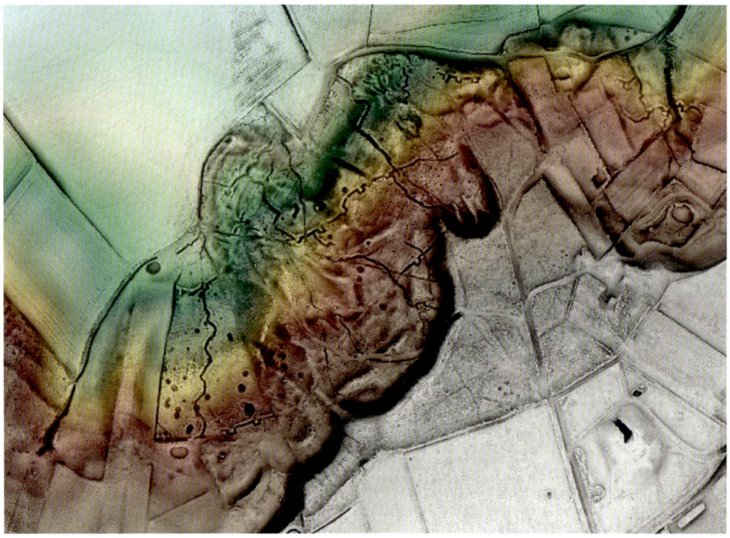

R

Researchers are using laser scanners to scan the ground from the air. The resultant digital elevation models are revealing many new sites, often in unexpected places. On the wooded slopes of the Koppenberg to the south of Oudenaarde, for example, an extensive trench system has been found, with traces of deep trenches running for hundreds of metres. This is what is left of a training ground for German storm troopers.

Metres
0 50 100 150 200

FIG. 161

A large number of plots in the Heuvelland region still show traces of the war. The preservation status of above-ground traces is seen on the Lidar images: green (good), orange (average) and red (vague). The war landscape around the Kemmelberg and Rodeberg is well preserved. The Flemish government's inventory list features just two 'war landscapes': a plot of land in the Kattekerkhofstraat featuring a zigzag trench, and a plot in the Schommelinkstraat.

How well above-ground remains are preserved depends on how the land has been used since the war. Through mapping land usage, we can study how the landscape has evolved over the last century and what impact this has had on the heritage. Many wooded plots of lands have been left relatively untouched, meaning that in nearly all woods the war heritage seems well preserved. Pastures that have not seen a plough since the reconstruction period also show unmistakable scars dating back to the war. Somewhat unexpectedly, even agricultural land reveal clear traces of the war, especially in cases where the land remained uncultivated until the 1960s. Even on fields cultivated just after the First World War or in the 1940s, some remains can still be seen in a micro-topography.

161

10 Using geophysical sensors to look under the ground

Wouter Gheyle
Nicolas Note
Timothy Saey
Hanne Van den Berghe
Marc Van Meirvenne
Veerle Van Eetvelde
Jean Bourgeois
Birger Stichelbaut

Geophysical sensors allow archaeological traces below ground to be mapped from above ground[1]. The one major advantage of this method is that no excavation is needed. A further benefit is that large areas can be surveyed, giving archaeologists a good look at what exists under the surface.

Geophysical sensors measure the magnetic and electrical properties of the subsoil. They can detect archaeological remains by distinguishing between their characteristics and those of everything else beneath the ground. In Belgium, researchers from Ghent University's Department of Soil Management, together with archaeologists and geographers, are studying places where underground war remains are suspected. In most cases they are using historical aerial photos as their starting point.

162

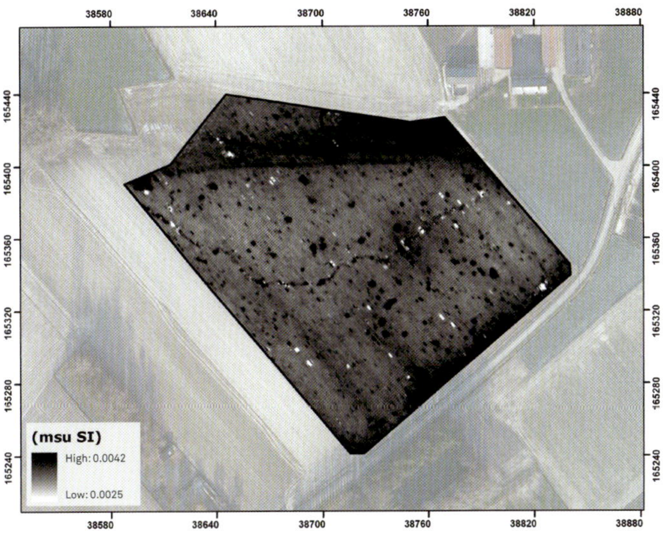

163A

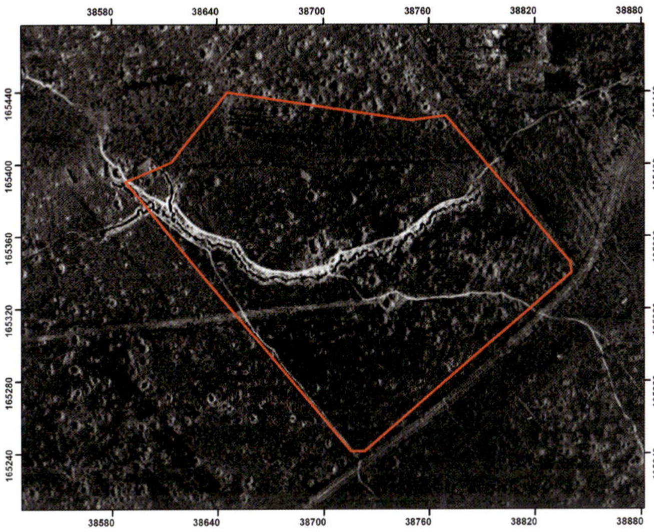

163B

FIG. 162

A quad bike fitted with a GPS antenna towing a cylindrical sensor in parallel lines across a field.

1 4x4 with a guidance system
2 GPS antenna
3 On-board computer (for recording the data)
4 Sledge with the EMI-sensor

FIG. 163A

Geophysical soil sensing revealed the trench and a large number of buried objects, recognisable as black or white spots.

FIG. 163B

British aerial photo taken on 18 July 1918, with the investigated trench in the centre.

[1] Saey et al. 2013, Stichelbaut et al. 2011
[2] Saey et al. 2013

SCANNING VIA ELECTROMAGNETIC INDUCTION

To scan the ground, researchers are using electromagnetic induction (EMI) sensors. A quad bike is used to tow a cylindrical EMI sensor across the ground (**FIG. 162**). The sensor contains one transmitter coil and several spaced-out receiving coils, allowing it to scan both surface and underground soil strata at the same time. The sensor measures both the soil's electrical conductivity and its magnetic flux.

Disturbances (excavations, pits, ditches and other human interventions) are registered as distinctive changes or 'anomalies' of the signal, with the magnetic flux reacting markedly to such disturbances. Electrical conductivity is used mainly to detect physical soil features: moisture and salt content, texture and so on. Both are very suitable for tracing buried metal artefacts.

By combining the sensor measurements with very accurate GPS coordinates, it is possible to spatially map what is beneath the ground. In processing the data, the researchers draw on historical aerial photos to link indications made visible by the geophysical measurements to wartime remains (see Chapter 8). Integrating the two sources provides an interpretation and evaluation of the remains still in the ground. Such preliminary studies allow an estimate to be made of the extant wartime heritage. The added value of such geophysical surveys can be seen through the following examples.

TRACES OF THE GERMAN SPRING OFFENSIVE IN LOKER (HEUVELLAND)

Researchers applied the technique to the southeast of Loker on a 3.2-hectare site at the foot of the Kemmelberg. Historical aerial photos showed that this had been a quiet sector behind the British lines until spring 1918. During the German spring offensive, German troops managed to advance further than ever in a westerly direction, capturing the Kemmelberg on 25 April 1918. An aerial photo of July 1918 shows the site as a devastated battlefield, littered with hundreds of shell craters (**FIG. 163B**). In the middle a bow-shaped trench some 250 metres long can be seen. The front-line itself ran about half a kilometre further south.

The geophysical sensor revealed a large number of traces still in the ground (**FIG. 163A**)[2]. The route of the trench can be clearly distinguished as a succession of geophysical anomalies. The sensor detected the trench mainly through

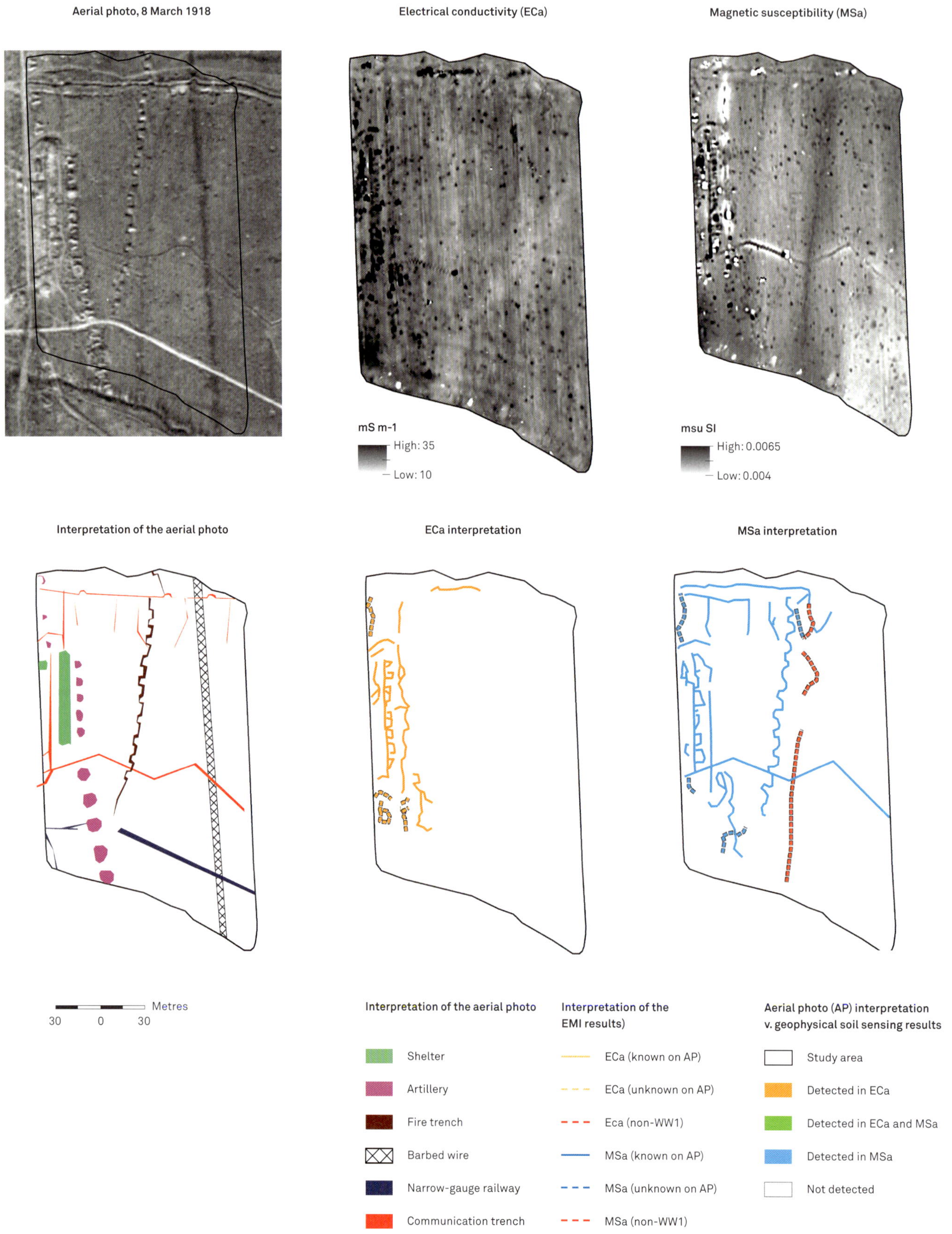
Aerial photo, 8 March 1918
Electrical conductivity (ECa)
Magnetic susceptibility (MSa)
mS m-1
High: 35
Low: 10
msu SI
High: 0.0065
Low: 0.004
Interpretation of the aerial photo
ECa interpretation
MSa interpretation
Metres
30 0 30
Interpretation of the aerial photo
Shelter
Artillery
Fire trench
Barbed wire
Narrow-gauge railway
Communication trench
Interpretation of the EMI results
ECa (known on AP)
ECa (unknown on AP)
Eca (non-WW1)
MSa (known on AP)
MSa (unknown on AP)
MSa (non-WW1)
Aerial photo (AP) interpretation v. geophysical soil sensing results
Study area
Detected in ECa
Detected in ECa and MSa
Detected in MSa
Not detected

FIG. 164
Interpretation of aerial photos taken during the war compared with the result of geophysical electromagnetic induction (EMI) sensing on the La Plus Douve site.

the presence of metal: perhaps the side of the trench had been reinforced with metal plates or wire mesh. The soil scans also show the large spread of metal objects. The ground is full of metal fragments, visible as extremely positive or negative anomalies in black or white, representing countless pieces of shrapnel, but also objects of daily use, metal poles and rolls of barbed wire. Unexploded shells are undoubtedly also present, as is the case everywhere along the front.

LA PLUS DOUVE

Though trenches are what is uppermost in our minds when thinking about the First World War, they are only part of the wide variety of WW1 heritage.

To the south-east of the village centre of Wulvergem (Heuvelland) lies La Plus Douve, which was 600 metres behind the British front line between November 1914 and June 1917. Due to its position behind a ridge, it was out of sight of the German front line. Historical aerial photos show a wide variety of remains, including trenches, barbed wire barriers, shelters and a well-camouflaged artillery battery facing north with a dozen gun emplacements (**FIG. 164**).

About 3 hectares of the site were scanned by geophysical sensors. The analysis of the data and its comparison with the analysis of the aerial photos reveal that almost 89 percent of the fighting trenches and 76 percent of the communication trenches visible on the aerial photos were picked up by the scan[3]. This basically means that they are still there in the ground. We are also noticing this trend at other sites, making one wonder just how much of the war heritage is still in the ground.

Our case study shows not only that trenches can be clearly detected, but also other structures such as gun emplacements and shelters. On the left-hand side of the aerial photo, we can see a long line stretching from the south to the north which looks like a raised bank of earth. The geophysical measurements unveiled a series of small chambers in the bank. These were shelters, probably constructed of wood and earth and offering protection against shells, but obviously not as strong as concrete bunkers.

THE TOR TOP DEEP DUGOUT

To the east of Ypres lies the strategic Hill 62 or Tor Top, one of the few places from where the Allies could observe the German lines. This was the reason why the hill was a great annoyance to the Germans. On 2 June 1916, they launched a major attack on Hill 62 and nearby Mount Sorrel, forcing the Canadian troops holding the line to retreat by a kilometre. After repeated counter-attacks, the Battle of Mount Sorrel ended ten days later with the lost area being recaptured. In this short period, the region was pounded by one of the war's most devastating bouts of shelling on Belgian territory.

The destructive power of the artillery forced both sides to seek shelter in concrete bunkers. An underground network of tunnels and shelters was also built, out of sight of the observers and deep enough in the ground to provide safety against the shelling. Allied tunnellers and German *Mineure* dug so-called 'deep dugouts', tunnels and shelters up to 14 metres deep, ranging from simple underground corridors with a few chambers to complex underground villages for hundreds of troops[4].

Dozens of such dugouts were constructed along the front on both sides. In some places on the front line, they were linked by tunnels and connected to underground listening posts beneath no-man's-land. Some of the tunnels were used to undermine enemy positions. Following the fighting in 1916, Tor Top was also equipped with underground shelters.

In November 2015, researchers from Ghent University carried out a scan of the ground to find out to what extent the trenches were preserved[5]. They also checked whether the heavy shelling during the First World War had had an influence on the state of preservation. In the top layers of soil, they found a lunar landscape scarred with hundreds of shell craters (**FIG. 165**). Yet despite the shelling, the scan revealed trenches, a bunker and even narrow-gauge railway lines in the ground.

In the deeper layers, several straight lines were revealed, none of which was visible on the historical aerial photos (**FIG. 167A**). Two sets of Canadian construction plans drawn up in 1917 solved the mystery (**FIG. 166**), revealing an underground shelter and entrances to the tunnel system. In addition, the trenches on the surface are also visible. By combining the geophysical scan with the trenches visible on the old aerial photographs, the dugout seems to be in just the right location, as are the galleries on the plan (**FIG. 167B**).

To verify these findings, soil probes were taken to determine how deep the gallery was in the ground. The tunnel's ceiling is about

[3] Gheyle et al. 2016b
[4] Barton et al. 2005
[5] Stichelbaut et al. 2017b

165A

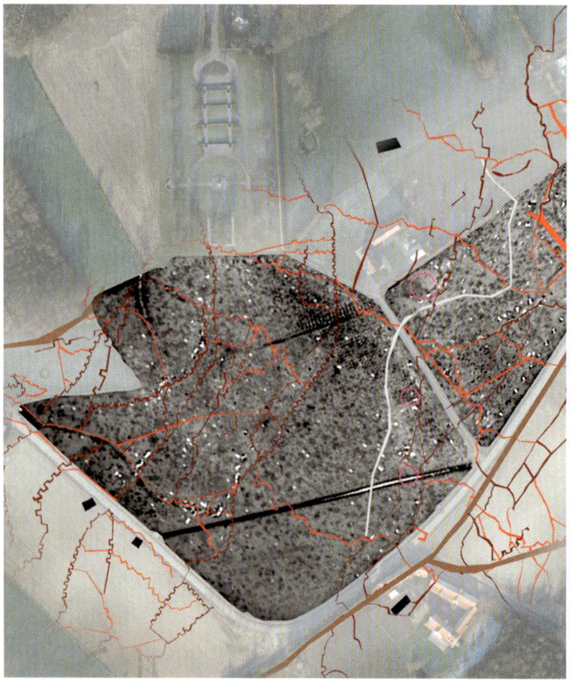

165B

166

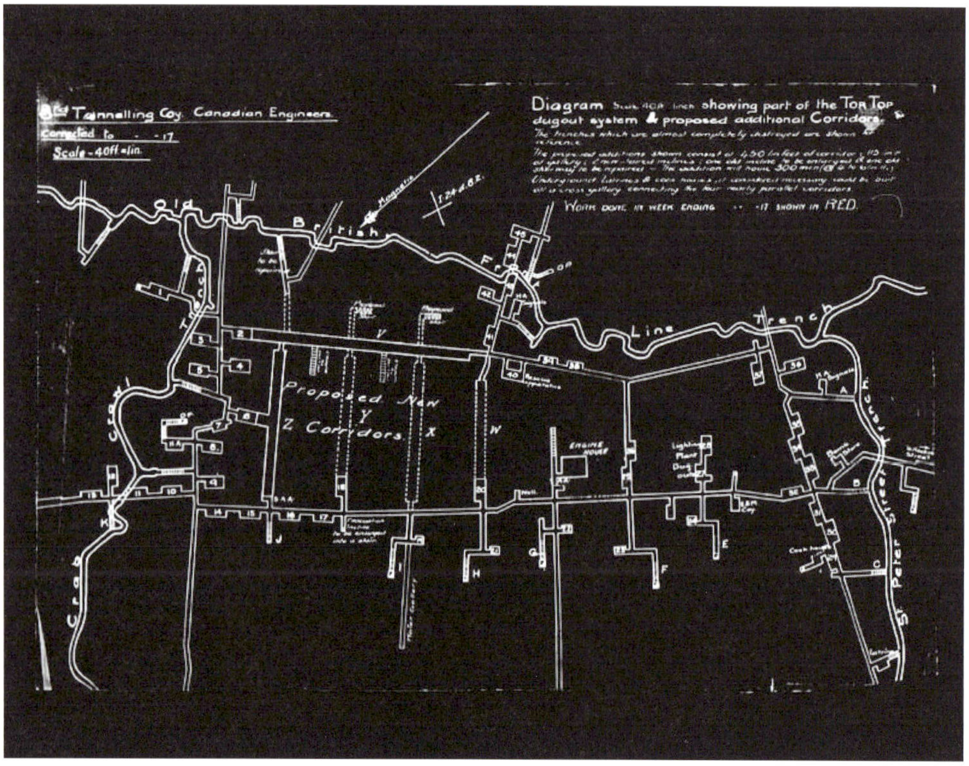

FIG. 165A

Overview of the geophysical EMI sensing results from the two plots on Tor Top.

FIG. 165B

Tor Top: geophysical sensing results combined with the structures found on historical aerial photos.

FIG. 166

Canadian plan of the tunnel system in Tor Top, made in 1917.

FIG. 167A

Tor Top: geophysical soil sensing results of the deeper ground levels with a distinctive pattern of lines.

FIG. 167B

The digitised plans of the Tor Top dugout projected on to the geophysical soil sensing results.

167A

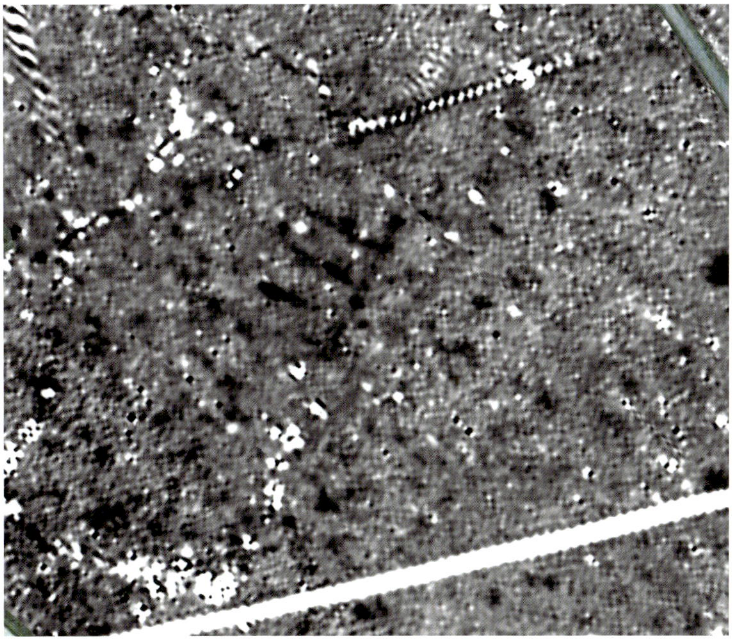

167B

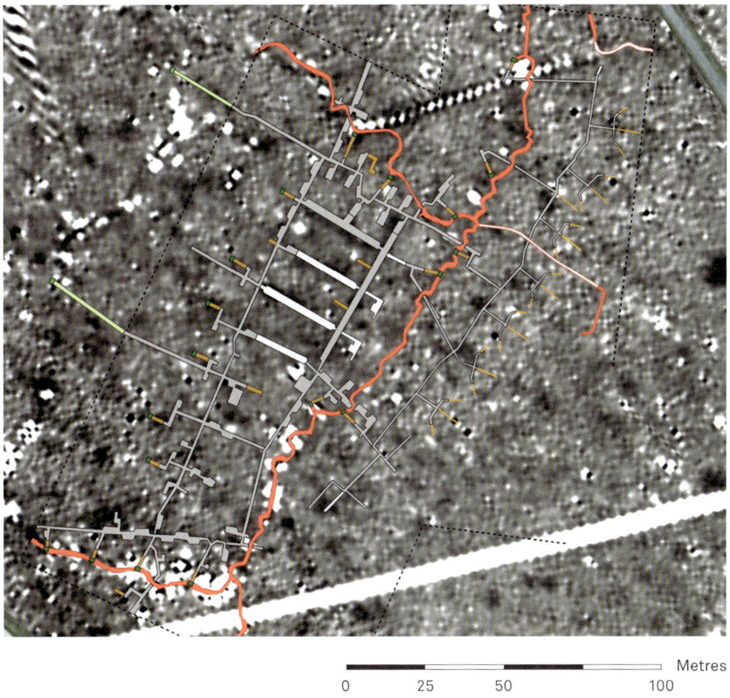

3.5 metres beneath the present-day ground level. Pieces of wood from the tunnel floor were found 5.2 metres down. In other places, the tunnel had completely caved in.

The detected dugout system was found to be the Tor Top dugout and the Crab Crawl dugout, named after the trenches at the surface. The 2nd Canadian Tunnelling Company started work on them at the beginning of October 1916. Their diaries speak of a gallery connecting three blocks of dugouts. Following the Third Battle of Ypres, the front was pushed further east. As a result, the dugouts were converted into a brigade headquarters offering shelter for 500 men in rooms full of bunk beds.

In charge of the use and upkeep of the dugout in October 1917, the English war poet Edmund Blunden described the dugout with a mixture of abhorrence and admiration as a "dirty but precious underworld," with "canals of foul water which stank along the passages" and a "black lattice of flies which hung to warm [light] bulbs".[6]

[6] Blunden 1929

11 Protecting the scars: a century of heritage policy

Koen Himpe

168

169

170

FIG. 168
Cover of the book *Les Sites de Guerre, campagne 1914-1918*, published by the Belgian army.

FIG. 169
The Pill-boxes of Flanders, compiled by Colonel Edward G. L. Thurlow.

FIG. 170
The Newfoundland Memorial on the border between Harelbeke and Kortrijk.

[1] Vaesen 2008
[2] Thurlow 1933
[3] This protected landscape (BSG 23/12/1942, later additionally protected as monument MB 26/03/2010) contains one of the five bronze Caribou Memorials (the others are in Marcoing-Masnières, Gueudecourt, Monchy-Le-Preux and Beaumont-Hamel, France, giving the landscape an international dimension). The R8 ring road around Kortrijk, construction of which started in 1967, cuts across the landscape without much care.

When hostilities finally ended in November 1918, large stretches of the Westhoek had been transformed into a lunar landscape. Even after the post-WW1 reconstruction work, scars still remained in the landscape. But even these are fading away over time. What was our policy towards these traumatic reminders of the war in the last century? What did the government do, and what is it doing, to preserve this war heritage?

The Westhoek landscape, in particular, bears many scars, witnesses to what the region went through in the First World War. The 65-kilometre front line ran from the River Leie (Lys in French) via Messines, Heuvelland, Ypres, Langemark, Houthulst and Diksmuide to Nieuwpoort and Middelkerke. The front line shifted back and forth in the hillier southern stretch, but was more or less static in the – to a great extent flooded – northern Yser plain. The whole front line was heavily fortified, with trenches, barbed wire barriers, concrete bunkers and various shelters everywhere. But it was not just the front line that was transformed. The hinterland was similarly changed by the military infrastructure needed to support the troops at the front, as seen in Wervik, Menin, Ledegem, Moorslede, Poperinge, Vleteren, Alveringem, Lo-Reninge, Staden, Koekelare and Koksijde. In both the Allied and German hinterlands, right up to the frontiers, from De Panne to Zeebrugge and from Knokke-Heist via Antwerp to Turnhout, military fortifications – command and observation posts, coastal batteries and lines of bunkers – bear witness to the war. Even the areas which only saw fighting in the first or last months of the war, such as the valleys of the Velp or the Gete, the defence ring around Antwerp and the valleys of the Leie and the Schelde, still bear scars.

Material traces are to be found all over the territory occupied by the Germans: mansions in which officers were billeted, woods used by the military for training purposes or for supplying firewood, fields turned into airfields and so on. And then there are the places where the dead were (re)buried during and after the war. Reminders of the war are never far away in Flanders.

1922: THE FIRST ATTEMPT TO PROTECT THE WAR HERITAGE

Belgium and later Flanders took a long time to recognise the heritage value of all the WW1 traces. In 1922, the Belgian Ministry of Defence presented a plan to protect the various war sites (the so-called *sites de guerre*), mainly in the Yser section of the front line. Some 25 sites were selected, to be turned into open-air museums[1]. The selection included both Allied positions (among them, Grand Redan in Nieuwpoort, the Belgian observation post in Pervijze, the ruins of the church tower of the Oud-Stuivekenskerke and the Trench of Death/*Dodengang* in Kaaskerke) and German ones (the Lange Max cannon in Koekelare, the Tirpitz Battery in Ostend and the Wilhelm II Battery in Knokke).

A few years earlier, Winston Churchill had come up with the idea of turning the Cloth Hall/*Lakenhallen* and St Martin's Church in Ypres, and possibly the whole town centre of Ypres, then in ruins, into a memorial to the war. And from 1933 onwards there was also a strong plea from the British side to prevent the demolition of bunkers (aka pillboxes) in the Ypres and Messines Salients **(FIG. 168 & 169)**[2].

But it wasn't until the Second World War that the first measures to legally protect the remains of the First World War were introduced. Strangely enough, the first protected object lay outside the former front-line area: the landscape (protected since 1942) around the Newfoundland Memorial, which had been erected around 1924 on the border between Harelbeke and Kortrijk. The large sculpture commemorates the October 1918 offensive and marks the place where the Newfoundland Regiment crossed the River Leie **(FIG. 170)**.[3]

A second – this time German-controlled – initiative in 1943 targeted the legendary *Studentenfriedhof* in Langemark **(FIG. 171)**.[4] It wasn't until after the Second World War that the first Belgian war landscape was put under protection: the ruins of the shelled church tower of the Oud-Stuivekenskerke, along with the nearby Our Lady of Zege chapel and the 'demarcation stone" installed by the Touring Club de Belgique. The symbolic initiative was launched in 1959 by various associations organising battlefield pilgrimages. Around 1924 the road users' association in Oud-Stuivekenskerke had erected a granite column to mark the spot where the German advance was stopped in 1914.[5]

'EXPLORATORY' INITIATIVES (1980-2004)

Between 1980 and the turn of the millennium, influenced by the increased importance of the WW1 heritage, a series of 'exploratory' protections were enacted, all of them from a fortification or industrial archaeology perspective. The sites concerned were, above all, of great symbolic value, such as the Menin Gate as part of the Ypres fortifications (1986); the German military cemetery in Vladslo with its Käthe Kollwitz sculpture (1997); the Ganzepoot (Dutch for 'goose foot') set of locks and spillways in the inner port of Nieuwpoort (1999); the British Bedford House Cemetery in Zillebeke (2002); the large Tyne Cot New British Cemetery in Passchendaele (2003); and Talbot House with its garden and former bathhouse in Poperinge (2004).

In 1992, a proposal for a specific thematic protection package for West Flanders was put forward, containing some of the original *sites de guerre*: the Belgian Trench of Death/*Dodengang* trench network on the Yser dyke in Kaaskerke; the John McCrae site with its casemates along the Ypres-Yser Canal in Boezinge; a few front-line landscapes at Sanctuary Wood and casemates at Lankhof Farm in Zillebeke; the Spanbroek mine crater or Pool of Peace in Wijtschate; and a Belgian observation post in Ramskapelle. Somewhat later, a factory chimney used as a Belgian observation post in Ramskapelle was put under protection, as well as the Yser Tower complex with the Pax Gate and pilgrimage site in Kaaskerke[6].

[4] Following the German capitulation in May 1945, the Belgian government, via a Decree of the then Regent (RB 11/12/1945), immediately declared this protection to be null and void. Half a century later, the cemetery again achieved protected status, this time as a monument (MB 06/09/2002).

[5] It was one of the original 22 demarcation stones in Flanders installed in remembrance of the Allied troops and as a way of promoting war tourism between 1921 and 1927. The very symbolic design of the low columns in red Alsatian granite, with similar ones installed in France, is the work of French sculptor and ex-soldier Paul Moreau-Vauthier.

171

172

FIG. 171
The German cemetery in Langemark.

FIG. 172
Temporary housing in Reninge.

FIG. 173 (pp. 174-175)
Two of the remaining Kruisstraat mine craters which left deep scars in the landscape.

Other cases came about more by chance in the context of (re)development projects, such as the Frontzate, the ultimate line of defence along the former railway line between Nieuwpoort and Diksmuide (1999). The protection extended not only to the Belgian trench and shelter infrastructure, but also to the dyke itself, constructed to prevent any flooding of the western Yser plain[7]. A further example was the German *Bayernwald* trench site in Wijtschate (2002).

Endangered sites were also nominated for protection. One curious example was the Bremen Redoubt (1994), an underground shelter, which, on losing its protected status a short time later, soon became a victim of redevelopment. Geographical inventory packages (selections from specific municipal inventory campaigns) also provided some protection, for example the semi-permanent emergency quarters in the village centre of Reninge (2005) (**FIG. 172**).

INVENTORYING THE FRONT-LINE REGION (2002-2006)

To preserve remains along the front line and in the non-occupied part of West Flanders, in November 2002 the government launched a project aimed at inventorying the First World War remains in the Westhoek. The Province of West Flanders and the Flemish government made an inventory of the material traces of the First World War in the Westhoek, recording bunkers, above-ground and underground shelters and depots, field kitchens, war landscapes and mine craters, war monuments, military cemeteries and commemorative gardens, emergency quarters, and so on[8]. Since then the results have been used by both governments as a policy instrument. The project's starting point was the recognition of the Westhoek battlefields as a UNESCO World Heritage Site.

THEMATIC PROTECTION (SINCE 2008)

Following the inventory of the front-line region, the campaign was extended to cover the rest of Flanders with a view to continuing the protection policy. Since 2008, there have been a number of thematic protection initiatives targeting military cemeteries; for a few commemorative gardens, monuments (such as sculptures commemorating civilian and military victims), bunkers and shelters; for various war-related infrastructures (mine shafts, trench structures, military kitchens, barracks, water towers); and for post-WW1 infrastructures in the devastated regions (emergency quarters, reception centres, hospitals). Task forces made up of specialists and other stakeholders advised the Flemish government to extend the selections to the whole of Flanders. This led to protection being extended to 162 military cemeteries (both Allied and German); more than 200 monuments throughout Flanders; and more than 175 shelters and bunkers, both in the front-line zone and in the hinterland, including the *Hollandstellung* along the east coast, the Ghent-Terneuzen Canal and the Schelde at Antwerp[9]. A number of other cases are currently being prepared or are already earmarked for protection.

Historical, architectural and artistic merits, in many cases context-sensitive, were important arguments for protection. But account was also taken of the social and cultural merits of the war heritage: the international aspect, the Flemish question, the impact on the civilian population,

[7] Debeil & Hulstaert 2011
[8] The remains are listed in: https://inventaris.onroerenderfgoed.be and in https://inventaris.onroerenderfgoed.be/dibe/relict/zoeken.
[9] Decoodt 2014, Decoodt 2007
[10] Chielens et al. 2006, Chielens 2006

Bunker/shelter

Memorial

Military cemetery

Mine crater

Mine shafts

Wijtschate Salient

British front line
November 1914 – June 1917

German front line
November 1914 – June 1917

FIG. 174
Extract from the supplementary investigation of archaeologically valuable landscapes – *lieux de mémoire* – Wijtschate Salient–Messines Ridge, showing the front lines and the associated war remains.

the commemoration of a collective trauma, devotion, etc. Several remains have become part of the landscape, witnesses to the past. The enthusiasm aroused by the In Flanders Fields Museum in Ypres and certainly by the publication of the book *De laatste getuige. Het landschap van Wereldoorlog I in Vlaanderen*[10] have led to deeper insights (FIG. 173).

SPATIAL COMMEMORATION (SINCE 2010)

Between 2010 and 2012, further research was carried out on archaeologically valuable landscapes. This led to 28 landscapes being ring-fenced as commemoration grounds or so-called *lieux de mémoire*[11], with a focus on battlefields, viewpoints and archaeological remains[12]. One new aspect here was the archaeological trench probe at eighteen specific and intrinsically varied locations, such as mine crater sites covered with woods or under grassland, long-lost camps and both German and Allied trench sites from various sections of the front, both on the inundated polder plains and in the Ypres Salient. The results provided a better insight into the presence and state of preservation of the underground heritage.

All these sites formed the basis for a spatial form of commemoration. The goal of these planning initiatives was to better protect the spatial context of the WW1 remains and battlefields, in preparation for a proper management of valuable landscapes. Focusing on the heritage of the First World War, the Landscape Atlas published in 2001[13] did little to delineate certain areas, for instance clustering Kemmelberg-Rodeberg-Vidaigneberg-Scherpenberg as one area, as was also done with the valley of the Douve in Ypres, Heuvelland and Poperinge. The same happened with three areas around the Ypres Fortresses, the Drowned Meadows/*Verdronken Weiden*, the Gasthuisbossen and the Wijtschate-Messines Ridge, Heuvelland, Messines and Zonnebeke and the area surrounding Polygon Wood and the valley of the Reutelbeek in Zonnebeke. Between 2012 and 2013 the Minister officially designated these areas in the southern Ypres Salient as commemorative sites. Improved demarcations of these areas were then enacted on the basis of remaining WW1 traces (FIG. 174).

Due to their unique value, a proposal was made to add the following battlefield landscapes to the Landscape Atlas: the battlefield in Halen (from the Battle of the Silver Helmets), the Gete valley battlefield near Sint-Margriete-Houtem in Tienen, Linter, Zoutleeuw and Geetbets, the Passchendaele battlefield in Zonnebeke, and the Pilkem Ridge battlefield in Ypres and Langemark-Poelkapelle. More were to follow: with the addition of the Ypres-Yser Canal in Ypres, Langemark, Poelkapelle, Houthulst and Lo-Reninge, the First World War received extensive attention. Due to its unique value as a line of fortification and the exceptional state of preservation of the extensive tranches and bunkers, an area around the anti-tank ditches in Stabroek, Kapellen, Brasschaat, Schoten, Schilde and Ranst (including parts of the German *Stellung Antwerpen-Turnhout* was also listed[14]. Several initiatives have been through the required procedure, while others have been temporarily added to the landscape heritage list.

These approval procedures constitute a first step in spatially translating these places into heritage landscapes, a process using spatial planning instruments. In concrete terms, this involves taking account of specific heritage values and characteristics, with the aim of protecting them spatially. The spatial implementation plans are generally drawn up at regional level, in consultation with the heritage agencies and local authorities. This results in an integrated heritage plan giving a prominent place to protection, valuation and exploitation and access to the war heritage without compromising environmental, agricultural, economic, tourist or housing considerations – no self-evident goal. The present-day landscape of the Ypres Salient is not only shaped by the war but is also the result of the intensive reconstruction work carried out in the early inter-war years which unavoidably destroyed many traces of the war. As a result, any specific preservation of what is left becomes a delicate exercise, especially when a sensitive archaeological component is involved: zones with a war-related micro-topology (FIG. 175), known locations of underground shelters and mine shafts, often chance concentrations of material remains or ammunition, etc.

In the areas covered by the Landscape Atlas, scientific, historical, aesthetic, social, cultural and spatial considerations are, inter alia, taken into account. In particular among the historical, social and cultural elements, the importance of WW1 relics is mentioned, precisely due to the continuing strong bonds with the numerous places of remembrance. Aesthetic considerations play a similar role, especially in the hillier region to the south of the Ypres Salient, with views (including over the centre of Ypres) often coinciding with former military-strategic perspectives.

[11] Nora 1984-1992
[12] Verboven 2012
[13] https://inventaris.onroerenderfgoed.be/
[14] Gheyle et al. 2013, Gheyle & Bourgeois 2013

175

176

The specific commemorative and experiential value of the Westhoek landscape attracts thousands of visitors each year, with a particular focus on the British cemeteries and the scattered remains of the military infrastructure. Similarly, the long line of mine craters on the ridge between Hill 60, St-Eloi, Wijtschate and Messines, a reminder of the Mine Battle of 7 June 1917, contributes to the social and cultural importance. Flooded craters such as the Spanbroek Mill crater (Pool of Peace) form quiet places of remembrance. The enormous Menin Gate in Ypres, where every evening the Last Post ceremony takes place, is a very special monument, calling on visitors to reflect on the terrible outcome of the war.

Post-WW1 reconstruction

The many futile attacks and counter-attacks, coupled with the specific topography of the Westhoek (the hills and ridges to the south of Ypres and the lower plain of the Yser valley) made the region the scene of a long-standing trench war. Towns like Ypres and Diksmuide were reduced to rubble, as were many villages in the surrounding area. In 1919, the ministry department responsible for the devastated regions (Dienst der Verwoeste Gewesten) listed 61 completely destroyed and 33 partially destroyed West Flemish towns and villages.

After the war, most of the landscape features were reconstructed in accordance with their pre-WW1 design. Roads, woods, fields and farms were re-established in their former locations. Town and village centres were similarly systematically reconstructed. The materials used, the building topologies, styles and spatial planning principles were closely linked with the ideology and pragmatism of the planned reconstruction. The result was a coherent reconstruction landscape, based on pre-WW1 landscape patterns. Together with the many war memorials, military cemeteries, mine craters and remains in the pock-marked war landscape, the reconstructed landscape is a reminder of the area's strategic importance. All buildings erected at that time tell us something about the reconstruction project, its practical implementation and the underlying ideas (**FIG. 176**). The share of the inter-war heritage dating from the 1919-1945 reconstruction period in the current housing stock is (according to 2004 figures) so substantial that the entire front zone in Belgium can be distinguished via its spatial distribution. A number of reconstructed buildings possess a marked commemorative value and were indeed erected with a specific view to commemorating the war. A number of remaining war memorials have great artistic value due to their authenticity, monumental form and position. The many striking British cemeteries with their timeless neoclassical architecture play an important role in the experiential value of the landscape (**FIG. 177 & 178**)[15].

[15] Cosyns et al. 2012

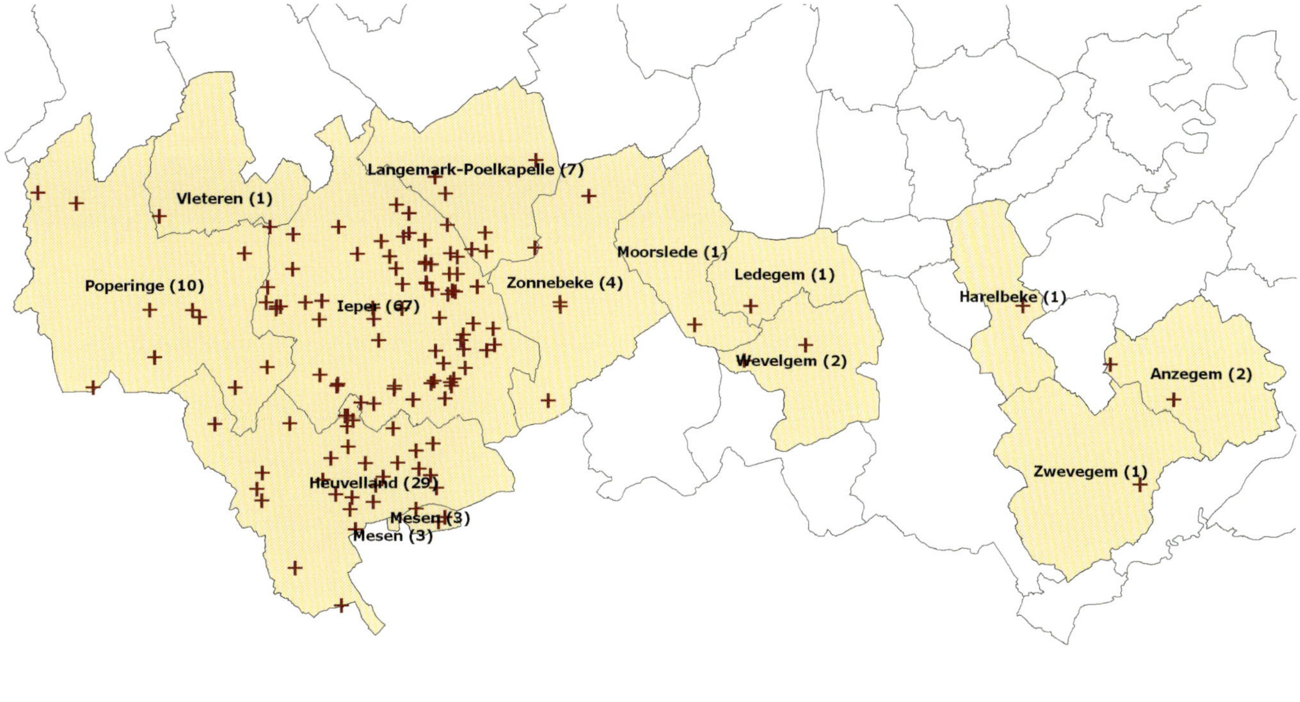

177

178

FIG. 175

Micro-topology in Heuvelland shaped by the war.

FIG. 176

Reconstructed farm in the Komenseweg in Zillebeke.

FIG. 177

Protected British military cemeteries in the south of West Flanders.

FIG. 178

Buttes New British Cemetery in Zonnebeke.

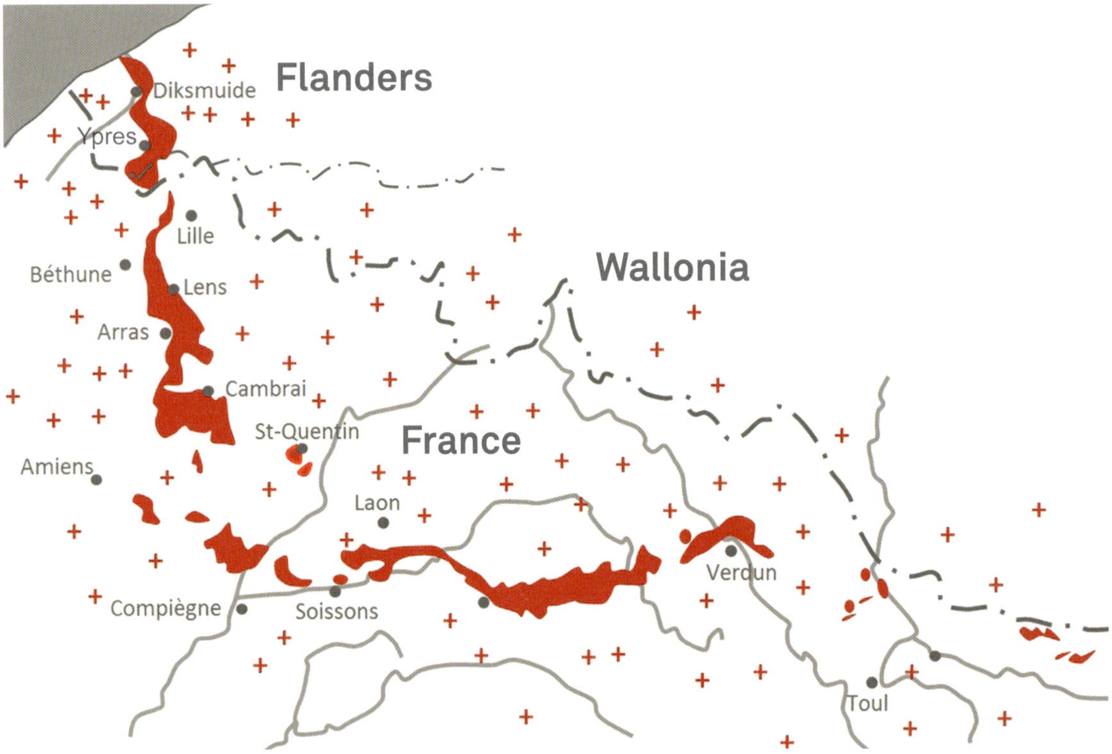

179

UNESCO WORLD HERITAGE

The extensive inventory carried out by the Flemish government and external bodies between 2002 and 2011 enabled a mapping of the diverse and sensitive WW1 heritage. As a next step, a sector protection policy is currently being compiled for military cemeteries, memorials, bunkers and shelters, archaeological hotspots and commemorative landscapes. Initially rather hesitant and little structured, the policy has since been refined and thematically deepened (**FIG. 179**).

Regional-level protection is a stepping stone for having a selection of WW1 sites recognised as a UNESCO World Heritage Site. To underline the international dimension of the nomination, the Flemish Region drew it up in close collaboration with the Walloon Region and an association of 14 northern French *départements*. In Belgium, 26 sites, 19 of them in Flanders, have been proposed for UNESCO recognition. A further 70 sites have been provisionally selected in France, along the long Western Front. A buffer zone is proposed around the selected sites to ensure their sustainable spatial embedding. The final selection is part of a focused heritage strategy commemorating the 100th anniversary of the First World War as a crucial moment in our collective memory[16].

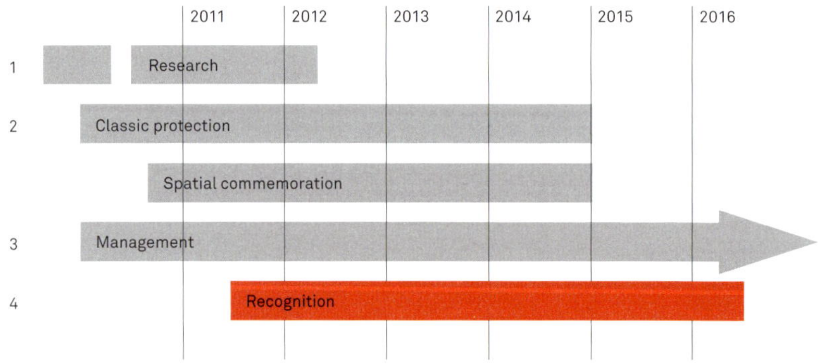

[16] Article based on the lecture given in 2012 by Koen Himpe in collaboration with Hannelore Decoodt entitled 'Protection of First World War Heritage' on the traces of the war. Colloquium 'Het erfgoed van de Eerste Wereldoorlog in een ruimtelijk perspectief' (The First World War from a spatial perspective), 1-2 March 2012, reproduced as Himpe (2014).

FIG. 179
Area covered by the research into First World War heritage, its protection and UNESCO recognition.

FIG. 180 (pp. 182-183)
Aerial photo of the Belgian-German front line along the Yser, 12 November 1917.

The military cemeteries and memorials to the missing in the Westhoek front-line region constitute the main focus of the UNESCO World Heritage application, to a great extent representing the sublimation of the First World War. They are the most important remaining witnesses of the cataclysmic war. The 'landscape of death' makes the war visible, there to touch. The selection constitutes above all an ethical appeal, both collectively and individually.

The following sites have been proposed:

1. The Nieuwpoort Memorial to the Missing (Nieuwpoort)
2. The German military cemetery in Vladslo (Diksmuide)
3. The crypt of the Yser Tower in Diksmuide (Diksmuide)
4. The Belgian military cemetery in Oeren (Alveringem)
5. The Belgian military cemetery in Houthulst (Houthulst)
6. The German military cemetery in Langemark (Langemark Poelkapelle)
7. The Canadian monument 'The Brooding Soldier' in Langemark (Langemark-Poelkapelle)
8. The Tyne Cot New British Cemetery in Passchendaele (Zonnebeke)
9. A cluster of Commonwealth military cemeteries around Doelbos including the Polygon Wood Cemetery and Buttes New British Cemetery in Zonnebeke (Zonnebeke)
10. The Commonwealth military cemetery Essex Farm Cemetery in Boezinge (Ypres)
11. A cluster of Commonwealth military cemeteries around Pilkem including the Welsh Cemetery Caesar's Nose, No Man's Cot Cemetery, Track X Cemetery and Buffs Road Cemetery in Boezinge, in Sint-Jan (Ypres)
12. The Menin Gate Memorial to the Missing in Ypres (Ypres)
13. The Commonwealth military cemetery Bedford House Cemetery in Zillebeke (Ypres)
14. A cluster of Commonwealth military cemeteries around Palingbeek including the Larch Wood Cemetery, Woods Cemetery, 1st D.C.L.I. Cemetery The Bluff and Hedge Row Trench Cemetery in Zillebeke (Ypres)
15. The French Kemmelberg Ossuary with the Den Engel war memorial in Loker (Heuvelland)
16. A cluster of Commonwealth military cemeteries around Spanbroekmolenkrater (Pool of Peace) including Spanbroekmolen British Cemetery and Lone Tree Cemetery in Wijtschate (Heuvelland)
17. The Island of Ireland Peace Tower in Messines (Messines)
18. The Commonwealth military cemetery Lijssenthoek Military Cemetery in Poperinge (Poperinge)
19. The French military cemetery Saint-Charles de Potyse in Ypres (Ypres)

The military cemeteries and memorials to the missing bear witness to a new attitude towards death, with soldiers killed in combat being remembered for the first time individually. While the war had no place for individuals, they found their place in death. Their remains were entrusted to individual graves with great care and on an unprecedented scale, wherever possible (that is, when identified) with their name inscribed on a headstone. The names of the missing are inscribed in lists of memorials to the missing. The recognition and personal identification of the dead was done in a spirit of equality, with no account taken of rank, class, culture or nationality.

The military cemeteries and memorials to the missing are unique, displaying exceptionally high quality in their architectural form and the way they merge into the landscape. They symbolise the former Western Front, a concrete reminder of an unprecedented conflict. The sheer number and concentration of both graves and cemeteries bear witness to the intensity and scale of the fighting 100 years ago. The many nationalities recorded on the headstones and memorials remind us of the world-wide scale of the Great War, reflecting its enormity.

The military cemeteries and memorials to the missing are no relics of the past, as burials of recently unearthed human remains still take place there. They are also visited by thousands of people from all over the world every year, in many cases in search of a fallen relative. Visits are sometimes formal, with politicians and diplomats paying their respects to the dead, but in most cases the visitors are just ordinary citizens and families, showing a will for continuity at an individual and collective level.

The cemeteries and memorials are constant present-day reminders of the past, showing how universal the post-WW1 remembrance still is. They have also become places of reflection, timeless sites forcing us to stand still and reflect on the meaning of war and its inevitable corollary of death. They represent a lasting and living veneration of remembrance, a universal call for peace and cooperation.

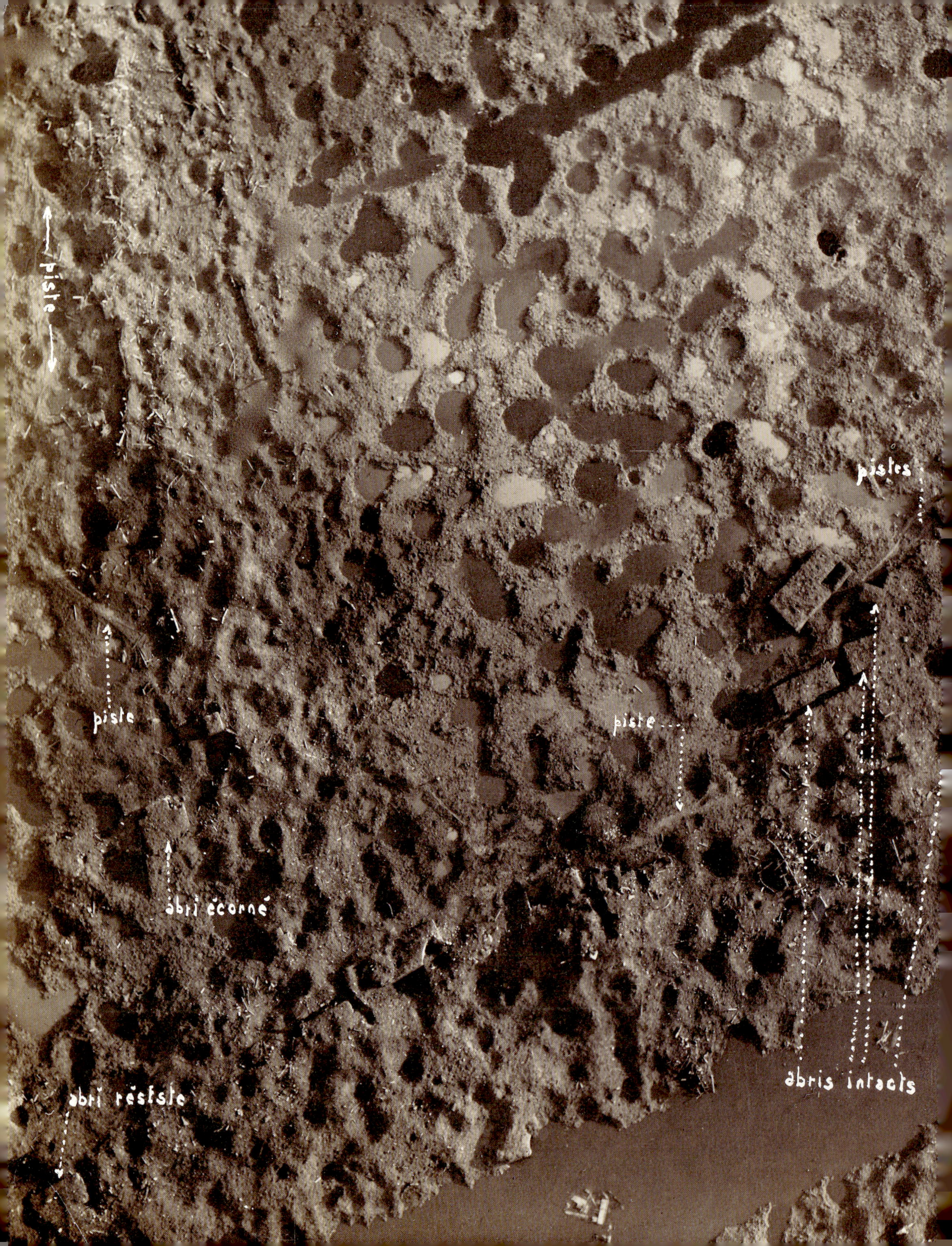
piste
pistes
piste
piste
abri écorné
abris intacts
abri résiste

piste
abris résistent
A.V.M.B 2550 12-11-17 800m 12h
MINOTERIE . C.31.
P: Adj. Ledure O: Lt Verelst.

Flanders Heritage Agency 2016a, *Duits oefenterrein Eerste Wereldoorlog*. Inventaris Onroerend Erfgoed. https://id.erfgoed.net/erfgoedobjecten/126614, 12 juni 2016.

Flanders Heritage Agency 2016b, *Oorlogslandschap Kattekerkhofstraat 1 (Kemmel, WO I)*. Inventaris Onroerend Erfgoed. https://id.erfgoed.net/erfgoedobjecten/96056, 12 juni 2016.

Animals in War Memorial Fund 2016, *The Animals in War Memorial*, Brook Gate, Park Lane, London W1. www.animalsinwar.org.uk, 6 June 2016.

Apers T. & Bracke M. In voorbereiding, *Archeologische opgraving Watou, Oude Provenstraat*, Ingelmunster, Monument Vandekerckhove nv.

Apers T. & Heyvaert B. 2013, Outpost Wieltje: vroege Britse stellingbouw in de Ieperboog (Ieper, West-Vlaanderen). In: *Conflict in Contact* 1, 14-18.

Arthur M. 2014, *Last Post: The Final Word from Our First World War Soldiers*, London, Orion Publishing Co.

Baratay E. 2013, *Bêtes des tranchées. Des vécus oubliés*, Paris, CNRS Editions.

Barton P., Doyle P. & Vandewalle J. 2004, *Beneath Flanders Fields: The Tunnellers' War 1914-1918*, Staplehurst, Spellmount.

Barton P., Doyle P. & Vandewalle J. 2005, *Beneath Flanders Fields. Tunnels en mijnen 1914-1918*, Zonnebeke, Johan Vandewalle.

Bax R. & Smeets M. 2014, Een loopgraaf uit de beginmaanden van de Eerste Wereldoorlog te Boortmeerbeek (Vlaams-Brabant). In: *Conflict in Contact* 2, 4-9.

Beazeley G.A. 1919, Air Photography in Archaeology. In: *The Geographical Journal* 53, 5, 330-335.

Beke F. 2013, Archeologische opgraving te Sappenleen (Poperinge, West-Vlaanderen). In: *Conflict in Contact* 1, 24-29.

Bewley R. 1997, From Military to Civilian: A Brief History of the Early Development of Aerial Photography for Archaeology. In: Oexle J. (ed.), *Aus der Luft. Bilder unserer Geschichte. Luftbildarchäologie in Zentraleuropa*, Dresden, Landesamt für Archäologie, 10-21.

Bewley R. 2002, Aerial Survey: Learning from a Hundred Years of Experience? In: Bewley R. & Raczkowski W. (ed.), *Aerial Archaeology. Developing Future Practice. NATO Science Series vol. 337*, Amsterdam, IOS Press, 11-18.

Blunden E. 1929, *Undertones of War*, New York, The Country Life Press.

Bot B., Kelner T. & Bracke M. 2012, *Archeologische prospectie Poperinge uitbreiding Ringweg. Basisrapport*, Ingelmunster, Monument Vandekerckhove nv.

Bouckaert K., Bracke M., Medinilla A. & Verwerft D. 2009, *Archeologisch onderzoek aan de Kriekestraat te Reningelst*, Mechelen, Archaeological Solutions.

Bourgeois J., Stichelbaut B., De Reu J. & Semey J. 2010, Drie decennia archeologische luchtfotografie in Vlaanderen: retrospectief en prospectief. In: *Cultureel Jaarboek van de Provincie Oost-Vlaanderen 2008*, Gent, Provinciebestuur Oost-Vlaanderen, 103-113.

Bracke M. 2010, *Koksijde, Hof Ter Hille. Een blik op het leven achter het front tijdens de Eerste Wereldoorlog (1914-18). 'Nonnenhof'. Conceptverslag*, Ingelmunster, Monument Vandekerckhove nv.

Bracke M. 2011, *Archeologische opgraving Lijssenthoek (Boescheepseweg), Poperinge. Basisrapport oktober 2011*, Ingelmunster, Monument Vandekerckhove nv.

Bracke M. 2012, *Archeologische opgraving Poperinge, Lijssenthoek (Boescheepseweg). Basisrapport juni 2012*, Ingelmunster, Monument Vandekerckhove nv.

Bracke M. 2013, Een hospitaalsite uit de Eerste Wereldoorlog archeologisch bekeken (provincie West-Vlaanderen). In: *Conflict in Contact* 1, 40-45.

Bracke M., Heyvaert B., Roelens F. & Vanhoutte C. 2012, *Archeologisch onderzoek Wienerberger, Zonnebeke (provincie West-Vlaanderen). Basisrapport januari 2012*, Ingelmunster, Monument Vandekerckhove nv.

Bracke M., Scheltjens S. & Wyns G. 2015, *Archeologische opgraving Oostvleteren, Veurnestraat. Basisrapport conceptversie*, Ingelmunster, Monument Vandekerckhove nv.

Bracke M. & Verdegem S. 2015, *Archeologische prospectie/opgraving Fluxys-Frontzone Pijpegale-Staden (provincie West-Vlaanderen). Evaluatienota*, Ingelmunster, THV MRG (Monument Vandekerckhove nv, Ruben Willaert bvba, Gate bvba).

Bracke M., Verwerft D., Medinilla A. & Bouckaert K. 2013, *Afvalkuilen, krengenbegravingen en munitiedumps uit WO I in Reningelst, Kriekstraat (provincie West-Vlaanderen).* In: *Conflict in Contact* 1, 50-53.

Brereton J.M. 1976, *The Horse in War*, Newton Abbot, Devon, David & Charles.

Bruneau R. 2005, Les équidés dans la Grande Guerre. In: *Bulletin de la Société Française d'Histoire et de Médecine Vétérinaire* 4, 1, 20-33.

Bucholz A. 1991, *Moltke, Schlieffen and Prussian War Planning*, New York, Berg Publishers.

Chevallier R. 1971, *La Photographie Aérienne*, Paris, Librairie Armand Colin.

Chielens P. 2006, De laatste getuige. Het landschap meer dan ooit. In: Chielens P., Dendooven D. & Decoodt H. (ed.), *De laatste getuige. Het landschap van Wereldoorlog I in Vlaanderen*,Tielt, Lannoo, 9-11.

Chielens P., Dendooven D. & Decoodt H. (ed.) 2006, *De laatste getuige. Het landschap van Wereldoorlog I in Vlaanderen*, Tielt, Lannoo.

Chielens P., Dendooven D. & Vandenbilcke A. 2012, *In Flanders Fields Museum, Museum Guide*, Ieper, In Flanders Fields Museum.

Clarke B. 1917, The Story of the British War-Horse from Prairie to Battlefield. In: Wilson H.W. & Hammerton J.A. (ed.), *The Great War. The Standard History of the All Europe Conflict*, London, Amalgamated Press.

Clutton-Brock J. 1999, *A Natural History of Domesticated Mammals*, Cambridge, Cambridge University Press.

Cooper J. 2000, *Animals in War (new ed.)*, London, Corgi Books.

Corfield R. 2010, Identifying the Lost Soldiers of Fromelles. In: *Chemistry World*, February, 1-5.

Cosyns E., De Moor J. & Saelens S. 2012, *Geclusterde ankerplaatsen Ieperse regio, met aanvullende inventarisatieronde wederopbouwarchitectuur*, West-Vlaamse Intercommunale in opdracht van het agentschap Onroerend Erfgoed.

Crawford O.G.S. 1954, A Century of Air-Photography. In: *Antiquity* 28, 206-210.

Dalle S. 2013, Wereldoorlog I-sporen in Emblem nabij het Fort van Broechem (Broechem, Antwerpen). In: *Conflict in Contact* 1, 68-73.

De Diggers 2001, The/De Diggers website. http://www.mausershooters.org/diggers/, 20 November 2014.

De Meyer M. 2009, World War 1 Battlefields of the Ypres Salient Mapped and Analysed with Aerial Photographs. A Confrontation with the Current Landscape and Archaeology. In: Stichelbaut B., Bourgeois J., Saunders N. & Chielens P. (ed.), *Images of Conflict. Aerial Photography and Archaeology*, Newcastle-upon-Tyne, Cambridge Scholars Publishing, 203-220.

Debaeke S. 2010, *Oud ijzer: de frontstreek bedolven onder levensgevaarlijke oorlogs-munitie,* Brugge, De Klaproos.

Debeil F. & Hulstaert W. 2011, Consolidatieproject restanten Eerste Wereldoorlog. In: *M&L, Monumenten, Landschappen en Archeologie* 30, 5, 24-67.

Decoodt H. 2007, De Sporen van 'Den Grooten Oorlog'. In: *M&L, Monumenten, Landschappen en Archeologie* 26, 1, 4-36.

Decoodt H. 2014, Belgische en Franse militaire posten aan het IJzerfront. In: *M&L, Monumenten, Landschappen en Archeologie* 33, 4, 4-23.

Delepierre A.-M. & Huys M. 1995, De Westhoek en de 'Groote Oorlog': restanten, toeristen en de officiële erkenning. In: *M&L, Monumenten, Landschappen en Archeologie* 14, 4, 50-63.

Delve K. 1997, *World War One in the Air,* Wiltshire, The Crowood Press Ltd.

Demey D. 2013, *Archeologisch onderzoek Oostvleteren, Kasteelweg, Nieuwe Begraafplaats. Rapport 62*, Sijsele, Ruben Willaert.

Demeyere F. 2010, *Sappenleen (Poperinge). Rapport historisch vooronderzoek*, Diksmuide, Alfa Erfgoedprojecten.

Desfossés Y. 1998, Préserver les traces. In: *L'Archéologie et la Grande Guerre 14-18 aujourd'hui*, Paris, La Cigogne, 36-51.

Desfossés Y., Jacques A. & Prilaux G. 2007, Les vestiges de la Première Guerre dans le nord de la France. Cas d'Etudes et Perspectives. In: *Les Cahiers de l'Urbanisme* 65, septembre 2007, 93-97.

Desfossés Y., Jacques A. & Prilaux G. 2008. In: *L'Archéologie de la Grande Guerre,* S.l., INRAP.

Deuel L. 1969, *Flights into Yesterday. The Story of Aerial Archaeology,* Suffolk, Penguin Books.

Dewilde M. 2006, De Eerste Wereldoorlog en archeologie. In: Chielens P., Dendooven D. & Decoodt H. (ed.), *De laatste getuige. Het landschap van Wereldoorlog I in Vlaanderen*, Tielt, Lannoo, 137-142.

Dewilde M., Brown M. & Wyffels F. 2015a, De sporen van de 'Groote Oorlog' archeologisch onderzocht. Proefsleuvenonderzoek in een Duitse WO I trainingssite in Koekelare, Welfvenestbos (provincie West-Vlaanderen). In: *Onderzoeksrapporten agentschap Onroerend Erfgoed,* Brussel, Agentschap Onroerend Erfgoed.

Dewilde M., De Meyer M. & Saunders N. 2007, Archeologie van de 'Groote Oorlog'. De Vlaamse situatie. In: *M&L, Monument, Landschappen en Archeologie* 26, 1, 37-54.

Dewilde M., Stichelbaut B., Van Hollebeeke Y., Verboven H. & Wyffels F. 2014, Bellewaarde en zijn turbulent oorlogsverleden. In: *M&L, Monumenten, Landschappen en Archeologie* 33, 3, 30-47.

Dewilde M., Vanhoutte S. & Wyffels F. 2015b, Preventief archeologisch onderzoek in de 'leege platse' Beselare, 2011-2013. In: *Onderzoeksrapporten Agentschap Onroerend Erfgoed*, Brussel, Agentschap Onroerend Erfgoed.

Dewilde M. & Wyffels F. 2015, Een ongewone vondst van Duitse gesneuvelden in Wijtschate, Galgestraat (West-Vlaanderen). In: *Conflict in Contact* 3, 48-51.

Dhanens P. 2008, *Een eeuw luchtvaart boven Gent. Deel I: 1785-1939,* Erembodegem, Flying Pencil.

Doyle P., Barton P. & Vandewalle J. 2006, Archaeology of a Great War Dugout: Beecham Farm, Passchendaele, Belgium. In: *Journal of Conflict Archaeology* 1, 45-66.

Duco D. 2004, *Century of Change, the European Clay Pipe, Its Final Flourish and Ultimate Fall, 1830-1940,* Amsterdam, Pijpenkabinet.

Ervynck A. & Lentacker A. 2014, They shoot horses, don't they? Skeletten van paarden en muildieren als erfgoed uit de Groote Oorlog. In: *M&L, Monumenten, Landschappen en Archeologie* 33, 2, 6-21.

Galtrey S. 1918, *The Horse and the War,* London, Country Life.

Gardiner J. 2006, *The Animals' War: Animals in Wartime from the First World War to the Present Day,* London, Portrait/Piatkus Books.

Gheyle W. & Bourgeois I. 2013, *Vergeten Linies. Antwerpse bunkers en loopgraven door de lens van Leutnant Zimmermann (1918),* Antwerpen, provincie Antwerpen.

Gheyle W., Bourgeois J., Bracke M., Dalle S., Deconynck J., Decorte J., De Langhe K., De Mulder G., Hanssens D., Heyvaert B., Note N., Saey T., Stichelbaut B., Van den Berghe H., Van Eetvelde V., Van Hollebeeke Y., Van Meirvenne M. & Verdegem S. 2016a, Interdisciplinair onderzoek naar een Brits-Australisch barakkenkamp in het niemandsland te Kemmel (West-Vlaanderen). In: *Conflict in Contact* 4, 36-46.

Gheyle W., Dossche R., Bourgeois J., Stichelbaut B. & Van Eetvelde V. 2013, Integrating Archaeology and Landscape Analysis for the Cultural Heritage Management of a World War I Militarised Landscape: The German Field Defences in Antwerp. In: *Landscape Research* 39, 5, 502-522.

Gheyle W., Saey T., Van Hollebeeke Y., Verplaetse S., Note N., Bourgeois J., Van Meirvenne M., Van Eetvelde V. & Stichelbaut B. 2016b, Historical Aerial Photography and Multi-Receiver EMI Soil Sensing, Complementing Techniques For the Study of a Great War Conflict Landscape. In: *Archaeological Prospection* 23, 3, 149-164.

Gierath G. 1928, *Geschichte des reserve-Infanterie-Regiments Nr. 210 und seiner Grenzschutz-Formationen (1914-1920)*, Oldenburg-Berlin, Gernard Stalling.

Grand Quartier Général des Armées 1916, *Notes sur l'Interprétation des Photographies Aériennes*, S.l.

Haneca K. 2014, Groene veteranen. Levende getuigen van de eerste wereldbrand. In: *M&L, Monument, Landschappen en Archeologie* 33, 6, 6-17.

Hauser K. 2008, *Bloody Old Britain: O.G.S. Crawford and the Archaeology of Modern Life*, London, Granta Books.

Heyvaert B. & Bracke M. 2011, *Archeologische opgraving Poperinge, Sint-Jansstraat (provincie West-Vlaanderen). Basisrapport*, Ingelmunster, Monument Vandekerckhove nv.

Hibbard B.H. 1919, *Effects of the Great War upon Agriculture in the United States and Great Britain*, New York, Oxford University Press.

Himpe K. 2014, De zorg voor littekens. In: *Ruimte* 20, 1, 12-19.

His Majesty's Stationery Office 1922, *Statistics of the Military Effort of the British Empire during the Great War 1914-1920*, London, His Majesty's Stationery Office.

Holste W. 1934, *Goslarer Jäger im Weltkriege: Das reserve-Jägerbataillon Nr. 23*, Hildesheim, August Lax.

Kokalj Z., Zakšck K. & Oštir K. 2011, Application of Sky-View Factor for the Visualisation of Historic Landscape Features in Lidar-Derived Relief Model. In: *Antiquity* 3, 85, 263-373.

Kokalj Z., Zakšek K. & Oštir K. 2013, Visualizations of Lidar Derived Relief Models. In: Opitz R. & Cowley D. (ed.), *Interpreting Archaeological Topography. Airborne Laser Scanning, Aerial Photographs and Ground Observation*, Oxford, Oxbow Books.

Laffin J. 1987, *Battlefield Archaeology*, Hersham, Ian Allen.

Laloo P., Cryns J., Van Goidsenhove W., De Brant R., Bourgeois I. & Gheyle W. 2013, Loopgraven uit de begindagen van de Eerste Wereldoorlog te Lier, Duwijck (provincie Antwerpen). In: *Conflict in Contact* 1, 97-101.

Lee A. 2014, *The Battle to Feed Tommy: New Exhibition Looks At the Diet Of a WW1 Soldier.* http://www.express.co.uk/news/world-war-1/502452/The-Battle-to-feed-Tommy-The-diet-of-a-WW1-soldier, 10 June 2016.

Lefere M. 2014, *Archeologische opgraving Elewijt Molenveld, School De Regenboog, Fase 2 (provincie Vlaams-Brabant). Basisrapport*, Ingelmunster, Monument Vandekerckhove nv.

Leggat R. 2000, *A History of Photography: The Beginnings of Photography*. http://www.rleggat.com/photohistory, 14 August 2008.

Lepetz S. 1996, L'animal dans la société gallo-romaine de la France du nord. In: *Revue Archéologique de Picardie*, Numéro Spécial 12, 58-59.

Lyddon W.G. 1938, *British War Missions to the United States, 1914-18*, London/New York, Oxford University Press.

Makoben E. 1933, *Geschichte des Reserve-Infanterie-Regiments Nr. 212 im Weltkriege 1914-1918: nach den Kriegsakten des Regiments und der 45. Res.-Division und nach den im Verzeichnis genannten Quellen*, Oldenburg, Gerhard Stalling.

Murray T. 2007, *Milestones in Archaeology: A Chronological Encyclopedia*, Santa Barbara, ABC-Clio.

Nel D. 1922, *Boesinghe ou les combats de la 87e Division Territoriale sur l'Yser*, Rennes, Imprimerie du Nouvelliste de Bretagne.

Newhall B. 1982, *The History of Photography From 1839 To the Present*, New York, The Museum of Modern Art.

Nora P. (ed.), 1984-1992, *Les lieux de mémoire*, Paris, Editions Quarto Gallimard.

Robertshaw A. & Kenyon D. 2008, *Digging the Trenches. The Archaeology of the Western Front*, Barnsley, Pen & Swords Military.

Saey T., Stichelbaut B., Bourgeois J., Van Eetvelde V. & Van Meirvenne M. 2013, An Interdisciplinary Non-Invasive Approach to Landscape Archaeology of the Great War. In: *Archaeological Prospection* 20, 1, 39-44.

Sakkers H., Den Hollander J. & Murk R. 2011, *De Hollandstellung van Knokke tot Antwerpen. Stille getuige van de Eerste Wereldoorlog*, Antwerpen, Witsand.

Saunders N. 2002, Excavating Memories: Archaeology and the Great War, 1914-2001. In: *Antiquity* 76, 101-108.

Saunders N. 2007, *Killing Time. Archaeology and the First World War*, Gloucestershire, Sutton.

Schulz E., Kissler A. & Schulz P. 1930, *Geschichte des Reserve-Infanterie-Regiments Nr. 209 im Weltkriege 1914-1918*, Berlin, Gerhard Stalling.

Scott M. 1992, *The Ypres Salient: A Guide to the Cemeteries and Memorials of the Salient*, Brooke, Gliddon Books.

Scully J. & Woodward W. 2012, Naming the Unknown of Fromelles: DNA Profiling, Ethics and the Identification of First World War Bodies. In: *Journal of War & Culture Studies* 5, 1, 59-72.

Simkin J. 2015, *Trench Food.* http://spartacus-educational.com/FWWtrenchfood.htm, 10 June 2016.

Singleton J. 1993, Britain's Military Use of Horses 1914-1918. In: *Past & Present* 139, 178-203.

Spillebeen W. 2014, *Oorlogsdagboeken 1914-1918 / Achiel Van Walleghem; Nederlandse hertaling van het integrale manuscript door Willy Spillebeen*, Tielt, Lannoo.

Steel N. & Hart P. 2001, *Passchendaele: The Sacrificial Ground*, London, Cassell Military.

Stichelbaut B. 2004, Belgische militaire luchtfotografie tijdens de Eerste Wereldoorlog, historische studie, luchtfoto-interpretatie en inventarisatie van zichtbare sporen. Een bijdrage tot de Vlaamse Battlefield Archaeology. *Vakgroep Archeologie*, Gent, Universiteit Gent.

Stichelbaut B. 2015, *Forgotten and Lost? Archival Research of Aerial Photographic Collections of the Western Front 1914-1918: A Guide To the Archives,* Ljubljana, Založba ZRC.

Stichelbaut B., Gheyle W., Saey T., Van Eetvelde V., Van Meirvenne M., Note N., Van den Berghe H. & Bourgeois J. 2016, The First World War from Above and Below. Historical Aerial Photographs and Mine Craters in the Ypres Salient. In: *Applied Geography* 66, 64-72.

Stichelbaut B., Gheyle W., Van Eetvelde V., Van Meirvenne M., Saey T., Note N., Van den Berghe H. & Bourgeois J. 2017a, The Ypres Salient 1914-1918: Historical Aerial Photography and the Landscape of War. In: *Antiquity* 91, 355, 235-249.

Stichelbaut B., Note N., Saey T., Hanssens D., Van den Berghe H., Bourgeois J., Van Meirvenne M., Van Eetvelde V. & Gheyle W. 2017b, Non-Invasive Research of Tunneling Heritage in the Ypres Salient (1914-1918): Research of the Tor Top Tunnel System. In: *Journal of Cultural Heritage,* 26, 109-117.

Stichelbaut B., Saey T., Meeuws F., Bourgeois J. & Van Meirvenne M. 2011, World War One Heritage in Belgium: Combining Historical Aerial Photography and EMI. In: Cowley D. (ed.), *Remote Sensing for Archaeological Heritage Management.* Budapest, Archaeolingua, 265-273.

The War Office 1922, *Statistics of the Military Effort of the British Empire During the Great War 1914-1920,* London, His Majesty's Stationery Office.

Thurlow E. 1933, *The Pill-Boxes of Flanders,* London, Ivor Nicholson and Watson Ltd.

Trueman C.N. 2016, *Soldiers' Food in the Trenches*. http://www.historylearningsite.co.uk/world-war-one/the-western-front-in-world-war-one/soldiers-food-in-the-trenches, 10 June 2016.

Vaesen J. 2008, Hergebruik of oorlogstoerisme? De omgang met Belgische militaire sites als sporen van de strijd, 1914-1940. In: Pallier P.-A. & Nefors P. (ed.), *Quand les canons se taisent. En toen zwegen de kanonnen. When the Guns Fall Silent*, Brussel, Algemeen Rijksarchief en Koninklijk Legermuseum Brussel, 483-518.

Van Campenhout K. & Alma X. 2014, IJzertijdbewoning en gevechtslinies uit WO I. Een opgraving van twee vondstzones te Beveren, KMO-zone Doornpark. In: *Vlaams Erfgoed Centrum Rapport*, Leuven, Vlaams Erfgoed Centrum.

Van Couwenberghe B., Ryssaert C. & Demey D. 2011. *Archeologisch vooronderzoek Poperinge Bedrijventerrein Sappenleen. Archeologisch proefsleuvenonderzoek, definitief rapport*, Antwerpen, Antea Group.

Van Creveld M. 1977, *Supplying War: Logistics from Wallenstein to Patton,* Cambridge, Cambridge University Press.

Van Emden R. 2010, *Tommy's Ark: Soldiers and Their Animals in the Great War,* London/New York, Bloomsbury.

Van Hollebeeke Y., Stichelbaut B. & Bourgeois J. 2014, From Landscape of War to Archaeological Report: Ten Years of Professional World War I Archaeology in Flanders (Belgium). In: *European Journal of Archaeology* 17, 4, 702-719.

Vancoillie J. 2002, De Duitse begraafplaatsen in Zonnebeke en zijn deelgemeenten. In: *Het Zonneheem* 31, 2, 31.

Vancoillie J. 2013, *De Duitse begraafplaats Menen-Wald. Geschiedenis van de Duitse militaire graven van de Eerste Wereldoorlog in Zuid-West-Vlaanderen,* Wevelgem, Jan Vancoillie.

Vancoillie J. & Blieck K. 2016, *Bouwen aan het front. Loopgraven, schuilplaatsen en betonbunkers van het Duitse leger aan het Ieperfront 1914-1918,* Zonnebeke, Memorial Museum Passchendaele 1917.

Verboven H. 2012, *Syntheserapport over de aanpak, methodiek, resultaten en aanbevelingen van het WO I-erfgoedonderzoek, onuitgegeven rapport Onroerend Erfgoed,* Brussel, agentschap Onroerend Erfgoed.

Verdegem S. 2007, Caesar's Nose, 1914-1918. Archeologisch onderzoek van oorlogspatrimonium langs de Ieperboog. *Vakgroep Archeologie*, Gent, Universiteit Gent.

Verdegem S., Billemont J. & Genbrugge S. 2013a, Archeologisch onderzoek Mesen Aquafin Collector, Rapport 28. In: *Adede Archeologische rapporten*, Gent, Adede.

Verdegem S. & De Decker S. 2014, Archeologisch onderzoek bij drie grachten. In: *M&L, Monumenten, Landschappen en Archeologie* 33, 2, 24.

Verdegem S. & Van Goidsenhove W. 2016, *Archeologisch onderzoek Ieper, Kleine Poezelstraat, VEC Rapport 25*, Sijsele, Vlaams Erfgoed Centrum.

Verdegem S., Van Goidsenhove W., Ryckebusch L. & Teetaert D. 2014a, *Archeologische opgraving Noordschoteplein (Lo-Reninge, West-Vlaanderen), VEC Rapport 70*, Sijsele, Ruben Willaert.

Verdegem S., Van Goidsenhove W., Ryckebusch L., Teetaert D., Smet J. & Herreman D. 2014b, Een Franse loopgraaf uit de begindagen van de stellingenoorlog (Lo-Reninge, West-Vlaanderen). In: *Conflict in Contact* 2, 78-83.

Verdegem S., Vervoort R., Tombeur L. & De Smaele B. 2013b, Resten van vesten te Ieper (Maarschalk Frenchlaan, Rudyard Kiplinglaan, Gildenstraat), Rapport 32. In: *Adede Archeologische rapporten*, Gent, Adede.

Wackenier W. 2004, Archeologie van staal en beton. Bunkers en minierte Unterständte uit de Eerste Wereldoorlog in Staden, Westrozebeke en Oostnieuwkerke. *Vakgroep Archeologie*, Gent, Universiteit Gent.

Wikipedia 2016, Kommissbrot. https://de.wikipedia.org/wiki/Kommissbrot, 10 June 2016.

Willers H. & Mangels M. 1926, *Königlich Preussisches Reserve-Infanterie-Regiment Nr. 215,* Berlin, G. Stalling.

Xingqing G. 1938, *Herinneringen aan mijn werk tijdens de oorlog in Europa. Oorspronkelijk in het Chinees, vertaald door Philip Vanhaelemeersch.*

FIG. 181
British trenches and barbed wire barriers in the snow in Ypres Salient.

PHOTOGRAPHY CREDITS

ALEXANDER TURNBULL LIBRARY
118

AUCKLAND MUSEUM
75

AUSTRALIAN WAR MEMORIAL
46, 73, 119, 150D

BAAC-VLAANDEREN
126

BAVARIAN STATE ARCHIVES, MUNICH
143

BIRGER STICHELBAUT, GHENT UNIVERSITY
B, C, E, F, I, M, P, 1, 6, 7, 8, 14, 21, 22, 24, 25, 27, 37, 53, 56, 64, 65, 67, 76, 94, 95, 98, 101, 104, 130, 133, 138, 144, 147, 150E, 151, 152, 153, 154, 159A, 171, 173, 175

CENTRE FOR HISTORICAL DOCUMENTATION OF THE ARMY
125

DE LOGI & HOORNE ARCHAEOLOGY
140

DEFENCE HISTORICAL SERVICE
33

ESRI, OPEN STREET MAP
25 base layer

F.C.LAMA //FOTO & CREATIESTAL
D, J ,99, 103

FRANKY WYFFELS, FLANDERS HERITAGE AGENCY
G, H, Q, R, 15, 47, 55, 83, 85, 86, 87, 136

GDI-FLANDERS
F orthophoto, P orthophoto, 17B, 27 orthophoto, 37 orthophoto, 56 orthophoto, 64 orthophoto, 67 orthophoto, 89 orthophoto, 139B, 150A & 150E orthophoto, 151 orthophoto, 154 orthophoto, 156 orthophoto, 157, 158, 159 orthophoto, 160 orthophoto, 165 orthophoto, 174 orthophoto

HANNELORE DECOODT, FLANDERS HERITAGE AGENCY
172, 178

HANS DENIS, FLANDERS HERITAGE AGENCY
K, 112, 114, 120, 121, 123

HILDE VERBOVEN, MOIRA HEYN FLANDERS HERITAGE AGENCY & BIRGER STICHELBAUT, GHENT UNIVERSITY
174

IMPERIAL WAR MUSEUM
52, 66, 81, 96, 124, 150A, 150B, 150C, 154 historical photo, 163B

IN FLANDERS FIELDS MUSEUM
A, 2, 3, 4, 5, 10, 17A, 19, 26, 35B, 36, 39, 43, 44, 45, 48, 49, 59, 63, 69, 70, 78, 79, 80, 84, 89, 90, 91, 93, 106, 107, 116, 117, 122, 141, 142, 145, 146, 148, 149, 180, 181

J. DE MOOR, FLANDERS HERITAGE AGENCY
176

JACQUES SEMEY, GHENT UNIVERSITY
O, 138A

KOEN HIMPE, FLANDERS HERITAGE AGENCY
170

KRIS VANDEVORST, FLANDERS HERITAGE AGENCY
109, 110, 115

LIBRARY AND ARCHIVES CANADA
166

LUC VANDAEL, FLANDERS HERITAGE AGENCY
179

MONUMENT VANDEKERCKHOVE
57, 58, 92, 100, 102, 111, 129

NATIONAL ARCHIVES KEW
F historical map, 77

NATIONAL ARCHIVES THE NETHERLANDS
105

NATIONAL LIBRARY OF SCOTLAND
113

ORBIT, GHENT UNIVERSITY
162, 163A, 164, 165, 165, 167

PATRICK VAN WANZEELE
11, 12

PAUL REED
18

PRIVATE COLLECTION DENIS PIETERS
134

PRIVATE COLLECTION JAN VANCOILLIE
88

PROVINCE OF ANTWERP
N

PUBLICATION LES SITES DE GUERRE
168

PUBLICATION NEL (1922) BOESINGHE OU LES COMBATS DE LA 87E DIVISION TERRITORIALE SUR L'YSER
38

PUBLICATION PILL-BOXES OF FLANDERS
169

ROYAL MUSEUM OF THE ARMED FORCES AND MILITARY HISTORY BRUSSELS
128, 135, 138B

RUBEN WILLAERT
54, 60, 71, 82

SIMON VERDEGEM, ADEDE
13

STUDIEBUREAU ARCHEOLOGIE
127

THV GATE / RUBEN WILLAERT / MONUMENT VANDEKERCKHOVE
9, 16, 20, 23, 28, 29, 30, 31, 32, 34, 35A, 40, 41, 42, 50, 51, 61, 62, 72, 74, 97, 108

UNIVERSITY OF TEXAS AT DALLAS, FERKO COLLECTION
137, 139A

VLAAMS ERFGOED CENTRUM
131

WOUTER GHEYLE, GHENT UNIVERSITY
132, 155, 156, 160, 161, 163

COLOPHON

This book is published on the occasion of the exhibition *Traces of War – The Archaeology of the First World War*, which runs from 17 February to 30 September 2018

at the In Flanders Fields Museum in Ypres.

EDITOR
Birger Stichelbaut

TEXTS
Thomas Apers
Jean Bourgeois
Maarten Bracke
Piet Chielens
Jan Decorte
Marc Dewilde
Anton Ervynck
Wouter Gheyle
Bert Heyvaert
Koen Himpe
Johan Hoorne
An Lentacker
Nicolas Note
Timothy Saey
Birger Stichelbaut
Hanne Van den Berghe
Veerle Van Eetvelde
Yannick Van Hollebeeke
Marc Van Meirvenne
Simon Verdegem
Franky Wyffels

FOREWORD
Piet Chielens
Annick Vandenbilcke

FINAL EDITING
Bart Biesbrouck

TRANSLATION
Richard Lomax

TEXT EDITING
Cath Phillips

PHOTO SELECTION
Birger Stichelbaut

PHOTO PROCESSING
Séverine Lacante

PROJECT COORDINATION
Hadewych Van den Bossche

DESIGN
Tim Bisschop

PRINTING
die Keure, Brugge

BINDING
Brepols, Turnhout

ISBN 978 94 9267 751 8
D/2018/11922/17
NUR 682/689

Hannibal Publishing is part of Cannibal Publishing
www.hannibalpublishing.com
www.inflandersfields.be